Britannia
Britannia
2000
Auto Windscreens
SHIELD
SGFC

TWINNED WITH REYKJAVÍK

TWINNED WITH REYKJAVÍK

STOKE CITY
THE ICELANDIC YEARS

LIAM BULLOCK

pitch

First published by Pitch Publishing, 2021

Pitch Publishing
A2 Yeoman Gate
Yeoman Way
Worthing
Sussex
BN13 3QZ
www.pitchpublishing.co.uk
info@pitchpublishing.co.uk

A CIP catalogue record is available for this book from the British Library.

ISBN 978 1 78531 780 4

Typesetting and origination by Pitch Publishing

Printed and bound in India by Replika Press Pvt. Ltd.

Contents

Foreword

Denis Smith

WITHIN FOOTBALL, the perception of what is going on behind the scenes from a supporter's point of view is usually what they glean from the media. After over 50 years in football, I have realised that things which are really happening in dressing rooms and boardrooms are usually very different from what the media and supporters think. That doesn't take anything away from these points of view; it is because there is always believed to be drama happening that makes football so entertaining.

When my cousin Dave Bullock, father of Liam, rang to ask me to write a foreword to this book, I was delighted to do so. I know, like me, Dave is a big Stoke City fan, and now I know that Liam is also a staunch Stoke City fan.

It is always a pleasure for me to read anything about the history of Stoke City, whether I am part of it or not. The club at the time that Liam is writing about was in the control of the Icelanders and, with a promotion in that time, was not short of enjoyment. As a manager myself of clubs that played against Stoke during this time, I obviously wanted to win these games. But I was also a Stoke City fan, and I wanted Stoke to finish second in the league behind the team I was managing at the time.

The pleasure that fans will get from this book is that you will be able to judge whether your opinions are the same as Liam's or are totally different. After all my time in football, I know how supporters' views differ, and that is the beauty of the game. I haven't had an input in the writing of this book, as I know that would spoil the concept of it being written solely from a supporter's point of view. The years Liam has written about are an interesting time for Stoke City, with plenty of excitement and drama.

Preface

ICELAND IS a small Nordic island nation in the middle of the North Atlantic Ocean, with a population of just over 360,000 – less than the combined population of Stoke-on-Trent and Newcastle-under-Lyme. The country is probably best known for its active volcanoes (everyone can still remember the name of Eyjafjallajökull, right?), its polar climate, literary sagas, the music of Björk and the physical prowess of strongman Hafþór Júlíus Björnsson (aka The Mountain from *Game of Thrones*).

However, in recent years, the Icelandic football team have been making global headlines, not least for their memorable 2-1 victory over England at the 2016 UEFA European Championship. They also became the smallest populated nation to qualify for the FIFA World Cup in 2018. While the national team has become a highly competitive outfit in recent years, at the end of the 20th century, Icelandic football was still trying to make its mark on the footballing world. However, in late 1999, Icelandic football was about to introduce itself to a certain Staffordshire club languishing in the third tier of the English footballing pyramid.

* * *

If there was ever an opportunity to go back in time and produce a Netflix-style, fly-on-the-wall football club documentary, I can't think of a more intriguing place or period than Stoke City FC during the Icelandic years. After Sir Stan's dribbling, Tony Waddington's cup winners and Mark Stein's heroics in front of the old Boothen End, and before Rory Delap bullet throws, Ricardo Fuller mazy runs and Mark Hughes's Stokealona, there was the Icelandic era of Stoke City. A short but memorable period between 1999 and 2006 which brought pulsating matches, one-of-a-kind players, perplexing managers and remarkable off-field decisions. For those of us who experienced it first-hand, some moments from this era will always be polarising. For those who weren't old enough to see it, it was a bumpy bridge between the old and new regimes, both led by businessman Peter Coates. One thing is for sure: it was an eventful time to be a Stokie!

It has never been an easy life as a fan of Stoke City Football Club. Fleeting moments of success and silverware are often separated by prolonged periods of failure and languishing in the second or third tiers of English football. Even during our recent Premier League boom period, we found ourselves constantly protecting our own players, managers, style of play and even the fan base itself. But we still love to be part of it, and we love the drama. We still rock up to the bet365 Stadium, have a couple of overpriced bottles of beer, find our seats with that annoying know-it-all sat behind, and we scream, shout, curse and sing for 90 minutes on a Saturday afternoon. For those of us who have a particular gluttony for punishment, you can jump on a train, climb in the car, or settle down for a five-hour official coach journey (if you're lucky, you might win a tenner on the team-name raffle) to see Stoke City on the road. And why do we love it? Because it's who we are, how we identify, it runs through our veins and it's our own little red and white world. *We* are Stoke City FC.

Occasionally, we'll get our moment in the sunshine. A generation will never forget the moment Tony Waddington's side lifted the League Cup trophy in 1972. Between 1991 and 1993, we were crowned Division Two (now known as League One) champions and we won the Autoglass Trophy (aka the Football League Trophy), and we were seemingly destined for bigger and better things. Eventually, those bigger and better things would arrive. A decade of Premier League football. A 5-0 win in the semi-final of the FA Cup. We even had a European tour and a trip to Valencia. At time of writing, things have certainly fallen from these dizzying heights, but there is always an underlying optimism that we'll be back, no matter how far we fall – we're back to being a sleeping monster!

* * *

So here I am, a Stoke fan from birth, born and raised in Fenton, currently sat at my desk in sunny Barcelona during a period of lockdown, trapped indoors with my wife Cris. It's March 2020, and the world has ground to a halt due to the coronavirus disease (Covid-19). There is no football being played and the pubs are closed. We can't even go outside to visit friends and family, so there is plenty of time to think about … well … everything. I've been thinking about my time as a Stoke fan, where it all began and what it was that truly captivated me. I'm 31 years old and I started attending Stoke games with my parents and my brother in the mid-90s. I was too young to remember the days of Mark Stein, and would typically be left at my nan's house on Forrester Street in Longton, watching the live scores change on Ceefax. There was nothing more tense than waiting for the pages to change on Teletext in the dying minutes of a match! My earliest memories attending games are of the Victoria Ground, stood on the paddock next to the dugout watching the likes of Mike Sheron, Richard Forsythe and Ray Wallace. I can still recall games from the 1996/97 season, beating Vale 2-0 at home thanks to Mike Sheron, and beating West Brom in the last game at the Vic. I remember enjoying it all, but I wasn't fully in tune with what was happening on the pitch and what it all meant. I wouldn't really 'get it' until the end of the 90s, in our new home – the Britannia Stadium, now known as the bet365.

My coming of age as a Stoke fan really happened around 1998, when I started to attend home and away games regularly. Family away games with my mum, dad and brother were always a treat. We would always pack in to our Vauxhall Cavalier and my dad would insist on parking in specific places that fit his own criteria – it had to be free to park, facing the right way back to Stoke and with quick access back on to the main road without any post-match queuing. Of course, this normally meant we would park at least a mile away from the stadium, spending more time walking (or even trying to find the car) than we would have spent queuing in traffic. It also led us to many a rough estate ... Manchester City's old ground at Maine Road was a particularly hairy away day in the car. We ended up in some half-boarded-up street in Moss Side, having to give a kid on a bike a couple of quid to not take the wheels or smash up the windows! Definitely a 'hide your Stoke shirt and scarf' type of situation. Still, cheaper than the £5 car park next to the ground.

I had my first season ticket with my brother, David, in the West Stand (then known as the McEwan's Stand) in the 1999/00 season. It was a bit of an odd choice for two teenagers to choose to sit in the McEwan's Stand rather than the Boothen End (the North Stand as it was originally known at the Brit).

The McEwan's was (and still is) known as a bit of a 'posh' stand, famed for the elder, quieter fans that would rather sip on their tartan flasks of whisky-laced coffee and complain about how the foreign players run funny (while mispronouncing their names) than vocally support the team. We had some characters in our block though, quite a few regulars from the Park Inn in Dresden who would also frequent Longton Cricket Club during the summer. They would also turn up 15 minutes late for night matches, complaining about traffic and parking. The McEwan's Stand would also occasionally play host to the Burberry-clad, youth-casual types that would suddenly emerge out of nowhere at the bottom of block 10 (next to the tunnel and the away end) at the slightest sniff of aggro. As unsavoury as they may have been, they did at least make a bit of noise and entertainment in an otherwise silent part of the ground! Despite not really fitting in, we made it our home for a good few seasons. My brother liked to sit with a side-on view of the pitch but would rather not sit with our parents in the Sentinel Stand. The McEwan's Stand also afforded a good view of the dugout antics. My brother is pretty much the know-it-all that sits behind you at games studying the play intently … although to be fair, he is the most knowledgeable Stoke fan that I know because of that. His incessant analysis and photographic memory were good for bringing me up to date with the circumstances that led to one of the most peculiar periods of Stoke City's modern history.

An Icelandic consortium, fronted by businessman Gunnar Gíslason, took over from directors Peter Coates and Keith Humphreys. This was the start of an exciting period as a young fan, following a new-look team in search of promotion. For the first time in my Stoke-supporting life, I was watching Stoke *win* games on a semi-regular basis. Not only were we winning games, we really stood out as a unique club in that old Division Two. We had a relatively new stadium, a foreign manager, 10,000+ crowds and a team of European imports from Scandinavia and beyond, none of which were typical of that time and place. After initially seeing the names of the incoming Icelandic players in *The Sentinel*, the first reaction was always 'how are we going to pronounce that or work that into a song?' Soon enough though, the shoe would be on the other foot, and Stoke fans would be the ones chortling at opposition tannoy announcers' feeble attempts to pronounce names like 'Ríkharður Daðason' and 'Tryggvi Guðmundsson'. This period was also the first time I saw us play at Wembley, win silverware and finally achieve promotion, and these are still amongst my best footballing memories.

I tend to think of that time as a successful period for Stoke City. But was it? Compared to the heyday of Sir Stanley Matthews, and the glory years with Hudson, Banks, Greenhoff ... no, and frankly there is no comparison. But even compared to the days of Lou Macari, Mark Stein, Ian Cranson, Wayne Biggins and Rooster Russell, many a fan would argue that the early 90s were a far superior experience for a Stoke fan compared with the early 2000s. Once the Icelandic project was over, we went on to a successful ten-year stay in the Premier League, so do I simply perceive the Icelandic years to be successful based on nostalgia? Is it due to the fact that it was my footballing introduction as a Stoke fan? Or did it just seem successful compared with the disappointment of the late 90s? Maybe it wasn't successful at all. Or maybe it was the foundations that led to the success that would follow.

* * *

Twinned with Reykjavík delves deeply into that ridiculous period for Stoke City FC between November 1999 and May. Through five managers with very different legacies, and a host of players who came with big reputations, promising futures or we simply had no idea about at all. Surprise sackings, shock appointments, walkouts, *very* public arguments, incredible debuts and some very special wins. During this chronological walk through the Icelandic era, the views of key players, media and fans of the time will be described to show the first-hand experiences from the people that lived through the time, including exclusive interviews with Chris Iwelumo, Clive Clarke, Lárus Sigurðsson and John Acres. For the good and the bad, the Icelandic years were some of the most important in the modern history of Stoke City, and some of the most entertaining. With that, I hope you enjoy this book, and remember the Icelandic proverb … *Blindur er bóklaus maður* (Blind is the bookless man).

Chapter 1

The Pre-Icelandic Icelanders

'There are plenty of boys in Iceland who have football in their blood … I've never been to a nation which has such potential to reach further if only appropriate conditions exist'
– Freddie Steele

THE STORY of Stoke City's relationship with the nation of Iceland actually begins before 1999. In fact, it began *long* before 1999. For many Stokies, our first introductions to Icelandic football came in 1993 and 1994, with the signings of Þorvaldur (Toddy) Örlygsson and Lárus Sigurðsson respectively. However, the Stoke–Iceland lineage goes back as far as 1946. Hanley-born Freddie Steele is a legendary figure in Stoke-on-Trent football, having played for both Stoke (from 1933 to 1949) and Port Vale (1951 to 1953). Steele racked up 152 goals for the two Potteries teams, ranking as Stoke City's second all-time goalscorer. He went on to manage the Vale during two different spells in the 50s and 60s. However, before his return to the Mother Town of Burslem, Steele managed Icelandic football club KR Reykjavík in 1946. KR Reykjavík was Steele's first managerial role, although it was only for the summer of 46. During that time, he took charge of five games, winning three, drawing one and losing the other, with the team finishing runners-up in the league. He went on to become the manager of the Icelandic national team for their first-ever international match, a 3-0 loss to Denmark.

Steele left Iceland in August of that year and returned to Stoke. He spoke fondly of his time in the land of fire and ice, stating upon his return, 'There are plenty of boys in Iceland who have football in their blood, and all they are missing are the conditions for the sport to really progress. Proper facilities, rather than playing on gravel, will lift the sport to a higher level. It isn't just about coaching a man to stop the ball but to work as a team. They are not 11 individuals but one whole. It is the main thing in every football match. My stay was a pleasure. I've never been to a nation which has such potential to reach further if only appropriate conditions exist.'

Like a sleeping Icelandic volcano, the Stoke–Iceland relationship would lie dormant for several decades, before bursting into life rapidly and dramatically. In 1993, Stoke manager Lou Macari brought the exciting midfielder Toddy Örlygsson to the club from Nottingham Forest to replace Kevin 'Rooster' Russell. Örlygsson, a player brought to English football by Brian Clough, left Forest at the end of his contract. During his two years at the club, Toddy was admired by fans and management alike. He scored some wonderful individual goals, including a sweet run and 20-yard finish against Sunderland that the man himself cites as one of his Stoke City highlights. In 2018, Toddy told *Duck Magazine*, 'My goal against Sunderland at home is one of my favourites. Running with the ball from the halfway line, going past a few players and a good strike! Okay, I know the keeper could have done better – but hey, it is a good goal!'

Toddy's spell at Stoke ended in 1995 on a bit of a sour note, culminating in contract disputes and an eventual move to Oldham Athletic for £180,000. However, time heals all wounds, and fans look fondly back on his spell, and the fan-favourite chant of 'Örlygsson, Örlygsson, running down the wing ...' was eventually revived for Matthew Etherington a couple of decades later. Ultimately, the signing of Örlygsson would be the start of a chain of events that ended with the Icelandic takeover in 1999. Before departing for Oldham, Toddy recommended another Icelander to Macari – his cousin Lárus Orri Sigurðsson.

Initially joining on trial from Þór Akureyri, youngster Sigurðsson impressed Macari and earned a contract for the 1994/95 season. He went on to win player of the year in his first full season at the club. Sigurðsson was a regular for several seasons, including the 1995/96 season when Stoke reached the Division One (now known as the Championship) play-offs. He was the last Stoke captain at the Victoria Ground in 1996/97, and played regularly during the ill-fated 1997/98 relegation season, the first at the Britannia Stadium. Lárus's brother, Kristján Örn Sigurðsson, was also on the books at Stoke between 1997 and 2001, though he never made it into the first team. During his five years and over 200 appearances at Stoke, Lárus Sigurðsson was a popular figure, and a particularly important player during his early years at the Vic. He even took a training session at my brother's Lads n Dads team on the pitch next to the Florence Social Club. The team manager had built the training session up all week, saying how lucky the lads were to be getting a professional to show the team how to train in an expert and sophisticated way. On the big day, Lárus turned up, told the boys to run five laps of the pitch, then left!

* * *

Lárus was a present senior figure through an intriguing time at Stoke City. The club was under the ownership of Peter Coates and Keith Humphreys, and in the summer of 1997, the club moved from the Stoke town centre-hosted Victoria Ground to the Britannia Stadium in the newly built Trentham Lakes estate. The imposing new purpose-built stadium had cast a long shadow from the side of the A50 over the Vic for several months during construction. Though the Vic had amassed a huge amount of sentimental value and fan adoration, the move, spearheaded by chief executive Jez Moxey, was seen as the next inevitable step in pursuit of top-flight football. The shiny new all-seater stadium came with all mod cons, a new bar, a flashy scoreboard … even cheerleaders ('The City Slickers') and a hippo mascot. The future looked bright. However, the departures of the hugely popular manager Lou Macari and top-scorer Mike Sheron prior to the move were the prerequisites to a massive downturn for the Potters. Following a prolonged period of increasingly poor results, questionable managerial selections and a perceived lack of investment into the squad, the fans turned on the board. This manifested as stay-away protests, organised campaigns, property damage and even death threats. Fans that weren't staying away from games stormed the pitch and the directors' box following a humiliating 7-0 defeat at the Brit in the 1997/98 season. The Britannia Stadium was feeling cursed and didn't feel like home.

The Coates and Humphreys regime oversaw the club's miserable relegation to Division Two in 1997/98, mainly thanks to a string of poor managerial appointments and weak squad additions following Macari's departure. The board had initially appointed Macari's former assistant manager Chic Bates as the Scot's replacement, before opting for former player Chris Kamara after a poor start. Kamara's performance was even more disastrous, winning only one of his 14 games, before being sacked and replaced by former manager Alan Durban. His caretaker position showed slight improvements, but he couldn't prevent relegation on the final day of the season. As well as the drubbing at the hands of Birmingham, the final -day 2-5 home defeat to fellow relegation-stricken Manchester City was particularly ugly, both on the pitch and in the stands. To make matters worse, one of the teams to beat the drop and seal Stoke's relegation on that final day was none other than Port Vale. The 'SOS – Save Our Stoke' campaign was launched to oust Coates, Humphreys and Jez Moxey. Even my own mild-mannered family had an 'Enough is Enough – COATES OUT' poster in the back window of the Cavalier. Things were really bad at the football club.

* * *

The Potters started 1998/99 back in Division Two. While the tensions between fans and the board kept rising, it seemed like maybe, just maybe, on the pitch, the team had finally turned a corner. The experienced Brian Little was appointed as manager, following a four-year stint at Premier League Aston Villa. Lárus Sigurðsson was still at the club and was part of Brian Little's team that started the season so well, winning our first six games, and 14 of the first 20. The fan chants of 'We're only here for the season' during the opening game at Northampton were perhaps slightly tongue in cheek, but it was impossible not to be optimistic when we were sitting pretty at the top of the table as summer turned to autumn. Needless to say, the season didn't end with promotion. We ended up missing out on the play-offs, finishing eighth following a calamitous second half of the season. The collapse included embarrassing defeats of 2-0 to nine-man Millwall, and a 4-1 loss at home to Bristol Rovers, met with yet more on-field protests against the board. Brian Little left at the end of the season, although he seemed to be mentally out of the door weeks before that formality. Perhaps the only rays of light in those two dismal seasons were the performances of Irish midfield talisman Graham Kavanagh and newly signed ex-Blackburn forward Peter Thorne, two of our better performers in an otherwise uninspiring squad.

Our failure to secure promotion back to Division One at the first attempt also meant the inevitable departure of Sigurðsson. In the summer of 1999, he moved to West Bromwich Albion for £350,000, eventually helping the Baggies win promotion to the Premier League. I spoke with Lárus, and he cited the 'fantastic, passionate supporters' as the main highlight of his time at Stoke. He also fondly remembers being voted player of the season in his first year and being made club captain at such a young age. He said, 'I came to Stoke as a young man, went through some great times and some difficult times, and these experiences stay with you forever. Stoke City and the supporters will always hold a special place in my heart. Thank you for the five years we had together.' Simon Lowe, editor and author of several Stoke City books including *Potters at War*, *Stoke City's Greatest Games*, *Delilah Roars Again*! and *Stoke City: A Nostalgic Look at a Century of the Club*, recounted the final months of the Coates-Humphreys regime: 'Selling Lárus Sigurdsson to rivals West Brom for a paltry £350,000 in August 1999 told us exactly where the incumbent board were in terms of ambition. The new Britannia Stadium had instantly become something of a noose around the club's neck. Fans were increasingly concerned that it was a bit of a white elephant, as crowds were often around 50% of its 28,500 capacity. Coates was still in the realms of selling pies through his company Stadia Catering at that point; not the multi-billionaire he would become through the arrival of the internet and online gambling when he returned.'

Managerless, a mess off and on the pitch, seemingly going nowhere in Division Two and a heavily damaged relationship between the club and the fans. How does all this directly relate to the now-departed Lárus Sigurðsson? Well, despite all his merits in the centre of defence, his true impact on Stoke City may have been even greater off the pitch, and it would only come to fruition after he had left.

Chapter 2

Winter Is Coming

'We are very excited about taking over a club with such tremendous potential. We are here to make Stoke City great again'
– Gunnar Gíslason

AT THE start of the 1999/00 season, Stoke City were in the familiar position of looking for a new manager. In reality, the club had never adequately replaced Lou Macari, a manager with the respect of the players, the admiration of the fans, an eye for a striker and his finger on the pulse of the expectations of the football club. The 1997 Chic Bates managerial experiment had failed, Chris Kamara's spell as manager was so bad it was unbelievable (Jeff), and Brian Little's heart just wasn't in it. Early signs were that the next appointment may turn out to be tricky too, as the first choice, a certain Anthony Richard Pulis, was reluctant to join due to the lack of board ambitions, and instead opted for Bristol City. Former Vale manager John Rudge was another name thrown around, but Rudgie would not take the hot seat, instead joining as director of football (after turning down the same position at the Valiants). Five weeks after Brian Little departed, the board finally found their man – former Norwich City, Blackpool and Stockport County manager Gary Megson.

Megson, appointed on a two-year deal, was the fifth full-time Stoke manager in two years, but at the time, he appeared to be a shrewd appointment. Former Carlisle manager Nigel Pearson also joined the club as Megson's new assistant. Despite the seemingly unenviable position, Megson seemed content working with no funds, instead drawing on his own experience in coaching and looking to the fans to revitalise the team. After his appointment, Megson told the press, 'It's going to be extremely tough, but passion, enthusiasm and desire don't cost anything. The biggest thing this club has going for it is the support. They can play an active part in getting us up.' The job he was facing was unattractive, as the off-field tensions continued between the fans and the board. The season also started in familiar fashion, with three defeats in the first four games. Lárus Sigurðsson had departed for the Hawthorns by the end of August 99, but this coincided with the team beginning a decent run of ten matches unbeaten, helped in part by Peter Thorne's goalscoring prowess. Even struggling striker Kyle Lightbourne was starting to justify his £500,000 price tag. The upturn in form took Stoke up to joint second and things were starting to look promising. But, as winter approached, something was about to happen that would change the club from top to bottom.

* * *

Prior to his departure, Lárus Sigurðsson was a key player in central defence, not just for Stoke, but for the Icelandic national team. During the mid-90s, when Sigurðsson was still plying his trade at the Victoria Ground, the then Iceland manager Guðjón Þórðarson (surname commonly spelled as

'Thórdarson' in English) would make regular trips over to see him play. These scouting trips continued as Stoke started to grow off the pitch, with the development of the Britannia Stadium, but were going backwards on the pitch. Thórdarson was impressed with what he saw, particularly off the field. He spied an opportunity, as the dissension grew to the point that Coates and Humphreys were ready to sell their majority shares in the club. While he didn't know any of the Icelandic investors personally, Sigurðsson was aware of the interest from his countrymen, and was even asked to meet representatives of the investors. After recognising the potential, in February 99, Guðjón took his idea of a Stoke City financial involvement back to Iceland, speaking with businessmen including Gunnar Þór Gíslason, Magnús Kristinsson, Elfar Adalsteinsson and Ásgeir Sigurvinsson, the 'Business Vikings' that could take their finances overseas to invest in such ventures.

Gunnar Gíslason, who was 33 at the time, would become the club chairman (the youngest in the league) and public face of the consortium. Gíslason was the head of a family-run fruit and vegetable distribution business and investment portfolio in Iceland, following English football from afar. Magnús Kristinsson, who looked like the Demon Headmaster with a bowl cut, ran a fishing company, and would become the consortium chairman, working quietly (at least initially) behind the scenes. Elfar Adalsteinsson was the director of a huge fish-freezing plant in the fjordside village of Eskifjörður, which was poetically described by *The Sentinel* at the time as 'one of the most prestigious seafood processing companies in Iceland'. Ásgeir Sigurvinsson perhaps had the most notable pedigree for running a football club, having played professional football in Germany, including for European giants Bayern Munich. The consortium comprised eight principal shareholders and over 350 smaller backers, and would become Stoke Holding

SA, a Luxembourg-based company created in the autumn of 99. Stoke Holding was to be funded by Icelandic business and banking, as well as venture capital company Uppspretta, formed by Kaupthing, a bank established in Luxembourg. Their initial attempts to seize majority control of Stoke City were unsuccessful and it seemed for a time like the takeover might not happen at all. The club's financial burdens, in part due to the move to the Britannia Stadium, were particularly unappealing to the consortium. The apparent collapse even prompted Port Vale chairman Bill Bell to call up the Icelandic group to try to lure the investors up the road to Vale Park. Interesting to think how things could have worked out had they been successful in their attempts! In the end, negotiations between Stoke and the Icelandic consortium reopened, and in October 99, a deal was reached. The newly formed Stoke Holding now owned a majority 66 per cent share in Stoke City FC for an initial figure of just over £3.5m (about the same cost as Marc Wilson from Portsmouth in 2011). The reign of Coates and Humphreys was over … well, more or less, at least. The pair's joint shareholding was shrunk from 95 per cent to around 29 per cent, meaning their command over the club was drastically diminished, but they kept a 'golden share', meaning they still had an important say in major club decisions. Jez Moxey would keep his position as chief executive for the time being.

The takeover was making headlines over in Iceland. Vidar Halldórsson, author of *Sport in Iceland: How Small Nations Achieve International Success*, spoke of the significance of the news in the nation: 'The takeover was widely recognised in Iceland, it was a big story. This was due to two main reasons. One is that the Icelandic nation is fanatical about English football. We started watching games in the 1970s, the national television station would show the full 90 minutes of week-old

English first division games. This was the first football we got to see. I did a survey in 2001 about English football with Icelandic men, and over 90% said that they had a favourite English football team. The survey also confirmed that over half of the respondents supported their English team more than their Icelandic team. The second reason is that Gudjón Thórdarson was a national treasure in Iceland. In terms of Icelandic football, his expertise was way ahead of his time. He was also a success with the national team, he was a legend with a lot of charisma. There was a strong belief in Thórdarson at the time. I think that he was the main reason for the takeover – to give him a bigger stage and a top job in English football.' Vidar added, 'The takeover happened because everyone had such a strong belief in Gudjón Thórdarson, it is part of the characteristic of Icelanders. We have so much confidence, we believe that we can conquer the world. The businesspeople believed that we had the best coach in the world, and that they would get rich as a result. Lots of Icelanders bought shares in Stoke City, they saw it as an opportunity to earn money. It seemed like a no-brainer that we would conquer English football and it would be a success.'

* * *

With the takeover came a wave of positivity and expectation, funnelled down from the new higher-ups. After the purchase, Gíslason stated, 'Our main target is to do well in the Premier League and that's something you can't achieve by taking half measures. Wins and more exciting play should bring in more crowds, thereby improving the club's financial position and raising the quality of the football. That's the kind of spiraling effect we're aiming for to send Stoke spinning to the top. We are very excited about taking over a club with such tremendous potential. We are here to *make Stoke City great again*.' Quite a catchy slogan that last sentence; Donald Trump must have been taking notes. Regarding the club finances, Gíslason said, 'There is no concern about the club's debt. We have spoken to our bankers and we will be restructuring the debt. It will not hinder us. If the manager comes to us wanting players, I am sure we will be able to accommodate him.' Ásgeir Sigurvinsson said at the time, 'Stoke are too big for the Second Division, a vintage club with loyal fans and Premier League potential.'

The prospect of squad investment and the numerous mentions of Premier League football, something yet to be witnessed in Stoke-on-Trent since the top division rebrand in 1992, was a teasing prospect. The Potters had not been in the top flight since 1985, meaning a generation of fans (including myself) had never seen Stoke dine at the top table. Plenty of fans were still happy to take these statements with a pinch of salt. The dust had barely settled on Chris Kamara referring to Stoke as a 'sleeping monster.' Author and lifelong fan Simon Lowe said of the changes at the club, 'There was some anticipation at this unknown foreign entity moving in to take over. This was as much because it heralded the end of the reign of the unpopular chairman Peter Coates (and a board which was seen very much as his cronies), as it was the excitement of what the Icelanders would do for the fortunes of the club. Deep cynicism ruled. Great changes of fortune like that just didn't happen at Stoke City.' Runar Kvernen, chair of the Norwegian supporters' branch and Stoke fan since 1970, has followed the ups and downs ('and downs again') of the club from Scandinavia. He spoke about the reaction in Norway to the purchase: 'The Icelandic takeover was exciting, a new energy after budget troubles and riots against Coates. I attended a couple of matches in the period, and even ran into Gunnar Gíslason and his crew at Quality Hotel in Hanley. We talked about it in Norway, as Iceland and Norway are well connected, but worries would come along the way. Did they have the finances and know-how …?' Questions would indeed arise about their finances and know-how, but at the time, the first objective was simple – get Stoke City back into Division One.

* * *

Before the Icelandic attempt to get us up could fully commence, there was one more bit of business that needed to be taken care of. Guðjón Thórdarson had initiated the idea to invest in Stoke City. He had brought the consortium together and was pivotal for making the deal happen. It was inevitable that he would be appointed as manager, meaning the popular (and thus far successful) Gary Megson would be out the door. During the negotiations and acquisition, the team had continued under Megson's stewardship, but the writing was very much on the wall. In his final game, at home to Bristol City in front of 10,775 fans, defender Nicky Mohan scored a 66th-minute equaliser, at which point the players ran to celebrate with Megson on the touchline. Thórdarson and Icelandic ambassador Þorsteinn Pálsson were in attendance at the Brit, watching from the stands. Megson would say of the player celebrations, 'I think they all put two and two together and came up with the right answer about my future. I am sorry to be going and it was an emotional occasion for me.' Megson's departure was described by Gíslason as 'a casualty of events'. After his dismissal on 15 November, Megson said, 'I'll be bitterly disappointed if the club don't pay me what I'd have earned over the two years. No one should come out of this feeling like a victim, but I will unless I'm treated honourably.'

There was disappointment amongst the team after Megson's dismissal. Clive Clarke, who debuted in 1999 and would remain a regular at the club until 2005, praised Megson and his short stint at the club, and spoke very highly of the team that he had put together. Clarke told me, 'When Gary Megson came in, I was used to training with all the senior players. He had enough faith in me and James O'Connor to make us regulars in a talented group of players. I was very disappointed when he was sacked. He was tough on me, but I needed it, and we all felt that we had a great chance of winning the league. We had a great team spirit and squad. It was the best Stoke team I played in.' Speaking about Gary Megson's departure with *Duck Magazine* in 2019, Peter Thorne reflected, 'Megson was alright with me and he got the players grafting for the shirt. He really was old school. To some players, maybe his approach might have offended a few. I think he pushed to get a rise and a reaction out of players. It was his way of motivating players. Some might shrink under that atmosphere, so you have to show what you're made of. Today, his style would annoy plenty of players and agents.' John Rudge and Nigel Pearson remained at the club after Megson's departure, meaning the new management team would retain a valuable amount of English footballing experience. Megson's short stint as manager is looked back on by most Stokies as the start of a period of high potential, with the consensus being that he was hard done by and that he could have been a success at the club. Megson would return to Stoke for another short stint two decades later, as a coach under the leadership of Tony Pulis.

* * *

The following day, after Megson was sacked, Guðjón Thórdarson would officially take over as Stoke City manager. For those keeping count, we were now up to six managers in two years. Thórdarson's managerial record was impressive, albeit garnered a world away from Division Two in England.

A player for his hometown club ÍA Akranes in the 70s and 80s, Thórdarson started his managerial career with KA Akureyri in northern Iceland ('Town of the Midnight Sun'), winning the title in 1989 despite the team being rank outsiders. He went on to guide ÍA Akranes to the Icelandic league title, the first of five consecutive titles between 1992 and 1996. He also won the Icelandic Cup twice with KR Reykjavík. In 1997, his impressive domestic record was rewarded, as he was appointed manager of the Icelandic national team. In the 25 games that he took charge, Iceland won 11, drew six and lost eight, which constituted Iceland's most successful international side at that time. During his tenure, Iceland came very close to qualifying for their first-ever major international tournament, losing out on Euro 2000 play-off qualification following a 3-2 defeat to world champions France in Paris.

Despite the feeling of injustice against Megson held by the fans, most Stokies were happy to give the new manager the benefit, given the circumstances of his arrival and the continual flow of positivity coming out of the club hierarchy. Thórdarson himself wasn't shy of talking himself up, nor the club prospects, commenting after his appointment, 'I am confident that I have the experience and knowledge to make Stoke City better, and hopefully we will eventually be playing amongst the best. I can make the players better. I believe I have the track record and knowledge to improve them, but, if they don't want to work with me, they will soon find out the consequences.' The feeling amongst supporters was a mixture of excitement and apprehension. We knew there would be new philosophies, new expectations and, crucially, new players … many of whom would be completely unknown to the average English fan. Stoke fan and writer of *The 90s Football Party Blog,* Rob Doolan summed up the reaction of the fans in that period, saying, 'The overwhelming feeling at the time was one of hope, of cautious optimism. It was clear that the only way was down under Coates Mk I and Humphreys, it genuinely felt like the vultures were circling and that all that awaited us was the basement and worse. The Icelanders appeared to have a vision, they were prepared to spend a decent amount of money (at first) by the standards of the third tier at the time, and we could start to look up again rather than down.' Neil James, Stoke fan and author of *Stoke and I: The Nineties*, also shared that optimism and reinvigoration, saying, 'The Icelandic years re-awoke an interest in Stoke that had been waning somewhat. It was the return of hope rather than anything else, as for the first time in a while, it seemed like we might want to be successful.'

* * *

We were now all set – the new board and new manager were in place. Stoke City's Icelandic saga was about to begin.

Chapter 3

The Icelandic Saga Begins

'Even though I dreamt about it, I couldn't imagine my start would be like that'
– Guðjón Thórdarson

THE ICELANDERS were welcomed to Staffordshire by Stoke fans in a variety of ways. There would, of course, be an official club-organised 'Meet the Manager' (and board) evening, as well as a display of A4-sized Icelandic flags for the first home game after their arrival. There was also a bloke who went to the ground dressed as a Viking, pinning a 'Twinned with Reykjavík' banner up on the fence behind the South Stand (thanks for the title inspiration!). Fans weren't the only ones happy with the arrival of the Icelanders. A few of my brother's friends (who weren't Stoke fans) were working in corporate hospitality in the executive boxes for matchdays. They loved the Nordic influx, as the Icelandic directors (and more typically, Icelandic guests) would often be *very* generous with their tips. Maybe they weren't fully aware of the conversion values of Icelandic króna to British pounds, or perhaps they had too much money (or too much drink). Either way, a 16-year-old from Longton who was regularly receiving £50+ tips wasn't going to question their generosity!

Fans didn't have to wait long for the first glimpse of the club's new transfer policies. It was no secret that the new board and manager were looking to exploit the Nordic market, citing the quality, character and commitment of undiscovered gems at discount prices as their justification. Joining on loan from Thórdarson's former club KR Reykjavík on 19 November 1999, Sigursteinn (Siggi) Gíslason and Einar Thór Daníelsson would be the first on-field Icelandic representatives of the new regime. Swedish right-back Mikael Hansson also joined from IFK Norrköping. The trio joined Norwegian centre-back Anders Jacobsen (who had already joined under Megson in July 99), bolstering the club's growing Scandinavian representation. Jacobsen was a particularly intriguing signing at the time, having bizarrely grown up as a Stoke fan in Oslo. He stated, 'When I was a young boy of about seven or eight, you either had a Liverpool or a Stoke shirt. Stoke were huge in Norway in the 70s. When I signed for Sheffield United there wasn't too much written back home, but when I joined Stoke, there were a lot of notices in the newspapers.' His sentiments are supported by Norwegian pop trio A-ha, who are also Stoke fans! Jacobsen is fondly remembered by members of the Stoke City Supporters Norwegian Branch, including Fredrikke Wongraven. He said, 'Anders Jacobsen was my favourite player at the time. He is one of the few Norwegians who have had the honour of playing for Stoke City, whilst also being a Stoke City fan. I bet this was a dream come true for him!'

Mikael Hansson would be by far the most successful of the three new Nordic signings, playing 65 games and scoring two league goals (both in one game vs. Bristol Rovers) for the Potters over a two-year spell. He endeared himself to the fans with his rapid swashbuckling runs down the right wing, the likes of which we aren't typically used to from a full-back in the red and white stripes. Along with John Halls and Carl Hoefkens, he's probably one of the most exciting attack-minded full-backs I've seen in my time as a Stoke fan (although Mame Biram Diouf's spell at right-back was certainly entertaining too).

* * *

Thórdarson's first game in charge came on 23 November 1999. Wycombe Wanderers were the opponents at Adams Park. Could Thórdarson's Stoke do it on a cold, rainy Tuesday night in Wycombe?

Thórdarson's first selected team was:

Gavin Ward, Anders Jacobsen, Clive Clarke, Nicky Mohan, Siggi Gíslason, Kevin Keen, Phil Robinson, James O'Connor, Graham Kavanagh, Peter Thorne, Kyle Lightbourne.

Substitutes: Ben Petty, David Oldfield, Einar Daníelsson.

Gíslason was handed a debut but suffered a dislocated shoulder after ten minutes. He was replaced by fellow newcomer Daníelsson. Graham Kavanagh continued to show that he was a player of high quality in Division Two, opening the scoring for Stoke just before half-time. A minute later, things got even better for Stoke and Thórdarson. A fine run through the Wycombe defence by the debuting substitute Einar Daníelsson saw him through on goal, before rounding the keeper to double the lead in wonderful style. The timing of the goals all but killed the contest, and after the break, Peter Thorne continued his fine goalscoring season to put Stoke three up. Captain and ex-Wycombe defender Nicky Mohan capped off the scoring, making it 4-0 to the visitors. The 500-odd Stokies who made the journey serenaded the new manager with the chant of 'It's just like watching Iceland'. A dream debut for the Iceman, inflicting Wycombe's worst-ever defeat in the Football League at the time. Thórdarson gleamed as he declared, 'I feel like I'm floating. It's unbelievable really. But I know I have to keep my feet on the ground. It would be too good to be true to carry on like this. Even though I dreamt about it, I couldn't imagine my start would be like that.' Thórdarson was right: it would be too good to be true to carry on in such a manner. The next three league games in the run-up to Christmas saw Stoke pick up just two points, although we did grab a win in the first round of the Auto Windscreens Shield (a variation of the Football League Trophy) at home to Darlington, thanks to an extra-time winner from Kyle Lightbourne.

Before carrying on, this is probably the right moment to talk about Sigursteinn Gíslason. In January 2012, at only 43 years old, Siggi died after an eight-month battle with cancer. During his fight, a charity game was held in his honour between two of his former clubs in Iceland, KR Reykjavík and ÍA, in front of almost 4,000 people, the fourth-highest-ever attendance at the home ground of ÍA. His death was mourned by the Icelandic football community, with many players and managers who knew him describing him as a great coach, a magnificent person and a popular leader who always had a positive attitude. He is survived by his wife Anna Elín Daníelsdóttir, his two sons, Magnús Sveinn and Teitur Leó, and daughter Unnur Elín. His stay at Stoke was short, featuring in only eight games, but he will go down in history as the first Icelander to start under the Icelandic regime, part of that night in Wycombe. He wore the red and white, and that makes him one of us – a Stokie. Rest in peace, Siggi.

* * *

Prior to the new millennium, the board took on a new director – Phil Rawlins. Stoke fan Rawlins had emailed chairman Gunnar Gíslason about investing in the club, and a meeting was set up by Jez Moxey. Rawlins had recently sold his international consulting company, earning himself a personal fortune of $259m. His intentions were to see Stoke return to the successes of his youth. In December 1999, Rawlins took a ten per cent stake in the club for $2m (about £1.2m at the time), with an added $1m loan to help the club's academy system. The new investment was a welcome sight for Peter Coates, who was excited to work closely with a businessman with Stoke's best interests at heart. Coates also felt that the Icelanders were more comfortable dealing with Rawlins than himself due to Coates's previous position as chairman, meaning he had a potential ally with some stroke in the boardroom. Rawlins stepped into what he saw was a club on the decline – attendances were down from previous seasons, turnover was down, marketing and PR were non-existent, and the club had lost its identity. His first move was to reinstate the name 'the Boothen End' for the North Stand behind the goal. The next steps from the board were to improve the playing squad.

Stoke would enter the transfer market and, once again, look to Scandinavia for a marquee signing. This time, the club wanted to show that it meant business. Stoke went out and broke their transfer record, spending £600,000 on Iceland international Brynjar Gunnarsson from Swedish club Örgryte IS. The transfer record would stand through to 2005, when Stoke paid around £950,000 for Sammy Bangoura. The 24-year-old Icelander was an impressive figure – over six feet tall, blond hair, blue eyes … if you were to build an Icelandic international from the ground up, he would probably look like Brynjar Gunnarsson. He was primarily a defensive midfielder for the Potters, though he played a number of games at centre-half early on in his Stoke career. I would argue that Gunnarsson was the best Icelandic signing the club made during the Icelandic years, although perhaps ranking third overall behind Toddy Örlygsson and Lárus Sigurðsson. He made 131 appearances between 1999 and 2003, and went on to play for Nottingham Forest, Watford and, most notably, Reading. He returned for a brief, low-key loan spell at Stoke in 2003/04, but he will mostly be remembered for his performances under Thórdarson.

As the 20th century turned to the 21st, Stoke's league form danced around through January to mid-February, going on a run of five games without losing, followed by four games without winning. After yet another two unremarkable League Cup and FA Cup efforts (losing to Sheffield Wednesday in round two and Blackpool in round one respectively), there was some promise of an early trip to Wembley Stadium brewing after progressing to the northern section semi-final of the Auto Windscreens Shield. An 82nd-minute winner from academy product and Irish midfield terrier James O'Connor saw Stoke pick up the win away at Chesterfield, setting up a two-legged northern section final against Rochdale. The winner would go on to the final at Wembley, the last Football League Trophy Final to be played there before the stadium closure and redevelopment. However, the footballing world was about to take a momentary pause for the passing of one of the all-time greats, a man with magic in his boots and Stoke City running through his veins.

* * *

On 23 February 2000, at the age of 85, Sir Stanley Matthews passed away, and the footballing world and city of Stoke-on-Trent grieved. Born in a terraced house in Seymour Street, Hanley, and known as 'The Wizard of the Dribble', Sir Stan's footballing accolades are numerous. Having made 697 senior appearances (318 for Stoke over two spells), he is still the only player to have been knighted while actively playing the game. He was the first Ballon d'Or winner, and the oldest player to play in England's top flight (50 years and five days), as well as the oldest to represent England (42 years and 104 days). He won the FA Cup for Blackpool in what would become known as the 'Matthews Final' of 1953. People who saw him play would describe him as one of the greatest of all time: a man who revolutionised football with his raw talent, his hard work and dedication to fitness and conditioning. Those who met him, and I count myself as fortunate enough to have met him at the last game at the Vic, knew him as a kind, generous gentleman, and a true ambassador for Stoke-on-Trent and Blackpool. In early March 2000, his life was honoured by our great city at his funeral at St Peter's Church, attended by the likes of Bobby and Jack Charlton, Gordon Banks, Nat Lofthouse and Tom Finney. Over 100,000 people lined the streets of Stoke-on-Trent to pay tribute. Sir Stan has two statues in the city – one in Hanley town centre, and an impressive three-part statue outside the bet365 Stadium, showing him dribbling the ball, which was unveiled in October 2001 by Kevin Keegan and Sir Stanley's daughter, Jean Gough. His ashes were buried beneath the centre circle.

Simon Lowe had worked with Sir Stan prior to his passing: 'I had the pleasure of getting to know Sir Stanley Matthews over the last few years of his life. We first met when I interviewed him for *The Official Video History of Stoke City FC*, commissioned by the club to produce this two-hour epic alongside renowned Potteries filmmakers Ray Johnson and Gary Kelsall. We were fortunate enough to then be asked to make his own, personal commemoration video of his life. Again, the same three of us produced and filmed a day-long interview with Sir Stan at his house in Penkhull. Les Scott of *The Sentinel* was the interviewer as he had ghostwritten Stan's best-selling autobiography with him.' Simon continued, 'As editing started on the video, we got news on 23 February 2000 that Stan had passed away. It was a real shock, although when we had done filming, we discussed how we felt he was going a bit downhill since his wife Mila had died just a few months earlier. I now think Stan wanted to get his life story down in book and video form as he knew his time was coming. At least we had been able to give his legions of fans something to remember him by.'

* * *

Three days after Sir Stan's death, the first game that Stoke encountered was a trip to the JJB Stadium to face Wigan Athletic. It was an ugly day, as Stoke took a huge following up the road to pay tribute and support the team at a critical part of the season. Trouble broke out between the two sets of supporters following a minute's silence for Matthews prior to kick-off, during which audible shouting could be heard from some Wigan fans, and Stoke fans in the home end would make themselves known. Once trouble erupted in the North Stand, a group of 100 or so Stoke fans would encroach on to the pitch to confront the home fans. The players were led off and the match was delayed for eight minutes. Blame and ill feeling has been thrown around from both sets of fans ever since, but it was an unfortunate and regrettable moment for all who witnessed it.

On the pitch, however, the game was a pivotal moment in the season for Stoke. After falling behind in the first half, Stoke talisman Graham Kavanagh brought the away side level just before half-time with a header from a James O'Connor cross. Super James would then score a dramatic 77th-minute winner after latching on to a through ball from Peter Thorne. What had started off as a grim tribute to Stoke's favourite son was to end in a much more poetic way. Stan's beloved Stoke had won, and the typical rendition of 'We love you City, we do' transformed into a teary 'We love you Stanley, we do'. This win would kick off another good run of league results for the Potters, as Thórdarson looked to mastermind promotion at his first attempt. Stoke also had a date with Rochdale, looking to make it to Wembley for the Auto Windscreens Shield Final and experience the first taste of silverware in almost a decade. Peter Thorne was in electric form in front of goal, and Stoke's Icelandic representation was growing even more. Perhaps there would be at least one more tribute to be paid to Sir Stan in the 1999/00 season.

Chapter 4

Que Será Será

'In that moment, joy. Just pure joy. It's why you play the game as a kid. That night there were a few beers in a London hotel to celebrate with our wives or girlfriends, but it was quite calm. The season was far from over, and we wanted promotion' – Peter Thorne

AS THE second half of the 1999/00 season rolled on, Stoke would add a couple more names to the growing portfolio of Icelandic players. In March 2000, attacking midfielder Arnar Gunnlaugsson joined the club on loan from Leicester City, where he had been a bit-part player in their League Cup-winning campaign but wasn't getting much Premier League pitch time. It was clear, though, that Gunnlaugsson had a bit of quality that was rare in Division Two, with an eye for a spectacular goal. The other new signing was more of an eyebrow raiser. Former Newcastle United winger Bjarni Guðjónsson joined from Belgian side Genk for a fee of £250,000. The reason that this transfer was so noteworthy was that Guðjónsson was the son of manager Guðjón Thórdarson. The manager had three sons who all played professional football – Bjarni, Þórður (or 'Thórdur') and Jóhannes ('Joey'). All three had respectable careers playing across Europe. It was at this point where most of us learnt that Icelandic surnames work differently to most Western countries – Icelanders typically take their fathers' (or less commonly their mothers') first name, followed by -son (literally meaning 'son') or -dóttir ('daughter').

Being the son of the manager meant that there was a light shone on Bjarni. He was quite short and stocky in stature, a Xherdan Shaqiri-like winger in some ways, with a full mop of brown hair and a baby face. Guðjónsson was quite a polarising figure at the time, as is often the case with some of our more creative players in recent history. A highly intelligent winger with a good cross on him, he could provide a goal from nowhere, but he could be a frustrating player too, and may just balloon the ball into touch. I personally felt he was an underrated member of the side. Arguably his greatest attribute was his attitude and hard-working nature, typical of most of our Nordic players at the time. Even under scrutiny and criticism, he didn't hide from the game, and would still stand up to take set pieces or try to put the ball into the mixer. I distinctly recall that Guðjónsson was always the first out to warm up before a match, spending ten minutes or more running squares of one half of the pitch (he must have been previously coached by Lárus Sigurðsson!). Guðjónsson and Gunnlaugsson both provided more quality to the team, slotting in alongside Gunnarsson and Hansson as regular Nordic starters in the 1999/00 run-in. By April 2000, the board, now reaping the benefits of input from experienced businessman Phil Rawlins, drew up a five-year plan to achieve Premier League football, to increase attendances to 30,000, increase youth prospects for first-team football and run the club at a profit. For squad matters, manager Thórdarson would confide in director of football John Rudge for knowledge of British football and domestic signings. Rudge had spotted a potential signing who was on trial at Preston North End after leaving Danish football. The player in question was striker Chris Iwelumo. The big Scot would join Stoke in early 2000, remaining at the club until 2004, witnessing many of the changes during the Icelandic era on and off the pitch. Big Chris spoke to me about many of his experiences at the club. Speaking about his initial signing at Stoke, Chris said, 'I was in English football on trial with Preston North End under David Moyes. My agent was Kenny Moyes, he brought me over from Denmark for a week's training at Preston. Four days into that, we played Port Vale at Vale Park and beat them 3-1. I scored a goal, and the next morning, John Rudge, who had watched the game, offered me a contract at Stoke. He liked what he saw and thought he'd get in there before Preston. I remember being sat in the car next to the Britannia Stadium on the Harvester car park. I asked my agent "what do you think?" He said that Preston were impressed with what they saw, they will offer a contract but a bird in the hand is worth two in the bush! Preston were in the Championship at the time and Stoke were in League One. I'd been at the Britannia Stadium all day with John Rudge; he offered me the contract, I went away to think about it and have some food, then came back and signed it. Preston offered a contract that evening after I'd signed.'

Iwelumo also reminisced, 'The next day I was put into a hotel, followed by training at Keele with the likes of Peter Thorne, Kyle Lightbourne and a fantastic group. I met Guðjón the afternoon that I signed. John Rudge was the main reason that I was there, and the relationship that Guðjón had with Rudge was great. Guðjón trusted John. When I came in, Thorney wasn't in the best form. Just after I signed, he scored two late goals and kicked on to unbelievable goalscoring form.' Iwelumo joined the club at an important point of the season, as Stoke were chasing down promotion and the Auto Windscreens Shield, with Peter Thorne back amongst the goals.

* * *

The first leg of the Auto Windscreens Shield Northern Area Final against Rochdale was at Spotland on 14 March 2000. Rochdale weren't exactly pulling up trees in Division Three (League Two), but there was still a feeling of apprehension … we don't often fare well against supposed 'lesser opposition' in cup competitions. Even so, the cup run had caught the imagination of Stokies, and another good following from the Potteries was well rewarded for their efforts after only four minutes, with unlikely goalscorer Mikael Hansson opening proceedings. That certainly settled any nerves and Stoke assumed control of the tie in the first half of the first leg. If Hansson was the unlikely scorer, Peter Thorne was not, scoring for fun at that stage of the season, including two goals in six first-half minutes at Rochdale. Before half an hour was played, Stoke were 3-0 up, and the tie was more or less over. Rochdale pulled one back in the second half to give themselves a glimmer of hope heading to the Brit eight days later. The second leg was played in front of the largest home crowd of the season thus far, 16,876. An 86th-minute goal from that man Peter Thorne secured a 4-1 aggregate victory for the Potters and Stoke were on their way to Wembley. The chants of 'que será será, whatever will be will be, we're going to Wembley' and 'we're the famous Stoke City and we're going to Wembley' had seldom been heard around ST4 but were ringing out on that night. To make it more appetising, fellow Division Two promotion hopefuls Bristol City had already secured their place in the final after a comfortable 5-1 aggregate win over Exeter. Bristol City were another well-supported team starved of success and cup final days out, so the tie promised to be an electric atmosphere under the twin towers of Wembley.

* * *

A cup final of any kind can often result in a distraction for league performances. However, Stoke were going from strength to strength in the league, having not lost since before the Wigan fixture in late February. Between the win against Rochdale and the final on 16 April 2000, Stoke and Bristol City would meet in the league at Ashton Gate, finishing 2-2 thanks to goals from Lightbourne and Kavanagh for Stoke, and making the final even more intriguing.

This was my first trip to Wembley, having been too young for the 1992 Autoglass Trophy Final win against Stockport, where Mark Stein was the hero for the victorious Potters. For us, it was a big family day out, although me, my mum Kath, my dad Dave and brother David used to go to away games as a family in any case. This was special though, which meant get there early, buy a jester's hat, grab a flag, painted face, red and white striped shirt and a march down Wembley Way singing 'Delilah'. There are certain things that stick in my mind from that day – seeing friends and relatives around the stadium and in our block, and I vaguely recall a charity game as prematch entertainment, in which Helen Chamberlain and Tim Lovejoy of *Soccer AM* fame were the managers of the Stoke team. The teams included the likes of TV personalities John Leslie, Angus Deayton, Ray Winstone, Chris Evans, Bradley Walsh and Ralf Little. Mick McCarthy and Mark Chamberlain also had a run-out. From memory … Bristol City won the charity match. There was, of course, a massive singalong of 'Delilah' during the build-up too. There was also another chance to formally pay tribute to Sir Stanley Matthews before the game, under much more suitable circumstances. What I mostly remember from this moment was the rendition of 'Abide with Me' before the game. It was spine-tingling, as it always is on the big occasions, but here it was extra special ... because it was for Sir Stan.

* * *

Perhaps for the first time in the Football League Trophy's history, the final garnered attention from media outlets outside of British shores, as several representatives of the Icelandic press descended upon London to cover the game. One of them was Víðir Sigurðsson, a journalist at Icelandic newspaper *Morgunblaðið*. Based on his good relations with coach Guðjón Thórdarson and the Icelandic board members, Víðir had stayed in the same hotel as the Stoke team in Watford prior to the game, following them on the team bus to the stadium. At the time, Víðir wrote, 'The stadium was crowded with about 76,000 people, which meant that almost 40,000 people came from each club. That alone is amazing, as both Stoke and Bristol City are considered "regional teams", and considerable travel would be required for supporters of both teams. The mood meant that the occasion could easily have been the FA Cup final of England itself, given the whole set and crowd.' The unique nature of Stoke City during this era was no more apparent than in this fixture looking at the two starting line-ups and substitutes. Of the 16 Bristol City players in the matchday squad, 15 were English, and the other was Scottish. Stoke's 16-man squad included six English, three Irish, three Icelandic, one Swedish, one Bermudan, one Norwegian and one Scot. Thórdarson's side lined up like this:

Gavin Ward, Mikael Hansson, Nicky Mohan, Clive Clarke, Brynjar Gunnarsson, Graham Kavanagh, James O'Connor,

Bjarni Guðjónsson, Arnar Gunnlaugsson, Peter Thorne, Kyle Lightbourne.

Substitutes: Carl Muggleton, Anders Jacobsen, Richard Dryden, Steve Melton, Chris Iwelumo.

Clive Clarke has admitted that, had that day been just a regular league game, he would have been ruled out for a hamstring injury, but was determined to play in the final. Iwelumo, who had made the bench, described the feelings of finding out the team news: 'I remember travelling down, no clue if I would be involved or not. When we got to Wembley, Guðjón put the team and the subs up on the board, and that's when I first found out I was going to be on the bench. I remember Paul Connor and Ben Petty were both in tears after being left out, and they walked out of the dressing room. That's what it meant just to be involved in the occasion. You've got your family and everyone down to watch, you just want to be involved in any way for such a game, so it was very understandable for Paul and Ben.'

Thórdarson, in a grey suit, yellow Stoke City tie and red-flower lapel, and captain Nicky Mohan led the team out on to the hallowed turf to a wall of noise and sea of flags from both sets of supporters. Wembley was sold out, 75,057 filling the stadium for one last Football League Trophy Final: 50 per cent Stoke City fans, 50 per cent Bristol City fans. The national anthem was played, the players took to the pitch, and we were ready to go.

Stoke started the brighter of the two teams. Brynjar Gunnarsson was looking particularly impressive with some confident runs and passes in a flashy pair of silver boots. After knocking at the door, Stoke took the lead on 32 minutes. Graham Kavanagh gathered a loose ball about 30 yards from goal, weaved through two Bristol City players and smashed the ball home, beating Bristol City goalkeeper Billy Mercer at the inside near post from about ten yards out. Stoke led at the break. A nervy second half saw the Robins grow into the game, with prolific striker Tony Thorpe posing a constant threat. The equaliser would eventually come in the 73rd minute. An inswinging Brian Tinnion corner from the right wasn't dealt with, leaving Paul Holland to head home with the aid of a deflection. The momentum was with Bristol City now, and the game seemed to be heading to extra time. In the 81st minute, Hansson played a diagonal ball over the top, which Guðjónsson shielded near the corner. Guðjónsson lured Bristol City defender Louis Carey into a challenge, bumbling Bjarni to the ground and gifting Stoke a soft free kick. Guðjónsson, who was clever enough to win the free kick in the first instance, then capitalised on Carey's protesting towards the referee to take the set piece quickly to Kavanagh. The Irishman pulled the cross back across the six-yard box, where you just knew Peter Thorne would be waiting to tap home like the goalscoring predator that he was. The intelligence of Guðjónsson to take the free kick while the Bristol City defenders were switched off (ensuring the ball wasn't rolling when he took it), and the alertness of Kavanagh and Thorne to exploit the situation, meant Stoke were again ahead and, this time, we weren't going to surrender the lead. A goal in front of the end where the Stokies were housed, it was pandemonium. The game finished 2-1 and Stoke City had won the Auto Windscreens Shield in Guðjón Thórdarson's first season in charge!

* * *

The celebrations were wild. There were iconic images of captain Mohan lifting that massive shield above his head atop the Wembley staircase, with England manager Kevin Keegan and chairman Gunnar Gíslason looking on. And they weren't the only ones watching over. Captured perfectly in the moment, with the sea of Stoke fans in the background, a banner of Sir Stanley Matthews was held up high as Mohan lifted the shield. Renditions of 'We're the famous Stoke City and we've won at Wembley' followed, along with several 'Delilah's and the standard 'Rocking All Over the World' and 'Simply the Best' singalongs. On the pitch, an emotional Thórdarson told Sky Sports, 'The fans are just superb, I mean come on, who could ask for more? I'm very proud of the fans, they also earned it. They stood behind us all of the time, and when we first spoke about Wembley, they were hungry for Wembley as well, so I hope they have enjoyed it.' Thórdarson would add, 'It was amazing to lead the team out to Wembley, the story was made and it was really fun to walk up these famous stairs to win the award.'

Chairman Gunnar Gíslason was equally as delighted with the outcome, telling Icelandic press outlet fótbolti.net, 'It was a lot of fun. It is not a big cup, but people are very happy with it. There is a tradition around finals in the UK. The players dress up in new clothes, men wear flowers and there is a lot of buzz about this lower league cup.' Looking back on the goal and the win, Peter Thorne told *Duck Mag*, 'Bjarni was great for me – he could whip a teasing cross in. He won a free kick, played in Kav who guided it into my path for an open goal – just up my street! I loved hanging around the back post then darting towards the ball. I'd just drift around and wait for a centre-half to switch off – then pounce. And in that moment, joy. Just pure joy. It's why you play the game as a kid.' Thorne added, 'That night there were a few beers in a London hotel to celebrate with our wives or girlfriends, but it was quite calm. The season was far from over, and we wanted promotion.'

Chris Iwelumo recounted the day's activities and post-match feelings: 'For me, it was good to be involved, get on the pitch, get my medal and lift the trophy. Amazing times! I remember the afterparty at the hotel, we had a fantastic night. Reserve players like Ashley Wooliscroft, Steven Taaffe and Dean Crowe came down with the fans in their suits and were jumping in players' rooms in the hotel that night.' The Wembley win was also a real peak in Stoke City interest for football fans in Iceland. Vidar Halldórsson commented, 'Most Icelanders watched the Auto Windscreens Shield Final on TV and supported Stoke. This was a big thing in Iceland, it felt like we had won the cup! We were very proud of the victory.' There was even a book published in Iceland after the triumph, entitled *Stoke City í máli og myndum*, meaning 'Stoke City in Case and Pictures'. The book gave a brief account of the club's history, with a detailed look at the takeover and reign of Gudjón Thórdarson … essentially like this book, only written in Icelandic!

Celebrations continued back in Stoke-on-Trent the very next day after the win. An open-top bus parade ended at the Brit, where well-known Stoke fan TJ was leading 'Delilah' in front of a full McEwan's Stand and a bouncing South Stand … we were singing in the rain. Gunnar Gíslason was there and received a great ovation. Even the Lord Mayor had turned up. The players took to the pitch in what was familiar fashion at the time … '2001: A Space Odyssey' played, followed by an alien-like voice counting down from ten, then the players entered to 'The Boys are Back in Town'. Graham Kavanagh did his best to start 'Delilah', though in the end he deferred to TJ as he didn't know the words. Not quite as impressive as Carl Dickinson's attempt would be a few years later. Icelandic journalist Víðir Sigurðsson again accompanied the team on the parade, recalling, 'In keeping with English tradition, the Stoke players drove the trophy on an open-top bus around the city the following day. The crowd that had cheered the team on during that run were absolutely incredible. I was thinking "what would happen if this club ever won a really big title?"' Gíslason and Thórdarson both addressed the fans, and the manager stressed to them that the season wasn't over. There was still one more objective to achieve … promotion. There were five league games remaining, and automatic promotion was still possible. Play-offs were probable. Could the season get even better?

Chapter 5

A Clash of Styles

'The almighty God was looking elsewhere. Even He can't put consistency into the referees. Only the FA can do that'
– Guðjón Thórdarson

IN A sea of positivity, one of the greatest impacts that the Auto Windscreens Shield win had on the club was that it brought fans back to Stoke City. Away attendances had remained high, but home crowds had dwindled over the years, particularly during the final months of the Coates and Humphreys regime. However, while the start of the season saw attendances of 10–11,000 (down to below 8,000 in some league games), post-Wembley attendances were up to 15,000-plus, helped no doubt by the feel-good factor, as well as a healthy league position and run of form. The Division Two season run-in promised to be an exciting one. There were still seven teams in with a realistic shout of automatic promotion with five games to play – Preston North End and Gillingham were in pole position for the top two places, but Stoke, along with Burnley, Wigan Athletic, Millwall and Bristol Rovers, were all in the running. Another long unbeaten run for Stoke was taking place, mostly due to Peter Thorne going into goalscoring overdrive. He hit four goals in a game against Chesterfield in early March, before scoring eight goals in five consecutive games in April (including a hat-trick against fellow promotion contenders Bristol Rovers). He would add yet another hat-trick in the penultimate game of the season, a 3-0 home win against Bury.

* * *

On the final day of the regular season, 6 May 2000, Stoke had one eye on the last automatic promotion spot, and another eye on the chasing pack looking to secure a play-off place, as we headed down to Reading. Preston had pulled away to be crowned champions, but six points separated second to seventh. Calculators out. Gillingham were in the best position to secure second place, level on 85 points with third-placed Burnley, but with a superior goal difference. Wigan and Stoke occupied fourth and fifth respectively on 82 points, with Bristol Rovers in sixth on 80 points and Millwall just outside the play-offs on 79. Rovers's goal difference was level with Stoke's, meaning a win for them and Millwall, and defeat for Stoke at Reading, would see the Potters drop out of the play-offs. Theoretically, Stoke could still finish second, but it would require a five-goal swing and all three of Gillingham, Burnley and Wigan to fail to win. A point would secure our play-off place.

The sun was shining on the Madejski Stadium, and the away end was obviously packed, resulting in the attendance swelling to Reading's second highest of the season. It was tense in that South Stand too. In the days before Twitter and Sky Sports apps, people were relying on wireless radios and Nokia 3210 phones. Reading, who had been relegated with Stoke in 1998, had nothing to play for but pride, having finished outside of the play-offs, but were in hot form at the end of the season. First half, as you might expect, Stoke were nervy, while Reading looked composed. Still, Stoke were in at the break level. Second half, news filtered through that Bristol Rovers were losing to Cardiff, easing the nerves amongst the mass of Stokies. As the game entered the last ten minutes, Stoke conceded a free kick which, after some deliberation between officials, was changed to a penalty to Reading. The penalty was converted by midfielder (and Championship Manager 2 legend) Darren Caskey. This certainly made the situation nervier, with Millwall winning against Oxford. However, as the clock ticked down at the Madejski, news was coming through from multiple sources – Bristol Rovers had lost, so a play-off place was guaranteed. It was party time in the away end!

The game ended with both sets of fans in a good mood; Reading had picked up another win in an impressive finish to the season, while Stoke were into the Division Two play-offs. Elsewhere, Gillingham surrendered second place to Burnley after losing at Wrexham. Wigan consolidated their play-off place with a draw at Bournemouth and Millwall leaped from seventh to fifth with a win against Oxford. The loss at Reading meant Stoke finished sixth and would face Peter Taylor's Gillingham. The Gills would have been smarting after missing out on automatic promotion, but they had also been a highly impressive outfit throughout the season. After a draw at the Brit back in the first league fixture in August 99, Gillingham ran out 3-0 winners in the return meeting at Priestfield in February 2000.

* * *

The defeat at Reading may have been a disappointing end to the season for Stoke, but spirits were high heading into the play-off semi-final first leg at the Brit. The Auto Windscreens Shield was fresh in our minds, Peter Thorne was in scintillating form, and the ground was set to be packed, with over 22,000 tickets sold for the clash on 13 May 2000. The prematch pomp and circumstance were set up to gee up the fans, including a booming 'Delilah'. The crowd was up for it; would the players be?

We would get our answer very quickly. Gillingham kicked off and hoofed the ball straight into touch. While fans were still taking their seats and the rendition of 'We are Stoke' was building, Kyle Lightbourne went on a mazy run that would have made Ricardo Fuller in his prime proud, dancing and jigging down the left towards the South Stand, before playing it inside to Arnar Gunnlaugsson. From the edge of the box, Gunnlaugsson produced a wonderful finish, curling it into the top-right corner past goalkeeper Vince Bartram. Gunnlaugsson was showing his quality and would be instrumental in Stoke doubling their lead on eight minutes. The original Stoke 'Arnie' carried the ball forward from his own half, before playing it to the marauding Brynjar Gunnarsson on the left of the Gills penalty area. His low cross was met by Lightbourne, who slotted home from ten yards out for his tenth goal of the season. The Brit was bouncing like we hadn't seen since its opening in 1997. After a shocking start, the Kent side would grow into the game drawing some good saves out of Gavin Ward. It wouldn't be long before Gillingham got a foothold in the tie, after some strong hold-up play from the ever-dangerous Iffy Onuora led to Ty Gooden prodding home past Ward on 18 minutes. The away side were now hunting for an equaliser and Stoke were grateful for Ward keeping the score at 2-1 going into the break.

Into the second half, and Gunnlaugsson continued to impress. His cross met the head of Peter Thorne, who beat the keeper, but somewhat surprisingly did not beat the post, as the ball bounced back out into the grateful hands of Bartram. Thorne wouldn't be denied though, as he latched on to the loose ball following a save from a James O'Connor header to prod home and restore Stoke's two-goal lead in the 67th minute. Thorne was always just in the right place at the right time to grab a goal. Gillingham kept pushing as the game passed 90 minutes. Four minutes were added on, in what would have been a massive result to take to Kent in the second leg for the Potters. As the Stoke fans whistled for full time, four minutes came and went, but the full-time whistle wasn't blown by referee Mike Dean (yes, him). Instead, the game continued past 94 minutes, and enter a name that still sends shudders down the spine of any Stoke fan that was in attendance that day – Andy Hessenthaler. The player-coach picked up the ball on the left wing, seemingly in an unthreatening position, cut inside and smashed the ball into the top right-hand corner from all of 25 yards. The game finished 3-2, meaning Stoke would take a slim lead to Priestfield in the second leg. However, the manner and importance of that second Gillingham goal meant that the win felt more like a defeat. The momentum had shifted from the team in red and white to the team in blue and black. Mike Dean's role in the outcome of the play-off semi-final is often overlooked in more modern recaps of the tie, but at the time it was a bitter blow to Stoke, and manager Thórdarson was seething.

Thórdarson confronted Dean on the pitch after the final whistle. He was holding up four fingers to the officials, clearly indicating that the game should have been finished after the allotted time. Speaking about Hessenthaler's thunderbolt, Thórdarson said, 'Obviously we were very disappointed with the goal. When the lads asked the referee on the pitch how many extra minutes he was going to play, he said three minutes, although certainly we got four minutes. When they scored the goal, I stopped the clock, and the official time was 00:49:56. So he gave them one extra minute. Under the circumstances, it's difficult to find out where he got that extra minute from.' To drill the point home, Thórdarson showed his stopwatch to the camera, still held on the time 00:49:56. Another massive blow for the Potters before the second leg came in the form of an injury to our key goalscorer. Peter Thorne picked up a knock in the first leg and was unable to recover before the trip to Priestfield. The team and management would need to regroup, regain their composure and go again at Priestfield if we were going to earn a place in the play-off final.

* * *

A trip to Priestfield is never a pleasant one, especially if you're a Stoke fan. Our record there is pretty grim, it's a long trip down to Kent and you're exposed to the elements in the roofless away end. The second leg was a night match on a barmy evening on 17 May 2000. The ground was filled to its relatively low capacity, just shy of 11,000, including a packed-in loyal Stoke following. For those who couldn't get tickets in the Potteries, a beamback was shown at the Brit, as thousands gathered to watch the game on a big screen.

Gillingham came out firing in a feisty clash in the South East. Andy Hessenthaler was once again tormenting the Stoke defence, cueing up Carl Asaba in front of goal, but the future City striker prodded wide when it seemed easier to score. Graham Kavanagh was fired up, going in hard on Hessenthaler in the middle of the pitch, as referee Rob Styles threatened to lose control of the game. That threat would soon come to fruition. After unleashing yellow cards for innocuous challenges in a game that needed a strong official, Styles would issue a second yellow card to defender Clive Clarke for angrily throwing the ball down on the spot after a throw-in decision went against him. Obviously, the Gillingham fans were up in arms at the dissent, and Styles barely gave it a second thought before producing the card. The game had now completely broken down, and a crowded scuffle in the penalty box saw a now-bloody Graham Kavanagh dragged out of the crowd by Styles, who flashed a straight red at the Irishman. The chances of Stoke getting out of Kent with a place in the play-off final had all but diminished at that point. On 55 minutes, Gillingham defender Barry Ashby headed home from a corner, and the tie was level at 3-3 on aggregate.

To Stoke's credit, the team kept on fighting, and managed to take the tie to extra time. Brynjar Gunnarsson deserves a lot of credit for his performance that night, stepping in to basically try to cover three positions as Gillingham set off on wave after wave of attack. Gillingham took an aggregate lead after 12 minutes of extra time thanks to Iffy Onuora. While the result now seemed inevitable, Stoke kept on battling, and a well-timed through ball from Nicky Mohan put striker Paul Connor through on goal. Devastatingly, Connor hit the post, and what could have been 2-1 on the night was soon 3-0 to the home team, when Paul Smith took advantage of a loose ball at the other end to put the tie to bed with two minutes remaining. Full time, the tie finished 5-3 to Gillingham. The Stoke players collapsed to the ground in exhaustion and disappointment, while Peter Taylor, the home team and fans celebrated. To make matters worse, Gillingham chairman Paul Scally was strutting around the pitch, grinning like a Cheshire cat. The Gills would go on to avenge their defeat in the previous year's final to Manchester City by beating Wigan this time round after extra time.

The ill feeling towards the officiating in both legs was felt at the time and has persisted ever since. Guðjón Thórdarson was highly emotional in the fallout of the game. After the match, Thórdarson had commented, 'The almighty God was looking elsewhere. Even He can't put consistency into the referees. Only the FA can do that.' In 2013, Chris Iwelumo said in an interview with Richard Forrester for the official website, 'At the time you couldn't believe it. It was such an important game in which he definitely got decisions wrong. I'm sure the fans are still holding a grudge against Rob Styles to this day. We managed to hold out until extra time but with nine men, it was a difficult task.' Reflecting on the dismal night, Clive Clarke said, 'I was gutted. The two yellow cards were poor decisions from the ref, but at the same time, I shouldn't have reacted the way I did. One was for challenging a decision for a throw-in that I won which clearly came off their man. The other was for sticking up for James O'Connor – I always had to look after him on the pitch. He was small but picked fights with the other team's so-called hardmen!'

In 2018, Thórdarson recalled both legs of the tie while speaking with #pottersmag contributor Dave Coxon. He recounted, 'My blood still boils when I think of that second leg! In that game we played well and handled ourselves just as I would have wanted us to, but I think the referee had another agenda and as a result we found ourselves down to nine men. Despite that setback we battled on and were so unlucky when Paul Connor hit both posts before the ball bounced out for Gillingham to clear. After Clarkey and Kav were sent off, we battled and took the game to extra time which in itself was quite an achievement, but I was livid particularly with how Kav was dismissed. He was punched and was bleeding so he retaliated and pushed the guy that punched him. Surprise surprise, only one incident was spotted. So, yes it was very hard to accept but that was just the nature of what we had to deal with.' Thórdarson also spoke about the first leg, stating, 'I also look back at the first leg when four minutes added time was announced on 90 minutes. We were leading 3-1 when in the 95th minute Andy Hessenthaler scored a screamer. A good goal but it was four and a half minutes over the 90. I asked the referee about the time, but he never explained where he got it from. What confused me was that in added time there were no stoppages and no substitutions were made. If the score would have stayed at 3-1, we would have been through to the final, but even so, I was proud of my players. They deserved so much more after putting together a terrific run of results to finish inside the top six in the first place.'

It was a heartbreaking end to the season for the Potters. The fans felt a great sense of injustice at the hands of Styles (and Dean) rather than any anger or disillusionment with the team. We were also without our main sources of goals for the crucial second leg. Thorne described the moments from the players' perspective, and even summed up the mood of the supporters after observing one of our more well-known fans. He told *Duck Mag*, 'I watched the game from the main stand and it was bloody painful. Horrendous. It just didn't seem right that we'd been on fire for all those months and then it ended like that. Just before getting on the coach to travel back up to Stoke I saw Nick Hancock: he looked distraught just before. He looked like he was about to cry. That long journey home was not nice.' The outpouring of love for the team at the final whistle, along with a chant of 'We're proud of you' showed that the fans were with this team every step along the way. We had shown that we were capable of sustaining a promotion charge for the duration of the season, we'd proven that we were capable of winning silverware, and we had an inspirational midfielder in Graham Kavanagh, a proven goalscorer in Peter Thorne and a manager who could spot a quality signing from distant lands. We would be ready to give it another go in the 2000/01 season.

Chapter 6

Daðason and the other Thórdarson

'Daðason is a born goal-getter – he instinctively knows how to find the right position. It is almost as though he smells when a chance is going to come' – Stig Nielssen

THE START of the 2000/01 season was accompanied by a feeling of optimism at the Britannia Stadium. The Icelandic era was well underway, and thus far the manager and incoming Nordic transfers had proven to be largely successful. Chairman Gunnar Gíslason laid down the gauntlet for the new season and for the future: 'We have to take it one division at a time. Our plan was to reach the Premier League in five years. That's four now, which is a tall order. We'll try to win the Second Division this season and take it from there.' A preseason tour of Iceland in mid-July saw successive draws against ÍA Akranes, KA Akureyri and Víkingur. A high-profile preseason friendly against Liverpool at the Brit attracted a crowd of 16,101 and saw Stoke victorious thanks to a goal from fresh Icelandic recruit Stefán Thórdarson. The new striker arrived from German side KFC Uerdingen 05, and had fans licking their lips as he continued to impress in preseason, as Stoke won five out of six of their domestic friendlies. The manager also brought in defender Wayne Thomas for £250,000 from Torquay, Danish midfielder Henrik Risom for £20,000 from Vejle, and experienced defender Tony Dorigo joined on a free.

Perhaps most exciting was the promised signing of Iceland international Ríkharður ('Rikki') Daðason, an imposing 28-year-old striker who had been scoring goals for fun for Norwegian outfit Viking Stavanger, netting 47 goals in 69 games. The signing caught the imagination of Stoke fans, even more so when word got around that he was dating Icelandic supermodel Asdis Maria Franklin. Stig Nielssen, sports editor of Stavanger newspaper *Rogalanas Avis*, had said of the new signing, 'Daðason is a born goal-getter – he instinctively knows how to find the right position. It is almost as though he smells when a chance is going to come.' Unfortunately, fans would have to wait until November to see the much-anticipated striker, as he was seeing out the Norwegian football season with Viking, which included a run to the Norwegian cup final. Prior to his arrival, Daðason spoke to *The Sentinel*. He said, 'I had several offers from other clubs. There was interest from a German First Division team and from another Scandinavian club as well as from Stoke. Financially, the deals were more or less the same, so my decision came down to gut feeling. Guðjón sold me on the idea Stoke City is a club going upwards, besides it is the dream of every kid in Iceland to play football in England.'

While we waited for Rikki's arrival, Thórdarson (the player, not the manager) was the one that was exciting the crowd in the early stages of the season. After an uninspiring 0-0 draw at home to Wycombe in the opening game, Stoke's form started to build, with Thórdarson netting against Reading, Peterborough, Oxford and in spectacular style against Premier League side Charlton in the League Cup. The Icelander had already netted a penalty in the first leg against the Addicks, as Stoke took a 2-1 lead to the Valley, but few have forgotten his 30-yard screamer in the second leg. Cutting in from the left but still at an acute angle, he arrowed his strike into the top-right corner, before casually strolling back to the halfway line. Even the referee seemed to congratulate him as he nonchalantly shrugged off a hug from Graham Kavanagh. Stoke would progress into the League Cup third round and a tie with Barnsley of Division One after the entertaining clash with Charlton finished 5-5 on aggregate, seeing the Potters go through on away goals.

* * *

September was a big month for Stoke in the 2000/01 season. Eight fixtures were played across league and cup competitions, including a Potteries derby in Burslem. Port Vale were relegated from Division One the prior season, and Stoke's failure to gain promotion meant that 'El Ceramico' was back after an absence of two seasons, and hostilities could be renewed. In the end, this first clash would be a relatively low-key affair, at least after a hot opening 15 minutes. Marc Bridge-Wilkinson, who had signed for the Vale on a free transfer from Derby that summer, put the Valiants ahead on 11 minutes. Fortunately, the lead only lasted four minutes before Lightbourne got on the end of a Kavanagh corner to level for Stoke. Lightbourne would hit the woodwork later in the game, as would new loan signing Marvin Robinson. There was a confrontation between Gunnarsson and Vale stalwart Tony Naylor, and Brian Horton's team would go close through Dave Brammer late on. Surprisingly, the crowd was relatively low for a Potteries derby (although still Vale's highest gate of the season); 8,948 were in attendance, including 4,500 Stoke fans. Stoke had asked for more tickets, but that request fell on deaf ears, despite Vale's financial plight at the time.

* * *

Stoke's league form had been steadily improving through the autumn, and the wins in rounds one and two of the League Cup against York and Charlton respectively had provided something of a rarity – a potential cup run (if you exclude Football League Trophy runs anyway). Next up in the cup on 1 November 2000 was the clash with Barnsley at the Brit. The exciting news for Stoke fans was that Rikki Daðason had finally arrived from Stavanger, having flown in the previous day, and was on the bench. It was another Icelander that had put Stoke in a good position in the tie, which was no longer a two-legged affair at this point of the competition. Bjarni Guðjónsson put Stoke ahead early on, and restored their lead early in the second half with a lovely 25-yard strike, after Mateo Corbo's free kick had earlier levelled for Barnsley. With five minutes remaining, Barnsley, who also had former Potters striker Mike Sheron and former Vale midfielder Robin van der Laan in their side, equalised through Lee Jones. The game seemed destined for extra time, as Guðjón rolled the dice and introduced Daðason to the Stoke faithful.

Rikki was met with a rapturous ovation, as the fans couldn't wait to see what our new signing could offer. In the 90th minute, having only been on the pitch for four minutes, Rikki headed home from right in front of goal to send the 10,000 Stokies in attendance into a frenzy. He had definitely arrived now! His timing couldn't have been better, not only for the goal, but for the team. Peter Thorne had started the season slowly (by his standards), and Stefán Thórdarson was going through a bit of a dry patch after his promising start. Backup striker Chris Iwelumo admitted that he knew that he would be in a fight to get a chance after Daðason's high-impact arrival, saying, 'Rikki scored on his debut, it absolutely killed me! Guðjón had been chasing him for six months before he joined. He was very relaxed, a big guy and spoke very good English. To get his goal on his debut, I thought "bloody hell, here he goes!" Even if me and him were on an even keel, you knew the manager would favour him after chasing him for so long, so it was an uphill battle, but competition gets the best out of you.'

The win against Barnsley set up a mouthwatering tie against Liverpool at the Britannia Stadium in round four. After his cup heroics, Daðason said, 'That was beyond my wildest expectations, it was just fantastic to get the winner. You've got nothing to lose when you go on with five minutes left and I got lucky. It was always going to be tough coming here and perhaps I've made it tougher for myself after scoring, but hopefully the fans will give me time. Liverpool will be great in the next round. I just hope the fans realise that I can't do that every game.' His words maybe seemed modest at the time, given his goalscoring reputation and his dramatic debut. However, his words would start to ring true as the season progressed. Fans would have to wait until Boxing Day for his next goal, and although he grabbed a few more as the season progressed, his return of eight goals in 18 appearances wasn't quite the impact some had maybe hoped for. The goal to game ratio was quite respectable, but his gangly frame and first touch, not to mention his lack of adaptability to the pace of the English game, meant he was soon finding himself as a regular substitute, as Peter Thorne and Andy Cooke led the attacking line.

* * *

Stefán Thórdarson and Rikki Daðason weren't the final Icelandic signings of the calendar year; 36-year-old international goalkeeper Birkir Kristinsson signed on loan from IBV as a replacement for regular choice Gavin Ward, who had suffered a back injury that would keep him out for a while. Kristinsson was another in a line of Icelanders who had a family relation to someone associated with the club, in this instance the new signing being the brother of director Magnús Kristinsson. The experienced keeper had a steady spell between the sticks, playing in 18 games that season, with the occasional howler such as against Northampton at home in the latter stage of the season. He certainly had a lot of personality and would typically shout and wave his arms towards the Boothen End to fire up the crowd prior to kick-off. Due to his family connections and own experience in banking, the consensus was that Kristinsson was also on the financial side of club dealings. Several years later, following the Icelandic banking collapse, Kristinsson would be sentenced to four years in prison for his role in the crisis, including gross breach of fiduciary duty and market manipulation.

* * *

In October 2000, the wins were coming regularly. Chris Iwelumo scored his first league goal for the club, a last-minute winner against Millwall. It was a special moment for the player and the fans, but it was one that wasn't originally meant to occur that day, as explained by the man himself: 'I wasn't even supposed to be on the bench for that game! I was up in the players' lounge after being left out, but Stefán Thórdarson went down injured during the warm-up. Stef Stefansson, the physio, came up to tell me that Thórdarson was injured and I needed to get myself down to the pitch and warmed up. It was about quarter to three and the players were coming back in, so I just warmed up at the side of the pitch. It was amazing to get my first league goal, and a big goal as well in a very tasty fixture. With the celebration, I just went absolutely mad! It just shows you how things can happen, with Stefán getting injured in the warm-up, giving me my chance off the bench. That put me more in the frame in the eyes of the management. Little things like that fell in my favour.' By late November 2000, and with the league form progressing at a steady pace, Stoke had turned their attention to two key upcoming cup ties – an FA Cup clash with non-league Nuneaton Borough, and the glamour fourth-round League Cup tie with Premier League giants Liverpool.

Chapter 7

Giant-Killings and Killing Giants

'Final whistle, Nuneaton Borough have done it! In classic FA Cup circumstances!'
– Martin Tyler

AN FA Cup first-round home tie to Conference side Nuneaton Borough on 18 November 2000 seemed like a good chance for the Potters to progress and possibly initiate another cup run, similar to the adventures of the League Cup. Our cup campaign so far in the season had led to toppling two teams from higher leagues, a glut of goals (including a banger from Stefán Thórdarson and a debut goal for Rikki Daðason) and a glamorous tie against four-time European champions Liverpool ahead. The clash with Nuneaton may have been an opportunity to progress, but it wasn't a particularly exciting tie for the fans, resulting in a crowd of only 8,437 (including over 2,000 that had journeyed up from Warwickshire).

Stoke went full strength against non-league Boro, hoping to avoid a historic cup upset akin to the 1978 defeat to lowly Blyth Spartans. The absence of No. 1 Gavin Ward meant veteran keeper Carl Muggleton was given the nod, ahead of loanee Kristinsson. The game was a dull affair, with little goalmouth action to report in the first half. However, three minutes before the break, Brynjar Gunnarsson received his second yellow card and his marching orders, meaning Stoke would have to play with ten men for the remaining 45 minutes, now hoping to avoid cup embarrassment. Nuneaton came out in the second half looking for a win, troubling Muggleton from crosses and forcing some goalmouth clearances from Mohan and Kavanagh. Stoke also went close through Thórdarson, Thorne and Clarke, but there was no way past inspired Boro keeper Chris McKenzie. The game finished 0-0, meaning a replay in front of the TV cameras.

The Sky Sports pundits, including a certain Chris Kamara, could smell an upset in the replay, on one of those typical FA Cup nights on a muddy pitch in front of a rowdy, packed-in crowd at Liberty Way. While Stoke started the better, and seemed to be in control of the game, it was the non-league side that went closest in the first half, rattling the crossbar after a 30-yard strike from Alex Sykes. Nuneaton were much improved in the second half, piling on the pressure and threatening the Stoke goal regularly. Delton Francis missed a golden opportunity for Nuneaton, fluffing his lines from two yards out. In the end, Boro would not be denied their moment, as in the 93rd minute, a low, pondering cross managed to find its way through two Stoke defenders, who watched on in what seemed like slow motion, falling to the feet of the grateful Marc McGregor. The striker placed the ball calmly past Muggleton to send the home fans wild. To make matters worse, with literally seconds remaining after the restart, Peter Thorne got his head on the end of a Henrik Risom cross, only for McKenzie to pull off a magnificent save, tipping it over the bar. Moments later, the game ended, as commentator Martin Tyler declared, 'Final whistle, Nuneaton Borough have done it!

In classic FA Cup circumstances!' Cue the pitch invasion, and there it was. Stoke were once again the victims of non-league opposition, and this time, in front of Sky Sports, meaning the highlights would be played annually for years to come.

* * *

The FA Cup exit was tough on the team. To their credit, the reaction was a 3-0 win at Swindon, mending some of the damage in the eyes of the supporters. A truly special way to put the Nuneaton debacle behind us would be to take the scalp of Liverpool in the League Cup. Stoke's big date with Gérard Houllier's Liverpool came on a Wednesday night on 29 November 2000 under the lights at the Brit. The stadium was completely sold out for the first time, making it the highest-attended game in the stadium's short history at the time. The Potters again went full strength, this time looking to score an unlikely upset rather than avoid one. Stoke had beaten Liverpool in a preseason friendly a few months earlier, though no one put much importance on that. Visitors Liverpool lined up with a mixture of regulars and fringe players, with a blend of youth and experience. It was still an expensively assembled team of household names and internationals, led by England forward Robbie Fowler, with Jamie Carragher curiously playing in midfield.

The game commenced, and it was Stoke who were presented with the first chance for a goal, falling to the one man you would want it to – Peter Thorne. Liverpool second-choice keeper Pegguy Arphexad took a heavy touch on a back pass from halfway and Thorne won the resulting 50-50 challenge. Thorne was presented with an unchallenged open goal, but somehow only managed to strike the post. From then on, it was all Liverpool, who went up the other end following Thorne's miss, with Fowler crossing for Christian Ziege to prod the Merseysiders ahead in front of the Boothen End. Vladimír Šmicer doubled the lead, latching on to a long ball forward from Markus Babbel, who also scored after more good work from Fowler. The England striker added a fourth before half-time, followed by second-half goals from Hyypiä, Murphy and two more from Fowler to complete his hat-trick. In a classic Stoke City moment, the scoreboard operators lost count and displayed a scoreline of 0-9. In the end, it was 0-8, enough to require the typewritten '(Eight)' on TV vidiprinters. Urgh; 8-0 to Liverpool. To think how different it might have been had Thorne scored that open goal ... it could have been 1-8! It was a horrible feeling. One of the few blessings about being in the lower leagues was that normally you wouldn't have to put up with glory hunters at school going on about beating Stoke. Not on this occasion though. There were plenty of Liverpool 'fans' at my school of St Thomas More in Longton, and they were all strutting their way into registration the next morning with their knock-off scarves procured from some Turkish bazaar from their last family holiday. Probably didn't help that I had previously milked the preseason friendly win as something more than it really was. It would take a while, but eventually we'd get our own back on Liverpool, hammering them 6-1 in Steven Gerrard's final game for the Reds in May 2015. I'm pretty sure a lot of the lads who were mocking me and my Stoke-supporting mates in school back in 2001 were Stoke season-ticket holders by 2015!

The cup defeats to Nuneaton and Liverpool were both grim moments in the modern history of Stoke City, remembered to this day. A 3-1 home defeat to Luton at the start of December seemed to indicate it was affecting the team at the time too. Stoke bounced back with a comprehensive 3-0 win at Bristol Rovers, thanks to a Thorne hat-trick. This was followed up by a draw at Wigan just before Christmas, a day that had been bigged up by the Latics for a 'live half-time performance from Bob the Builder!' Inevitably, it was just a bloke in a Bob the Builder suit walking around the pitch with Santa, while they played the theme tune from the kid's TV show. What a disappointment! Things on the pitch were not disappointing though. From the pre-Christmas period, Stoke would put together a run of results that would put them yet again in contention for promotion, and possibly yet another Football League Trophy.

Chapter 8
Déjà Vu

'The manager made some strange decisions for the second leg at Walsall … it wasn't something that any of us expected. The strangest thing was leaving Thorney out after he'd scored 19 goals for us that season. We were pros and did what we were asked, but it wasn't our best performance' – James O'Connor

CHRISTMAS OF 2000 saw Stoke find their form again, with Peter Thorne back amongst the goals. It was also the start of a 15-match unbeaten run up to 24 February 2001, seeing the Potters move into automatic promotion contention yet again, and progression to the Football League Trophy northern section semi-final, with the cup now rebranded as the LDV Vans Trophy. Stoke's Icelandic trio of Daðason, Gunnarsson and Guðjónsson were in goalscoring form, and Thorne and Cooke were forging a strong partnership up front. Notable wins included a 2-0 home win against fellow promotion contenders Wigan, a match refereed by Rob Styles who received torrents of abuse from as early as his prematch warm-ups, and an impressive 4-0 win away at Peterborough. The return league clash with Port Vale also took place during this period, finishing 1-1 on 17 February. After James O'Connor had given Stoke a second-half lead, Dave Brammer scored a 25-yard rocket to earn the Vale a point, in front of more than 22,000 fans at the Brit. Stoke's unbeaten run came to an end at Millmoor, as promotion-chasing Rotherham came from behind to win 2-1.

Stoke's efforts to retain the Football League Trophy led to a tasty encounter with the Vale for the third time that season. The match was scheduled to take place at Vale Park, but it was postponed, first due to frost, then waterlogging a fortnight later. Even a week later, the pitch wasn't fit for purpose, so the Football League made the unusual decision to switch the game to the Britannia Stadium. While Vale obviously went full strength, Guðjón Thórdarson decided to mix up the team by making five changes, with one eye on the run-in for promotion. The in-form Cooke, Gunnarsson and Guðjónsson were on the bench, and bit-part players Petty, Kippe, Risom and Goodfellow were given a run-out. In a drab opening hour, very little could separate the two sides. In the 64th minute, Vale took the lead through Micky Cummins, and they seemed to be heading for the victory. With three minutes left, Nicky Mohan turned home a cross from Wayne Thomas to force extra time. The competition was using the golden goal rule, meaning any goal in extra time would end the game and decide the winner. Mohan was to turn from hero to villain, handling the ball in the box to allow Marc Bridge-Wilkinson to fire past Birkir Kristinsson and send Vale through to the area final. Brian Horton immediately ran on the pitch to celebrate with his team and the 3,000 Vale fans at that end of the pitch. Despite it 'only' being the LDV Vans Trophy, in front of a modest crowd of 11,323, it was still a sickener to see the Vale players and fans celebrating on our pitch, especially after two draws in the league. I remember being so annoyed after the final whistle that I kicked the empty chair in front of me, sending a chunk of it flying down the rows. If you were sat in the Sentinel Stand in the 2000/01 season and found half your chair missing for a league game in mid-February, I can only apologise … send your hate mail to Marc Bridge-Wilkinson! Port Vale would go on to win the trophy at the Millennium Stadium in Cardiff. Stoke now turned their attention back to the league run-in.

* * *

Following the defeats to Rotherham and Vale, Stoke staggered towards the end of the season, only winning three of their next ten fixtures, losing five. On 17 April 2001, a 1-0 defeat to play-off-chasing Bournemouth thanks to 18-year-old Jermain Defoe (who had scored his first professional goal against Stoke earlier in the season) meant automatic promotion was now a distant thought, and our play-off place was in jeopardy. Fortunately, the Potters, now sporting a newly designed club badge (specifically designed to include the colours of the Icelandic flag), ended the season with three straight wins to secure a fifth-place finish, with Brynjar Gunnarsson scoring in all three games.

The penultimate game of the season was a trip to Oldham Athletic, and despite picking up a spirited 2-1 win which would be crucial for ensuring a play-off place, the day was a real ugly one, and brought out some of the worst people you're ever likely to encounter at a football match. The game formed an unwanted backdrop to the Oldham riots, a series of racially motivated crimes and outpourings of violence between gangs of white extremists and Asian communities in the Greater Manchester area. A large section of the away end was occupied by members of the BNP, National Front and other right-wing fascist organisations. It is estimated that more than 6,000 people made the journey to the town, many without tickets and with no intention of going to the game. Some of the travellers looking for trouble may have been Stoke-affiliated (we've had our fair share of unsavoury followers down the years), others may have been posing as Stoke fans. Some were forthright in why they were there, and it wasn't to support the team. Running battles were frequent before and after the game, and fighting was occurring in the away end between those who had come to incite violence and Stoke fans who wanted nothing to do with it. The not-so-subtle England chants quickly descended into more provocative 'If you all hate P**** clap your hands' chants, leading to scuffles in the stands. I was at the game with my family, and the racist chanting was like nothing I'd heard before. My dad hadn't helped by parking at least a mile away from the ground on some dodgy-looking estate (needed to be facing the right way, didn't want to pay, etc., etc.). On the pitch, late goals from Gunnarsson and Daðason gave Stoke a vital three points in their play-off bid, and we were all happy to get away from the match and move on. The final game of the regular season saw Stoke run out 4-1 winners at home to Swindon in front of 20,591, meaning it would be the Division Two play-offs yet again for Stoke City. This time, it'd be a relatively local clash with Walsall of the Black Country.

* * *

Walsall had shown their quality in the league meetings between the two sides, chalking up a comfortable 3-0 win at the Bescot Stadium back in October and holding out for a 0-0 draw at the Brit towards the end of the season. Once again, Stoke would be at home in the first leg, a Sunday afternoon kick-off on

13 May 2001. The crowd was bumper, over 21,000, and the build-up prior to kick-off included club legend Gordon Banks being unveiled as the new club president. Gavin Ward had returned to the side several weeks earlier, while the Icelandic pair of Stefán Thórdarson and Rikki Daðason were once again left on the bench in favour of the successful pairing of Peter Thorne and Andy Cooke.

Stoke were second best in the first leg, and Walsall would have considered themselves unlucky to not take a lead back down the M6 to the Bescot with them. The game ended 0-0, after Saddlers striker Don Goodman missed several chances for the visitors, and Thorne and Cooke failed to capitalise on the few chances that fell their way. Walsall almost snatched a first-leg lead late on, as Pedro Matías was sent through on goal. Minutes after coming on as a substitute, Stoke defender Ben Petty pulled Matías to the ground, taking the inevitable straight red card. The game ended goalless, with all to play for in the second leg. Manager Thórdarson was full of praise for his substitute Petty after the dismissal. After the first leg, the manager said, 'He needed to pull the lad down because it looked as though he was through on goal. It is better for me to get men sent off rather than lose the game.'

The second leg under the floodlights of the Bescot came three days later and, again, the away end was sold out. The atmosphere was positive, but team news before kick-off certainly raised eyebrows. Manager Thórdarson, who for the longest time had relentlessly stuck to 4-4-2 after altering from his original favourite of 3-5-2, changed formation to 4-5-1, leaving both Thorne and Cooke on the bench. The manager instead opted for Daðason up top with Kavanagh just behind, supporting the striker. Stoke started the game brightly. Tidy play across the pitch ended up with James O'Connor on halfway, who played a long ball up towards Daðason. The big Icelander won his aerial duel, cushioning the ball down to Kavanagh, who hit an unstoppable first-time volley from just outside the area to give Stoke the lead. It was a wonderful goal from Kav, who ran towards the Walsall fans in celebration, giving it the big shush symbol. Thórdarson's bold team line-up was looking like a masterstroke. Walsall battled for an equaliser in the first half, forcing a corner just a few minutes before the interval. The corner from Tom Bennett seemed innocuous but, catastrophically, Gavin Ward somehow let it slip through his fingers, gifting Walsall an equaliser in front of the travelling Stokies. An equaliser from such a howler just before half-time was massively deflating for both the Stoke players and fans.

Walsall looked to capitalise in the second half, and within two minutes of the restart, Stoke failed to deal with a headed defensive clearance forward. Pedro Matías waltzed in to fire home from a tight angle to make it 2-1 to the home side. Another huge confidence blow for Stoke, who already looked a defeated and beaten team. The Walsall fans were bouncing, and Ray Graydon's side smelt blood. Three minutes later, a free kick conceded by Gunnarsson on the right was whipped in by Dean Keates, and Don Goodman appeared to poke home from inside the six-yard box. As it turned out, the ball had gone straight in from the free kick, with Ward rooted to his line. The chants of 'dodgy keeper' were now ringing in his ears. Then 3-1 was soon 4-1, as Kavanagh played a troublesome pass to Wayne Thomas under pressure in his own box. Thomas failed to clear his lines and Matías intercepted the pass, deflecting the ball past Ward. With six minutes remaining, substitute Peter Thorne headed home a Kavanagh cross for a consolation, but the game was long over, and it finished 4-2 to Walsall. Again, Stoke had failed in the second leg, and watched on as the home fans poured on to the pitch to celebrate. Walsall would go on to beat Alan Pardew's Reading at the Millennium Stadium to secure promotion back to Division One. Stoke were once again left licking their wounds after consecutive play-off semi-final losses.

* * *

If the Gillingham game had felt like an injustice against a brave Potters performance, Walsall felt more like a let-down from the team and management. Promotion was expected more than imagined at the start of the season by the board, and the cup defeats to Nuneaton, Liverpool and Port Vale had angered and frustrated many during the year. Some would lay the blame at the manager's door. Looking back on the 2000/01 play-offs, James O'Connor would come to admit, 'The manager made some strange decisions for the second leg at Walsall. He put Graham Kavanagh, who I usually partnered in midfield, in behind the striker, he put me at right-back, where I hadn't played before, and he left out our striker, Peter Thorne, on the bench. It wasn't something that any of us expected. The strangest thing was leaving Thorney out after he'd scored 19 goals for us that season. We were pros and did what we were asked, but it wasn't our best performance.' Clive Clarke shared similar sentiments, saying, 'Gudjón got it totally wrong with the line-up. It was one of those nights where everything went for Walsall and in the end, we crumbled.' The decision to line up in such a way had seemed to have been working for 40 minutes or so, and you can't account for individual errors like Ward's. The second half, however, was a team capitulation, the likes of which we hadn't often seen from this side.

The failure to secure promotion at the second attempt (third if you include the pre-Icelandic Brian Little effort) was worrying to Stoke fans, some of whom saw fit to act for the good of the club. Simon Lowe, together with a group of supporters including his father Chris and actor Roger Martin, formed the supporters trust group otherwise known as 'The Friends of Stoke', with intentions to support the club, both for day-to-day running and financially. The group was set up as a safety net should the Icelanders suddenly decide to pull out, leaving Stoke in a fatal financial situation that the likes of York City and Stockport County had experienced at the time. Simon Lowe said of the group, 'It stemmed from pub conversations and grew until there were a core of people on a formal "committee" to publicise our existence and aims, which were simply to help the club as much as possible and be there in readiness for a fall.' Simon continued, 'I was invited into the boardroom to discuss my thoughts on the way things were going for the club. Mostly it was about how things were unfolding on the pitch. The board were speaking to various prominent supporters to gauge feelings at the time as they were well aware of the protests which had greeted men in their position in the not-too-distant past at Stoke. The board, including chairman Gunnar Gíslason and Magnús Kristinsson, fed me with a very nice prematch roast meal and chatted with me. I felt they were interested but a bit aloof. At this point I wasn't introduced to the English directors, so I also felt there was a significant division between them as had so often been reported by the local press.'

The growing concern was shared with members of the boardroom, both in the UK and in Iceland. Stoke fan Gary Mellor (founder and director of Beswicks Sports) and close friend Phil Rawlins were in attendance at the Bescot, with Rawlins in tears while being interviewed by BBC Radio Stoke afterwards. He, like many others, was frustrated at the prospect of another season in Division Two. Years later, Rawlins would say that the board deliberated on whether to sack the manager. It was actually members of the Icelandic consortium who had called for Thórdarson's dismissal, with Coates, Humphreys and Rawlins opting to stick with him. In the end, the board agreed to give Thórdarson one more year under close monitoring. The pressure was really on now – promotion was a must for Stoke in the 2001/02 season, as both the manager–board relationship and internal director factions were starting to show real signs of breaking. For Thórdarson and his squad, it was time for the last dance.

Chapter 9

Kavanagh, Thorne and Sam Hammam

'It's a great club with a great squad and great fans, so let's hope we can get promotion'
– Peter Thorne

JUNE AND July 2001 saw several ins and outs at the Brit. Stoke mainstays Nicky Mohan, Kyle Lightbourne, Henrik Risom, Ben Petty and Chris Short were amongst the names that were moved on. More significantly, star midfielder Graham Kavanagh left the Potters for newly promoted Cardiff City for £1m in a shock transfer that rocked the club. The Bluebirds had been taken over the previous year by Lebanese businessman Sam Hammam, who splashed the cash in a bid to move Cardiff swiftly up the English football pyramid. Prior to his move, Kavanagh had been synonymous with Stoke City. He scored the final goal at the Victoria Ground, the first goal at the Britannia Stadium, played over 200 games and had been at the club through relegation and two successive play-off defeats.

His move to Cardiff was indeed controversial. To really put the stamp on the ill feeling about the transfer, *The*

Sentinel had reported that Kav made comments after the transfer inferring that Cardiff were a bigger club with more realistic chances of promotion, and the move would help his international career to blossom (these comments were later denied by the man himself). Not only had he moved to a high-spending promotion rival, Cardiff were a team with a reputation for having somewhat 'boisterous' support. Their attendances were high, with the potential to be much higher, and their home support at Ninian Park was famed for creating a hostile atmosphere for away supporters. Their travelling fans were no angels either, having clashed violently with Stoke fans throughout the day before and after a league game in April 2000. Ironically, during the game in 2000, the referee had to bring a halt to proceedings as Cardiff fans were throwing chairs at the Stoke City corner taker ... Graham Kavanagh.

The Irishman's perceived comments, though likely misquoted, may have wrangled more with the Stoke faithful as there was plenty of evidence to back up the claims, particularly regarding Cardiff's ambition. They were clearly punting for successive promotions with their aggressive transfer strategy. Cardiff's flamboyant owner was ahead of his time in many ways, not least in his desire to be involved in all manners of the club, from free-spending money man, through joining management on the bench and even joining in with the fans celebratory 'Ayatollah' head-tapping. Everything about them at that time made them quite hateable.

There were positives to come out of the transfer from a Stoke point of view though. The money raised by selling one key player meant Guðjón Thórdarson could bring in several new players to freshen the squad up. Goalkeeper Neil Cutler was brought in, as well as Scots Dave Rowson and Peter Handyside; the latter would be made team captain. Stoke also entered the European market once again to look for quality at discount prices. Versatile Belgian midfielder Jurgen Vandeurzen was signed, and Guinean striker Souleymane Oularé joined from Spanish side Las Palmas. Thórdarson described Oularé as 'our Jimmy Floyd Hasselbaink', exclaiming, 'Second Division defences will soon find out what he's all about. His body strength is probably better than any of my players, so he will have no fears playing here in England.' Belarus international defender Sergei Shtanyuk also signed from Belgian club Royal Antwerp, an imposing mountain of a centre-half who looked like he could run through a brick wall or face off against Rocky or Hulk Hogan. Finally, Stoke made the intriguing and ambitious signing of former Dutch international Peter Hoekstra. The tall left-winger had an impressive pedigree, having played over 150 games for Dutch giants PSV and Ajax, with five caps at senior international level, including a start against England in Euro 96. Director of football John Rudge was pivotal in bringing Shtanyuk and Hoekstra to the Britannia Stadium, as Stoke widened their exploitation of the foreign market across Europe. The two signings would prove to be strokes of genius from Rudge and Thórdarson, as both players looked to be way ahead of the calibre of Division Two. Very few strikers could get the better of Shtanyuk, while Hoekstra's skill and intelligence on the ball at that level meant he was like caviar in a greasy spoon café.

* * *

Peter Hoekstra would grab his first Stoke goal in a friendly against the excellently named German outfit Wacker Burghausen. Preseason saw mixed results against Austrian and Turkish opposition during a European tour, with home friendlies against Leicester ending in a 2-1 defeat and Derby a 0-0 draw. After an opening-day defeat to QPR at Loftus Road, Stoke started to pick up wins, as Cooke and Thorne looked to have found their best form as a partnership. In unfortunate circumstances, new signing Souleymane Oularé would be ruled out for the season having only played 30 minutes of football as a substitute. After being rushed to hospital in August 2001 with chest pains, Oularé was diagnosed with a blood clot, which could have been fatal for the 29-year-old. There had been no indication of ill health after his signing and medical, as John Rudge explained, 'There are various theories being considered, one being it could have been caused by flying. Souleymane had been doing a lot of air travel and doctors think it is possible the clot may have formed in one of his legs and then moved to the lungs. He underwent a thorough medical before he signed for us and nothing showed up.'

Despite the loss of the new striker, Peter Thorne was back amongst the goals for the Potters. At 28 years old, Thorne was still in his prime, with plenty of goals left in the tank. However, on 10 September 2001, news was breaking that Cardiff were planning to swoop for our star striker. Surely not!? The Bluebirds had already swiped our midfield general of the past five years. It was unthinkable that we would sell our primary source of goals to a top-six rival when we were supposedly going all out for promotion. Thorney was guaranteed goals, which made him pretty much irreplaceable. Soon enough, our worst fears were realised. Peter Thorne signed for Cardiff City for the substantial fee of £1.75m, smashing their own transfer record that they had only just set with the signing of Kavanagh. Our two Wembley heroes were now lining up for one of our main promotion rivals. Hell, excluding the Vale, arguably our biggest rivals of the time full stop.

I remember the time very vividly. I was 13 years old, and on 12 September 2001 (the day after the New York World Trade Center terrorist attacks), I was off on holiday to Greece with my family. Of course, I was wearing my brand-new Stoke City shirt. That summer, for the first time, I had decided to go with a name and number on the back and chose my favourite player. Yep, you guessed it … THORNE 9. He officially signed for Cardiff on the day we departed to Greece. Given the circumstances (albeit, some more grave than others), it wasn't an ideal holiday! I know I wasn't the only heartbroken little Stokie at the time. While there was a lot of anger and hatred directed towards Kavanagh (rightly or wrongly, and history would suggest that Kav was shown towards the door rather than pushing it open himself), there was a feeling of sadness and pain losing Thorney, essentially under the same circumstances. My mum was so angry that she wrote a letter of complaint to the club! Unfortunately, it didn't make a difference. He was gone. Seeing him in a blue shirt just felt wrong. His words, though not as cutting as quotes attributed to Kavanagh, still hit home. 'It's really exciting. I know what Sam [Hammam]'s done before. It's a great club with a great squad and great fans, so let's hope we can get promotion. It definitely helps going to a new club when you know somebody. Obviously, I have got Kav here, and that'll help me get to know the players better.'

Reminiscing about the move, Thorne told *Duck Magazine* in October 2019 that he didn't want to leave Stoke. He said, 'Over the years, plenty of Stoke fans have asked me if I left because me and Guðjón didn't get on after I was dropped for that game [Walsall away in the play-offs 2000/01]. That's 100% not true. I loved playing for him. My agent was onto me about interest from Cardiff, but I wasn't interested. I mean that. I was happy and I was desperate for my life to stay as it was. The speculation lasted ages, but I was ignoring it.' Thorne added, 'It all came to a head when I was called to a meeting with John Rudge. It was just us two in a room. He basically told me the club had to sell me because they needed the money. I was gutted. I did everything to stay but from that moment, I had little choice; £1.7 million was a lot of cash back then. I'm not driven massively by money, being happy meant a lot to me and I was scared I would regret changing anything. Looking back now, I have to say I'm grateful for the money I made from it for my family. It was a massive wage increase and with bonuses involved, I knew it would set me up for life. I'm retired at 46 because of that move. At the time though, all I felt was pressure. We weren't ones for the high life – we've never lived in a typical footballer's big house. I just felt tense, knowing I would be expected to repay the club with constant goals.' In the interview, Thorne went on to say, 'Stoke are my number one club and always will be.' Still gets me emotional. My favourite player as a kid.

* * *

With Kavanagh and Thorne gone, there was a growing resentment between fans and board. As Simon Lowe put it, 'Here were the club's Crown Jewels being sold (in this case unforgivably to a direct rival) to raise money, just like the likes of Mark Stein, Mike Sheron and Lárus Sigurdsson had under the previous regime. Nothing had seemingly changed.' Fortunately, the money raised was used to finance Thórdarson's last probable crack at promotion, and there was a feeling of a new side as we marched on through the autumn. Stoke would further strengthen the squad with the funds acquired from Hammam's raid, bringing in Allan Smart from Hibernian, and another Icelandic acquisition from Norway – versatile defender and defensive midfielder Pétur Marteinsson from Stabæk IF. Our first game post-Thorne was against fellow promotion contenders Reading. The Royals were a side that had shared a lot of familiarities with the Potters. Relegated together in 1998, both teams staggered initially in Division Two, before mounting viable promotion bids and experiencing play-off failure. Both clubs had moved into shiny new stadiums and were regularly clearing 10,000+ attendances. Managed by Alan Pardew, the Berkshire club had a number of high-profile players for Division Two, including the prolific forwards Nicky Forster and Jamie Cureton. The 15 September 2001 meeting between the two sides still had the large shadow of the Thorne transfer hanging over it. However, one of Stoke's new recruits would help to bring the fans fully on side with Thórdarson's rebuilt squad. After some early Reading pressure, Stoke took control of the game thanks to an inspired display from Peter Hoekstra. The Dutchman had shown glimpses of his quality in his earlier performances, but this was the first time he truly took hold of a game and turned on the style. It was first-half goals from Guðjónsson and Cooke that ensured victory for the Potters, but Hoekstra was easily man of the match.

A run of four straight wins in late September to early October saw Stoke climb the table, with first league goals for Vandeurzen and Hoekstra, as well as Stefán Thórdarson back amongst the goals. Without Thorne leading the line, the goals were now being shared out across the attacking options. Our first Potteries derby clash of the season came at Vale Park on a Sunday afternoon on 21 October 2001. After a tense opening 45, Vale came out strong in the second half, and took the lead through prolific striker Stephen McPhee. With time running out, manager Thórdarson made a double substitution, bringing on midfielder and youth-team product Lewis Neal, and the big Scottish forward Chris Iwelumo. The two combined to equalise for the Potters on 78 minutes, rescuing a point and avoiding defeat to the local rivals. Big Chris discussed the moment, saying, 'I think I'm still the last player to score for Stoke against the Vale, that's scary, but shows you how different the league positions have been. One of my closest friends, Sagi Burton, was the centre-back for Vale that day. We were signed around the same time – him for Port Vale and me for Stoke. We are still very close today and I still banter him because he was marking me. I never really knew how big the rivalry was until after I scored that goal. I never ripped up trees for Stoke but the fans have always been very appreciative and held me in high regard, as I do for them, because of goals like that. Fans say my best goal for Stoke was the volley against Wigan in the FA Cup. The Port Vale goal, when you look at what it meant and who it was against, is up there as my best goal.' It was now no wins in four attempts for Thórdarson against the Burslem boys, including three 1-1 draws in league meetings.

* * *

The draw at Vale Park formed part of a ten-match unbeaten run, with eight wins catapulting Stoke up the league towards the summit. Hoekstra had found his feet, Iwelumo was scoring regularly and the team was gelling nicely, built on a solid foundation enforced by Cutler in goal and Shtanyuk and Handyside in the middle of defence. The Potters had the chance to go top on a chilly Tuesday November night at the JJB Stadium against Wigan Athletic.

Chapter 10

Hit for Six

'We have found out this week how football can treat you if you are not fully focused, and no one wants to experience anything like that again because it badly hurts your pride'
– Guðjón Thórdarson

SPIRITS WERE high in mid-November, as Stoke stretched their unbeaten run to ten games with an impressive 3-2 win against high-flying Brentford, Shtanyuk grabbing a late winner in front of almost 18,000 at the Brit. The Potters headed up the road to Wigan Athletic on 13 November 2001 knowing a win would take them top of the league. The ugly scenes that had marred this fixture after Sir Stanley Matthew's death were a distant memory for both, but it had added a bit of spice to the fixture between the two sets of supporters. On the night, there were probably as many Stoke fans there as Wigan Athletic fans, with the familiar sight of a sea of empty seats visually overpowering the 7,047 in attendance in the striking JJB Stadium. The travelling Stoke fans were loud before kick-off, chanting 'We are going up' with optimism as the game got underway. It was Paul Jewell's Wigan that struck first on the night. First Jurgen Vandeurzen was dispossessed, and then James O'Connor failed to clear, allowing Tony Dinning to hit a grass cutter that seemed to take an age to nestle in the bottom corner of the Stoke net after just four minutes. The lead wouldn't last long, as Vandeurzen and O'Connor made amends by combining to draw Stoke level, as the Irishman crossed to Vandeurzen, who headed home within two minutes of the opener. Wigan retook the lead after a high ball into the box was fumbled by Neil Cutler, leaving Andy Liddell the simplest of tasks to slot home for the Latics. Wigan got a third before the break, as Arjan de Zeeuw powered home a header from a corner.

Into the second half, new signing Allan Smart was dispossessed on the edge of the Wigan box, before a long ball upfield was held up by Liddell. He played it wide to Paul Dalglish, son of Liverpool and Scotland hero Kenny, who finished sublimely from range, meaning the game was effectively over as a contest. Just after the hour mark, Wayne Thomas toppled Lee McCulloch to gift Wigan a penalty and a fifth goal, before a solo run and finish from Jeff Kenna completed the rout late on. The Potters had conceded only six goals in their previous ten games, but the unbeaten run came crashing to an end in spectacular style. Wigan Athletic 6-1 Stoke City.

* * *

Obviously, the game was a disaster. But weirdly, it still didn't feel like a 6-1 game. Just one of those nights where everything Wigan hit went in, and everything we did went wrong. There were some poor individual performances in there; Cutler, Thomas, Rowson and Smart were particularly bad. Chris Iwelumo mentioned that manager Thórdarson almost made the entire squad run around the city when the coach returned to Stoke-on-Trent *that night*, but the manager calmed down and changed his mind en route back. There was still hope that this would be a one-off and wouldn't affect the league form too much. There was also the small matter of the FA Cup first round which was on the horizon. Stoke were once again drawn against non-league opposition at home, this time in the form of Ryman League Second Division outfit Lewes. The defeat to Nuneaton was still fresh in the memory, and a defeat to the lowest-ranked team left in the competition was unthinkable. The fixture was initially meant to be played at the Sussex side's home ground 'The Dripping Pan', but the non-leaguers opted to switch the game to the Britannia Stadium in the hope of making a bit of money out of the tie.

Thórdarson, still smarting from the heavy defeat to Wigan, was out to make sure his side would not be on the end of yet another cup upset. Prior to the meeting with Lewes, Thórdarson said, 'We have found out this week how football can treat you if you are not fully focused, and no one wants to experience anything like that again because it badly hurts your pride. We know from last year (against Nuneaton) what can happen in the FA Cup and there is no way anyone would want to go through it again.' After the Wigan game, Thórdarson held a post-mortem meeting with his players. 'It wasn't a case of looking for scapegoats,' he explained. 'It was a case of discussing exactly what went wrong and how we can stop it happening again.'

Fortunately for Stoke, there would be no cup upset this time round, as the full-strength side proved too powerful for lowly Lewes, running out 2-0 winners thanks to a first-half goal from captain Peter Handyside and a second-half goal from Brynjar Gunnarsson. Lewes manager Jimmy Quinn was still in good spirits after the game, explaining that the money from the tie would be enough to improve the facilities and the ground. Coincidentally, Wigan, who had just battered Stoke in the league, lost their FA Cup first-round tie to non-league Canvey Island. Stoke's reward for beating Lewes was a second-round tie with Third Division Halifax Town, which Stoke would win in a replay thanks to goals from Guðjónsson, Iwelumo and Gunnarsson.

* * *

The 6-1 defeat to Wigan didn't have an adverse effect on league proceedings, as Stoke bounced back with two wins and a draw in their next three fixtures, including an impressive 5-1 win at home to Wycombe Wanderers. After the game, Wycombe manager Lawrie Sanchez accused Bjarni Guðjónsson of cheating to get Paul Emblen sent off for violent conduct. Sanchez said, 'He conned the referee and won them the game. Guðjónsson stumbled as though he had been hit by Tyson.' Thórdarson would jump to the defence of his son, exclaiming, 'If it is right for a manager to have a go at a player like that after a game there is something wrong. We have that on the video and I will be sending it to the FA.' This wasn't the first time the two managers had clashed, after Thórdarson accused Wycombe of kicking and time-wasting during their opening-day draw at the Brit in the prior season. Sanchez had also been outspoken at Stoke's preference for foreign signings rather than encouraging home-grown prospects. Oddly, Sanchez wasn't the only one to be outspoken about the Icelandic investment in Stoke City at the time. Peak weirdness relating to the takeover was arguably reached in December 2001 when Icelandic punk band Ceres Fjórir released a two-minute song entitled 'Stoke er djók' – which means 'Stoke is a Joke'! The video is still available on YouTube! The song is more a criticism of the business capitalism of the takeover of Stoke City at the expense of Icelandic football, rather than any real dig at the team or fans (although Gudjón Thórdarson is in part targeted in the lyrics). Singer of the band, Hlynur Áskelsson, said of the song, 'I spoke about Stoke a lot, and I have happy memories of the song "Stoke er djók". There was no malice, I didn't like the business idea as such, and that was the trigger for the lyrics, not that I had anything against Stoke, and I wish them all the best.' The singer also admitted that he just wanted the lyrics to rhyme, hence the song title!

The Christmas run-in saw the much-anticipated home clash with Cardiff City. Peter Thorne would miss out on a Britannia return due to injury, which meant the spotlight was firmly on the chosen villain of the saga, Graham Kavanagh. Stoke fans laid into the Irish midfielder from the very moment he came out to warm up. Every touch of the ball was greeted with a chorus of boos, the shouts of 'Judas!' and chants of 'There's only one greedy bastard'. Like many similar situations, such as the Mike Sheron departure in 1997, the causes and fallout from the original transfer were likely exaggerated after a game of Chinese whispers. Still, creating a hostile atmosphere for a player, referee or manager that may have wronged us is something Stoke fans do very well (just ask Arsène Wenger), and if it helps the team, even better! On this day, a late free kick from Dean Gordon earned Cardiff a point, after Stoke had taken the lead after 76 minutes thanks to a Danny Gabbidon own goal.

Stoke would go unbeaten until late January, ended by defeat to QPR. The return clash against Cardiff at Ninian Park also ended in defeat, in part thanks to an influential performance from Graham Kavanagh, which would initiate another staggered Stoke City run-in towards the end of the season. Rikki Daðason scored in three consecutive games, albeit including two penalties. One of the penalties was a consolation goal in a miserable 3-1 defeat at Bournemouth, my first away game without my family and with a group of schoolmates that would make for regular away days in the years to come (shout out to Sean Allen, Nathan Edwards, Adam Brannigan and Mark Dobson). A high-profile FA Cup third-round clash with Premier League side Everton at home saw the visitors work hard for their 1-0 win, thanks to an Alan Stubbs goal in front of a record gate of 28,218. Stoke's season had become very stop-start in January and February. There were dominant performances, such as a 5-0 win against Cambridge and 4-0 against Bury, but also abject defeats, none more so than on 10 February at the Brit. In front of more than 23,000, Stoke went down 1-0 to Port Vale thanks to a first-half goal from Micky Cummins. Towards the end of the game, the Vale fans were in full piss-take mode, ripping up seats and serenading Stoke corner taker Guðjónsson with a chant of 'Daddy's boy'.

The manner of the defeat was a real let down for Potters fans, as once again it seemed like the Vale had raised their game for the derby clash, while the Stoke team just hadn't turned up for the occasion. The defeat brought questions from the stands about Thórdarson's ability to emphasise the importance of the Potteries derby to the squad, particularly the mass of foreign players who had probably never even heard of Port Vale before signing for Stoke. There was a feeling that Brian Horton was getting the best out of his team of British talent, albeit originating from outside of Stoke-on-Trent. Chris Iwelumo, who started on the bench despite scoring in the fixture at Vale Park, suggested some reasons for our poor record in the Potteries derby: 'I think every footballer goes into a match to win it, but I think that rivalry had that bit of an edge that the British players understood. They're in and around the area, they read the newspapers, they speak with the fans, whereas I think the Scandinavians stayed with their families, not mixing with the community. The Vale players got that extra 15 per cent because of the atmosphere around the place. The build-up to the game, every time you go out for dinner, everyone spoke about it – "Are we going to get the win?" I don't think the Scandinavian players mixed in that environment, so the build-up may have been a little bit different for them.' The defeat was a bitter pill to swallow, coming amongst a period of inconsistency for the team. A loss to promotion contenders Reading later in the month, and now three games without a goal, meant Stoke were now looking below them rather than above. Reading moved 11 points clear of Stoke, and the play-offs were starting to seem like the most realistic chance of promotion.

* * *

As form ebbed and flowed in February, Thórdarson took the opportunity to bring in a few more new faces to try and achieve automatic promotion. Finnish goalkeeper Jani Viander joined the club (though he would never actually make a first-team appearance, despite warming the bench for several months), experienced defender Mike Flynn signed from Stockport, along with Ian Brightwell from Walsall and Tony Dinning (who scored in the 6-1 win for Wigan). Finally, Thórdarson took Jamaica international striker Deon Burton on loan from Derby, and he returned to an old face to fill in for the injury-prone Peter Hoekstra. Arnar Gunnlaugsson joined on loan for a second time under Thórdarson, hoping to go one better than his last stint which saw play-off defeat to Gillingham.

Arnie would be back in the team and back amongst the goals in March, helping to improve Stoke's erratic form by turning draws into victories. Burton chipped in with a couple of goals in an away win at Colchester, but he was otherwise drawing blanks in front of goal. The last 11 games of the season saw seven wins, one draw and three losses, including a defeat at Wycombe resulting in Lawrie Sanchez standing tall, staring towards Stoke fans who had been berating him all game. It was a frustrating game at Adams Park. Stoke seemed to be comfortably heading for a draw, with fans enjoying the tribal drums that were played every time Wycombe won a corner (met with Native American 'whooping' noises from the away section). Wycombe struck in the 83rd minute, and Sanchez couldn't help but direct his shit-eating grin towards the away section. With four games remaining, a 2-0 home win against Swindon moved the Potters within touching distance of the play-offs, but a defeat at Oldham meant automatic was now out of reach. Play-offs were guaranteed after a win in the penultimate game of the season, Andy Cooke scoring the only goal against Denis Smith's Wrexham at the Brit. The season ended with a draw at Bristol City, meaning Stoke would finish fifth for the second consecutive season, and would be in the play-offs for a third in a row. If it were to be third time lucky for the Potters, they'd need to do what they had failed to do the previous two seasons and win the semi-final tie. Stoke City's opponents in the play-offs in the 2001/02 season? Cardiff City.

Chapter 11

The Legend of Oularé's Arse

'At this stage, it's very tempting to think about the play-off final – especially when you can see the Millennium Stadium from our ground!'
– Spencer Prior

IT SEEMED like destiny that we would be paired with the Bluebirds in a play-off semi-final shoot-out. It was last chance saloon for Guðjón Thórdarson, and possibly Stoke City as a club, for promotion. The board were now demanding success, meaning any failure now would guarantee the manager would be shown the door, as well as possibly a number of players who would have been on sizeable contracts for Division Two standards. The board themselves may even walk rather than face another season in the third tier. A third successive play-off defeat would also be a huge disappointment to the fans, especially against Cardiff City. For Cardiff, it was a tantalising prospect to secure promotion at the first time of asking, and by doing it knocking out Stoke on their way to the final at the Millennium Stadium in their own city. Cardiff were unbeaten since Lenny Lawrence took over as manager three months prior to the play-off clash.

Former Stoke hero turned villain Graham Kavanagh was vocal in the run-up to the tie. 'Now that it's down to a two-legged tie against my former club, it makes it all that little bit interesting. And I feel we've got a great chance of winning. I would have preferred to play them in the final, but I don't feel I have anything to prove going back to Stoke.' Kavanagh also said, 'I certainly want to go back there and turn them over and I certainly want to get Cardiff City into the First Division. That means going back to Stoke and taking all the criticism and jibes. The last time I went back, I got absolutely slaughtered by their fans – which surprised me a bit. But it just makes it that little bit sweeter if we go through.' There was no chance of misquoting his words this time; the Irishman was up for the fight.

* * *

Once again, Stoke were at home for an afternoon kick-off in the first leg, held on 28 April 2002. By now, being at home for the first leg felt like a distinct disadvantage. The onus is on the home team to dictate how the game is played – do you go out and attack, hoping to put the game to bed in the first leg? Do you keep it tight and give yourself a clear plan for the second leg? So far, Stoke had narrowly beaten Gillingham and drawn with Walsall in the previous first legs, before coming unstuck away in the return fixtures. The atmosphere was once again electric, with the constant threat of boiling over as the bad blood between the supporters had reached fever pitch. Prior to kick-off, Cardiff chairman Sam Hammam rocked up to the stadium in typical ostentatious fashion, in a stretch limousine and brandishing a Cardiff City flag. Quite predictably, his ride wouldn't leave ST4 in the same condition it arrived in, particularly his windows. Thórdarson's chosen starting XI included the on-loan Tony Dinning and young striker/attacking winger Marc Goodfellow. Peter Thorne made his return to the Brit in the colours of Cardiff, while Kavanagh also started. Just to really rile the home fans up, Kavanagh would be the last Cardiff player to emerge from the tunnel for the prematch warm-up, provoking the predictable response from the Stokies who were in their seats early.

Cardiff settled into the game much more quickly than Stoke, and they took an early lead on 12 minutes. Kavanagh, still being booed every time he touched the ball, initiated a clever one-touch passing sequence that saw the prolific Robert Earnshaw put through on goal. Earnshaw confidently slid the ball past Cutler to make it 1-0 to the visitors. Stoke came back, forcing Bluebirds keeper Neil Alexander into action either side of half-time, first from Goodfellow, then from an O'Connor effort from distance. However, it was Cardiff who would strike again, as a free kick from Kavanagh into the box was headed towards goal by Spencer Prior. Cutler could only parry to Leo Fortune-West, who prodded home from a few yards out in front of the travelling fans. It was too much for some Stoke fans, as crowd trouble broke out in the West Stand block nearest to the away fans, where a section of Stoke casuals had congregated to provoke the visiting section. The game was held up for five minutes as stewards and police tried to restore control.

Once restarted, the game looked to be getting away from Stoke, and a two-goal deficit would be a mountain to climb in the second leg. Thórdarson threw on loanee Deon Burton in a last-ditch attempt to salvage something from the first leg. In the 84th minute, the manager was rewarded, as a corner from the left wasn't cleared. After bouncing around, the ball eventually fell to Burton, who was somehow given the time to bring it down eight yards in front of goal, before powering it past Alexander with the aid of a slight deflection. While it may not have been as spectacular or as late on as Andy Hessenthaler's late strike for Gillingham back in 2000, Stoke would hope that it would be just as important going into the second leg. It was still Cardiff that would leave the much happier of the two teams though after the first leg, taking a lead back to fortress Ninian. For Stoke, it seemed like the play-offs were getting worse with every passing season.

Kavanagh was once again making sounds in the press, and the former Stoke captain was confident looking forward to the game in the Welsh capital. He said, 'I was last to come out for the warm-up, which didn't help the reception I got from the Stoke fans, but the Cardiff fans made me feel relaxed. I was expecting a hostile reception; it happened last time I played at the Britannia Stadium. There were also a few quotes in the local paper which I didn't actually make and that didn't help things. During the game I didn't have my head down in fear or worry, but it's difficult to block everything out.' Kav admitted, 'It was a bit intimidating when I went to take the corners. I was wary of somebody coming on to the pitch. But I thought we coped well with the atmosphere, showed tremendous spirit and held on for a good result. Our supporters were magnificent throughout at Stoke and it will be a massive help if they can show the same kind of spirit on Wednesday. I'm sure they will create an intimidating atmosphere – as they did in the FA Cup game against Leeds – and see us through.' Following the game, Cardiff defender Spencer Prior also said, 'At this stage, it's very tempting to think about the play-off final – especially when you can see the Millennium Stadium from our ground! But we haven't achieved anything yet. And if we don't apply ourselves properly in the second leg, Stoke will turn it around and we won't get through.'

* * *

The second leg at Cardiff took place a few days later on the evening of 1 May 2002. Cardiff had completely sold out their allocation, as 800 hardy Stoke fans made the trip to South Wales, ferried in via official coaches under police escort, in the hope of witnessing a miracle. It would turn out to be one of the most dramatic nights in Stoke City's long history.

Guðjón Thórdarson did not ring wholesale changes to the starting line-up, opting for a couple of swaps with the additions of Gunnlaugsson and Burton for Goodfellow and Cooke. Forgotten man Souleymane Oularé was on the bench after recovering from his long-term illness. The players entered to a fiery cauldron, quite literally, as fireworks went off to greet the walk out from the tunnel. The packed terraced stands of Ninian Park were a sight to behold, as the chants of 'Bluebirds' rang around the old stadium. Stoke created the first clear-cut chance of the game in the first half. A ball over the top from Clive Clarke was controlled well by James O'Connor on the left. His cross fell perfectly to Chris Iwelumo, who somehow managed to miss the target from four yards when it seemed easier to score (a feat he would duplicate for Scotland some years later at Hampden Park).

As the darkness descended across Glamorgan, Cardiff would go close to opening the scoring in the second half. Peter Thorne was typically in the right place at the right time to get his head on a high cross to direct the ball towards the far post. The ball looped over Neil Cutler's shoulder in slow motion, before the Stoke keeper was able to scramble to prevent it from crossing the line. The home fans cheered as they thought the ball had gone in, but the score remained 0-0, and 2-1 on aggregate. Thórdarson decided to act, introducing Oularé with 20 minutes to go, and later throwing on Andy Cooke. With time ticking into the 90th minute, the Cardiff tannoy announcer began to instruct the home supporters to stay off the pitch, as the players would be doing a lap of honour after the game. In the third minute of injury time Stoke were, as Nigel Johnson put it, 'going like trains towards the penalty area'. The defiant Clive Clarke led one last attack down the left. His cross into the danger area was cleared to the right side of the penalty area, falling to Bjarni Guðjónsson. The manager's son poked the ball back towards the middle, where James O'Connor, who had performed admirably for 90 minutes, somehow steered the ball through a crowd of defenders (including straight through Kavanagh's open legs), and into the back of the net. The Stoke fans at the far end of the ground could barely believe it. The delayed reaction from the away end after the collective sigh of disappointment of the home fans was an incredible sound. O'Connor led the charge to celebrate in front of the travelling contingent. Back at the Britannia Stadium, fans watching on the big screen poured on to the pitch. Stoke were still in this and had forced extra time.

Cardiff players and fans were shell-shocked, having conceded such a late equaliser when the game seemed to be heading for 0-0. Stoke on the other hand were now revitalised, taking the game to the hosts. With the game heading towards penalties, in the 115th minute, Burton enticed Prior into a shove on the on-loan Derby man, granting Stoke a free kick on the edge of the Cardiff area. O'Connor, who was playing like a man possessed, stepped up to take the free kick at the end where he had equalised some 20 minutes earlier. It was an odd moment, as O'Connor never took attacking free kicks … he wasn't at all prolific in front of goal. The Irishman hit a rather tame effort towards the wall, which clattered off someone in the box, wrong-footing Alexander in the Cardiff goal before nestling in the net. Stoke were 2-0 up, and the Cardiff players collapsed to the ground. Super James was running towards the Stoke fans again, this time with his hands on his head in disbelief. The away end was going berserk. Replays showed the true source of the deflection, and it was a moment that would go down in Stoke City folklore. It had deflected in off Souleymane Ouláre's arse! Spencer Prior's protests saw him awarded a red card from referee Mike Dean, who was back for yet another memorable Stoke City play-off moment. As the game approached the 120th minute, Cardiff would muster one more chance. Kavanagh crossed to present Leo Fortune-West a golden opportunity from two yards out, but thankfully, he headed wide. The net at the away end of the ground had led a blessed life all night. With Stoke running down the clock in the corner, the travelling fans burst into the loudest 'Delilah' of the evening, coincidentally the song made famous by legendary Welsh crooner Tom Jones, which Cardiff fans had been mock-singing earlier in the evening. As 'Delilah' finished, so did the game, and the away end (and the 7,000 at the Britannia Stadium) erupted. There was the inevitable chant of 'Kavanagh, what's the score?' as he and Thorne congratulated their former team-mates and trudged off the pitch with their heads down. Peter Thorne reflected on the play-off defeat, saying, 'At the final whistle, I tried to block everything out. Kav was the same – it was just a weird feeling. I didn't go into the dressing room singing Delilah obviously, but there was a big part of me that was quietly pleased it was Stoke.' Chris Iwelumo also reflected on that night: 'We knew we were losing quality and our main sources of goals at the start of the season. Even the players were questioning with two big players lost, "Is That Our chance gone?" But it allowed players like me more opportunities. We also brought some players in, and we delivered. That first tie in the play-offs, the fans gave Kav and Thorney a lot of stick. They chose to go for the money and the big contracts, and Cardiff were big promotion favourites as well. The fans didn't look favourably on that, that's part and parcel of football and all part of the banter, and they got it all back at Ninian Park when we knocked them out.'

Iwelumo continued, 'Cardiff basically had our number that season on three previous occasions. They were comfortable in the first leg, then Deon Burton came off the bench and got us back into the match. We were told the day before how we were going to set up. We went down there and we went at it – 4-3-3 – and it was game on. The TV cameras were there, and the tension was there. I remember Cardiff had a corner, and Leo Fortune-West was trying to bully one of the centre-backs. Wayne Thomas walked up to him and punched him right in the centre of his back! I was thinking "Thommo, what are you doing?? If the referee sees that, it's a red card!" Leo squared up to him and Thommo just stood there.' Big Chris spoke highly of the team attitude and confidence, reflecting, 'We just had it that night. We just knew we were going to get the result; we had that edge about us. Souleymane Oularé – the ball came off his backside! What a goal that was! It was such an important goal. Ten minutes before the end of extra time, some Cardiff fans racially abused Wayne Thomas as he was about to take a throw-in. Thomas was just stood there, ball under his arm, refusing to do anything until the ref removed the fan. The Cardiff fans were going mad! We were at Ninian Park for four hours after that match because of all the trouble! When we knocked Cardiff out, Kavanagh and Thorney were the first players to come over to congratulate us, obviously with tears in their eyes. For us it was the final, we knew whoever won that match would win the final.' Clive Clarke echoed the sentiment that the team were confident in getting a result. Clarke admitted that the infamous tannoy announcement actually spurred him on to initiate the Stoke comeback: 'It was a great atmosphere and we were confident we could get a result going into the game. They spent big but we felt the expectations of the crowd might get to them. As the ball came to me at the end of the game, their stadium announcer came on the mic to say something about a lap of honour. I think that gave me the energy to make that run for the first goal!'

* * *

No one could believe we had done it. Stoke had beaten Cardiff 2-0 on the night, 3-2 on aggregate, thanks to the inspirational James O'Connor and, of course, Souleymane Oularé's backside! Gary Mellor of Beswicks Sports recalls the night very fondly, particularly the roles played by two of the Stoke players that he represented. Gary reflected, 'My favourite memory of this time has to be the away win at Cardiff City, and the role Clive Clarke and James O'Connor played. The leadership and desire James showed was an unbelievable testament to his character. Clive Clarke was as good as any young left back at the time.' Stoke were heading back to Cardiff for the Division Two play-off final. After the match, and despite Stoke fans being kept behind for an eternity, Cardiff fans had gathered to try to attack the leaving away fans and coaches. Even that couldn't dampen spirits. Angela Smith (KnotFM and Stoke City Fans Council) said, 'No one cared that we had no windows in the coach post-match! Long live Souleymane Oularé!'

Those not in attendance at Cardiff or the Britannia beam-back gathered around radios to ride the emotional rollercoaster, including Simon Lowe: 'I chose to spend one of the greatest nights in the club's recent history at that point at home, making a new bed which I'd just had delivered, listening to the commentary on the radio. I was in London, so I couldn't get Radio Stoke, and was listening to Radio 5, who were focusing on the much more interesting Championship play-off semi-final between Norwich City and Wolverhampton Wanderers. Right at the end of that game, with Norwich ahead on aggregate by just one goal and Wolves pounding them, the commentator switched to Cardiff, breathlessly segueing across by saying, "news of a goal at Ninian Park". Although there had been intermittent updates from the Stoke game, there had seemed little prospect of us scoring the two goals we needed to turn the tie around. I stopped making the bed and listened in anticipation, hairs on the back of my neck bristling, something was afoot. The commentator from Ninian Park was screaming something about a goal. For Stoke. We were level on aggregate somehow! Extra time would be played. I had no idea who scored until much later. Nor about the legendary "keep off the pitch" announcement that the Cardiff tannoy announcer made just before the goal went in.' Simon continued, 'On tenterhooks during extra time, I listened intently as the bed took second place to willing on the team remotely. As the Norwich game finished with them going through within 90 minutes commentary now switched to our game. Suddenly bedlam seemed to be let loose over the airways. O'Connor's strike had gone in. We were ahead! 3-2 on aggregate. I was so busy jumping around I didn't hear the detail that it had deflected in off Souleymane Oularé's backside! I had a beer, or two, to celebrate. I didn't finish making the bed until nearly midnight. I still have it. It's now known as the "Ninian Park bed".' What. A. Night.

* * *

Oularé was the unlikeliest of heroes for the Potters, having sat out the season after his life-threatening condition. Stoke's Icelandic physio Stefan Stefansson later commented on the moment, saying, 'I would never have believed back then he would make such a quick recovery and be back playing and scoring. But I am absolutely delighted for him after everything he's been through. There was a big, big smile on his face after the game. He hardly speaks any English, but he doesn't need to to know how important that goal was for us.'

Years later, Oularé recalled his time at Stoke for a newspaper in Belgium. He said, 'At Stoke I had medical problems that were life threatening. I could play in the play-offs, when Stoke competed for promotion to Division One. After five minutes of play, I headed in the winning goal. That was very nice. I forgot immediately all my misery.' Yes, he really said 'headed'! The Guinean would not make another appearance for Stoke and was released in 2003. However, his name, and his arse, have gone down in Stoke City legend.

Chapter 12

A Broken Curse

'These curses are there to be broken. It might have been playing on the Brentford minds as well because they had to maintain the record. But it didn't concern us' – Peter Handyside

IN SOME ways, the miracle of Ninian Park had felt like winning a final in itself. But there was still one more obstacle in the way of promotion for Stoke – Brentford at the Millennium Stadium. The Londoners had beaten Huddersfield on their way to the final, and they had only missed out on automatic promotion by one point from Reading. After the semi-final win, Thórdarson reflected, 'Cardiff were the team I wanted to avoid in the play-offs, so to beat them having lost at home is an outstanding achievement. After twice missing out on the play-off final, this is a sweet moment and the victory will make us stronger for Brentford next week.'

Stoke would not only have to contend with a dangerous Brentford side, but also would have to battle with the supernatural in the Welsh capital. The Millennium Stadium, which was hosting major English cup and play-off finals while Wembley was undergoing renovation, was producing a strange statistical anomaly for the eventual winners of each of the last 11 encounters over a three-year period. All 11 teams (plus another three in rugby) that had used the south-side facilities had lost their respective finals, leading to the christening of 'the South Stand dressing-room curse'. Chelsea, Manchester United, Arsenal and Tottenham Hotspur all fell foul of the curse. Although the jinx was just superstition, it didn't stop people from pulling out all the stops to exorcise the South Stand demons. In March 2002, prior to the LDV Vans Trophy Final, Nottingham-based feng shui expert Dr Paul Darby endeavoured to lift the hoodoo with a ceremony in the dressing room using Buddhist chanting, scattered incense and sea salt, blessings, bells and candles. He even went as far as leading a horse through the grounds to expel the 'negative energy'. In their FA Cup Final, Chelsea aimed to counter the curse by wearing their 'lucky' white socks. It was all to no avail, as north end-hosted Cambridge United went on to lift the LDV Vans Trophy and Arsenal took the FA Cup back to North London. It just goes to show – you can lead a horse to the Millennium Stadium, but you can't make it lift the curse.

Would Stoke rise above such daft gimmicks? Nah. Stoke would instigate their own feng shui experiment, under the supervision of 63-year-old Welsh multimillionaire artist Andrew Vicari. He was commissioned to paint a seven-feet-high red and yellow phoenix and sun design on the wall of the cursed dressing room, with the aim to improve the flow of energy in the area and exorcise the 'bad spirits'. Guðjón Thórdarson may have been praying to the Nordic Gods to break the jinx, but he was playing it cool in the run-up to the Brentford game. He remarked, 'Some of the players might be worried but I'm going to turn it into our favour, so we take our players down there and change the spirit inside the dressing room.'

* * *

The sun was shining on South Wales on 11 May 2002. Once again, an army of 30,000+ Stoke fans were making their way to a final under Guðjón Thórdarson, and the win at Cardiff had given everyone renewed positivity that this side could finally get the job done and seal promotion. There may have been a few concerns about a mass descending of Stoke fans on the Welsh capital, as once again the prior clash between Stoke and Cardiff had been marred by crowd trouble. It's intriguing to think how the day would have fared had we ended up playing Cardiff in the final rather than the semis. However, on this day, there was no apparent trouble to be witnessed, as Stoke fans swarmed the pubs and bars in the city prior to kick-off. I remember seeing plenty of old schoolmates walking through the streets before the game. The same ones that were supposed Liverpool, Man Utd and Chelsea fans … the very ones that had taken the piss after the 8-0 Liverpool defeat. They had suddenly dug out some old Broxap and Ansells-sponsored Stoke shirts for the occasion! While Stoke had sold their allocation, Brentford had not, bringing just over 11,000 fans from West London. Stoke's request for more tickets had seen a few more given up, but not as many as the club would have liked. I remember being sat in the lower tier, somewhere near one of the corners. The stadium is remarkable, but the view wasn't particularly great, especially with a lot of people standing throughout the match.

Thórdarson would go with the side that had started at Ninian Park ten days prior, captained by Peter Handyside:

Neil Cutler, Clive Clarke, Peter Handyside, Sergei Shtanyuk, Wayne Thomas, Bjarni Guðjónsson, James O'Connor, Tony

Dinning, Arnar Gunnlaugsson, Chris Iwelumo, Deon Burton. Substitutes: Jani Viander, Ian Brightwell, Jurgen Vandeurzen, Andy Cooke, Souleymane Oularé.

Brentford's line-up included the Icelandic international Ívar Ingimarsson, prolific goalscorer Lloyd Owusu and the midfield general Steve Sidwell, who would go on to play for Stoke under Mark Hughes in 2014. The prematch atmosphere was pretty much all Stoke, taking up three quarters of the 42,523 in attendance. While Brentford were given their moment to sing 'Hey Jude' (a rather typical and dreary chant for several sets of fans across the country), 'Delilah' was once again spine-tingling, as it always is on the big occasions. The game was live on the ill-fated ITV Digital, meaning finding decent highlights of the day are pretty much impossible, even now at time of writing!

The players entered to a chorus of cheers and fireworks in Cardiff. As the game got underway, Stoke settled quicker than the Bees, with Arnar Gunnlaugsson and Bjarni Guðjónsson pulling the strings in midfield and Deon Burton threatening up front. After 16 minutes, Stoke took the lead thanks to Burton, tapping home after Chris Iwelumo flicked on from Gunnlaugsson's corner. The goal put the Potters firmly in the ascendency, and Steve Coppell's side offered very little in reply. On 44 minutes, Guðjónsson's free kick was deflected into his own net by Brentford forward Ben Burgess, giving Stoke a two-goal cushion going into half-time. Neil Cutler was forced into action in the second half to thwart Lloyd Owusu and Mark McCammon but Stoke ran out comfortable 2-0 winners in the play-off final. Finally, *finally*, Stoke were promoted and back in Division One. Guðjón and his side had done it and made us proud. It was party time in Cardiff! Chants of 'Are you watching Kavanagh?' rang around the Millennium

Stadium, as a banner was unveiled in the upper tier which posed the same question.

As the players and staff lifted the play-off trophy and took a lap of honour, the celebrations commenced. Two more banners came out and ended up with the parading players – a pre-made official-looking 'What South Stand Jinx?' Nationwide Football League banner, and the more poetic, home-made 'Dressing Room Jinx My Arse'. Stoke had broken the curse! Thórdarson would say, 'I just looked forward to breaking the curse and was very pleased to get the South dressing-room. During the warm-up before the game, I was in there on my own, and I just spoke to the Almighty in the dressing-room. I think he must have listened!' Triumphant captain Peter Handyside also spoke of the jinx: 'It was discussed, but these curses are there to be broken. It might have been playing on the Brentford minds as well because they had to maintain the record. But it didn't concern us.' Reflecting on the day, Chris Iwelumo said, 'We made it to the final and we were all excited about that. I knew I was in with a very good chance of starting. We had just beaten Cardiff with an offensive formation, and Guðjón didn't often tinker with a winning side. So, if I stayed fit, I was playing at the Millennium Stadium in front of all those fans. Cardiff was the big one. We'd beaten Brentford in the league that season too, I scored a goal in the game at the Britannia.' On the game, Iwelumo commented, 'It was game over by half-time! Deon Burton was just alive in and around the box. The importance of a player like him coming in was big. He'd been there and done it. It didn't faze him playing in these occasions. In the game after half-time, I rocked my ankle and came off for Andy Cooke. Before the game, Cookie was raging, he was so annoyed not to be starting, the competition was big in the group. To go down and put the whole dressing room hoodoo to bed, and to get the result at the Millennium, was the highlight of my time at Stoke. I have been promoted five times in my career, and that's definitely right up there. A fantastic result and an occasion that all the players enjoyed and deserved.' Clive Clarke believes that, had Stoke kept Kavanagh and Thorne, they would have bypassed the play-offs altogether. He reflected, 'Gudjón was excellent that season, and the Icelandic players found their feet in terms of lasting a full English season. Some of the signings were very good, particularly Shtanyuk, Handyside and Hoekstra. Always thought that if you added Kav and Thorney in that team, we would have won the league, not just the play-offs.'

* * *

For many fans, the Brentford game was a great day, but not such a feeling of euphoria compared to what it could have been. Yes, it was a massive victory, celebrated passionately and it was a highly enjoyable day out, but coming after *that* win at Cardiff, there was a feeling of inevitability about it. You ask many a Stoke fan who was there that day, and they'll say, 'I knew we would win.' And they mean it too! To get past Cardiff at that time and in that way was huge for the football club, and James O'Connor should take so much credit for his performance. Deon Burton also deserves plenty of plaudits. He didn't make much impact during the regular season, but his goal in the first leg of the semi-final, winning the free kick in the second leg, and a goal in the final … these were invaluable contributions. The much-maligned Bjarni Guðjónsson, taunted as 'Daddy's boy' during the Potteries derby a few months prior, was superb in the semi-final second leg and in the final. Brynjar Gunnarsson had an excellent season in central midfield, Neil Cutler was dependable between the sticks, Peter Handyside and Sergei Shtanyuk were a formidable centre-half partnership, Wayne Thomas and Clive Clarke had made the full-back positions their own and Peter Hoekstra had shown some pure quality in an injury-ravaged season. Up front, Andy Cooke and Chris Iwelumo did an admirable job supplying the goals that Peter Thorne had often been required to produce single-handedly. Out of the ashes of the Kavanagh and Thorne transfers grew a team. John Rudge deserves a lot of credit too for his role in the incoming transfers, but there was one gentleman who had come through the bad moments to inspire the team to promotion – Guðjón Thórdarson.

Chapter 13

Goodbye Guðjón

'We have players here on short contracts who need decisions and I need a decision as well. They asked for results and I have delivered. Now they have to deliver a proper contract'
– Guðjón Thórdarson

THE CONFETTI had not even settled on the Millennium Stadium pitch following the play-off triumph before attentions turned to the new season, particularly for manager Guðjón Thórdarson, whose contract was up in a matter of days. His relationship with some members of the Icelandic consortium had soured over the past 15 months, which nearly saw him dismissed the previous summer. By the summer of 2002, Guðjón and chairman Gunnar Gíslason were no longer on speaking terms. Following the play-off final win, Thórdarson came out with fighting words directed towards his fellow countrymen. 'They can't sit in Iceland and wait to make decisions,' said Thórdarson. 'We have players here on short contracts who need decisions and I need a decision as well. They asked for results and I have delivered. Now they have to deliver a proper contract.' After the play-off win, Gíslason simply said, 'We need to look at who's the best man to manage the club.'

Many expected a new contract to be delivered, with personal relationships put aside in favour of the best intentions for the football club. As Thórdarson had stated, he was expected to deliver promotion, and he did. However, less than a week after steering the Potters to play-off victory, and 24 hours after the victory parade, Guðjón Thórdarson was sacked as Stoke City manager. It was quite a surprise, or as an Icelander may say, *Það er rúsínan í pylsuendanum* (which translates to 'That's a raisin at the end of the hot dog!'). The man who had brought the idea of buying the club to the Icelandic consortium was now axed by the very same men – the business Vikings had struck. The relationship had become 'untenable' according to the chairman. The official statement read, 'Whilst the board recognises the contribution of Guðjón Thórdarson in helping the club to promotion, it is felt that the long-term interests of the club will be best served by the appointment of a new manager. The manager has not always appreciated the financial constraints within which he has had to work, and it is felt by the board that this situation is unlikely to improve especially given the uncertainty regarding future income from television rights. We would like to place on record our thanks to Guðjón for initially bringing the Icelandic investors together and for his contribution to Stoke City FC overall. We wish him well in the future.'

Despite their initial support of Thórdarson, favouring him over the manager at the time Gary Megson, it seemed that the roles were now reversed in the boardroom. Phil Rawlins has since expressed that he had voted to keep the Icelander, confirming that Peter Coates also supported him. As quoted in Rawlins's biography *Defying Expectations*, Coates said,

'Although I wouldn't have appointed Thórdarson in the first place, he got better as he went on and had more experience with the English game. I actually got on with him quite well, in fact better than the Icelanders did. He used to moan and groan about them, but it was nothing I hadn't heard before from other managers. I was certainly surprised when they sacked him, and it was very curious timing.'

In his 2018 #pottersmag interview, Thórdarson admitted that he knew that his dismissal was coming, even after the Brentford win: 'I had a difficult time with the chairman from my very first day in Stoke, so it was nothing new. It goes back to the beginning but the strange thing for me was that with the Icelanders coming in, I thought that they would support me, I was wrong! Any support I had came from Peter Coates and Keith Humphreys. Yes, I had more support from them than my own people.' Thórdarson also said, 'Even when we won the game at the Millennium Stadium, I knew what was coming. I met the chairman after the game, and I saw his face. He didn't even enjoy the win, and that was sad because I knew what my destiny was, but we'd gained promotion and I thought we had a good team. A team that I knew could get promoted again if I could add two or three good players. For me, it was an unfinished job, but the decision had already been made.'

Chris Iwelumo spoke highly of his former boss: 'I had a feeling that all wasn't right that evening with Guðjón. I don't know what had happened, but I think that he knew that he was done and moving on. I don't know if there was a fallout, but the way that he held himself – he was proud of what he'd achieved but he kept himself to himself that evening. You could see that he was with his own thoughts.' Speaking of Thórdarson's dismissal, Iwelumo said, 'I was gutted, as were most of the squad, that he was let go. I always wonder what would have happened if we had kept Guðjón. He had gotten the best out of a great group, he had man-managed, motivated … he ticked all the boxes. I was at home when Guðjón was sacked. He called up all the players and explained the situation. I have had some experiences with Guðjón since then. He actually wanted me to be his assistant manager four years ago for a job in United Arab Emirates. Me and Guðjón had a very good, healthy relationship. He was very harsh when he needed to be. I think he knew the potential that I had, and whenever I was slacking, he made sure he came down hard on me. I thought he was a great manager. He gave me my chance to go and play football. He was exactly what I needed at that time. I can remember his team talks now, he was just a great character, he tried to simplify football and he wanted us to just go out there and enjoy how we played.'

Iwelumo continued, 'I remember once, Peter Hoekstra tried to throw his boot at Guðjón when he was taken off at half-time! We were getting beaten, so Guðjón took Peter off. Peter was swearing in Dutch and in English, and then he took his boot off and threw it at Guðjón during his team talk! He then stormed into the shower, still swearing. We won the game in the end, and Hoekstra would start the next game! Another time, when we were in Austria, he caught me, Clive Clarke, Wayne Thomas and Dean Crowe in a room at two o'clock in the morning playing poker. He made us run 25 400-metre laps at six o'clock in the morning and the same again at ten o'clock at night on the same day as punishment, with two double training sessions in between! After we got beat 6-1 at Wigan, we got on the bus and he said "when we get back, you're not going home. Go in, get some training kit on, and we're going running around the town. People are going to see you do this!" About six of the boys said, "you're not making me run". After Guðjón calmed down, he just told us to go home. He kept us on side. If he had made us run the city, he may have just lost the group. He could be harsh when he wanted to be! But he had that winning mentality.' Clive Clarke was also disappointed and surprised to see Thórdarson dismissed. He said, 'Gudjón came in and did well, but in his second season he was under pressure and it told, and he took it out on the team. I had my moments with Gudjón, but as time went on, the better we understood each other and got on really well. His sacking was crazy, and I felt for him. The board hadn't a clue about football at that level. Gudjón was fiery, as everyone knew he had crossed them, but to be sacked after selling two of your best players yet winning promotion was silly in my opinion. He was building something then and he should have been given his chance in the Championship.'

The impact of the sacking was also felt back in Iceland. Vidar Halldórsson said of the decision, 'This was a big let-down. When he left, the interest faded away for the general public. We lost faith in the project as a nation. Thórdarson was still a strong figure in the Icelandic football scene, so we were actually offended when he was sacked! We didn't support the businessmen – we supported the charisma and character of Gudjón Thórdarson. We have fond memories of Thórdarson's success at Stoke, especially the key moments winning the Auto Windscreens Shield and promotion.' The decision to part company with Thórdarson led some members of the Icelandic consortium to pull out, taking their financial backing with them at a time when the ITV Digital collapse was affecting clubs financially up and down the country.

The verdict was also met with much contempt from many Stoke fans. Some of the anger manifested as protests outside the Brit, with calls for the man to be reinstated. Fan Pat Bailey, one of the campaign's leaders, had said, 'We've seen three play-offs, two trophies, he has got us to the First Division, what more qualifications do you need? This man has fought for Stoke City Football Club and the fans, now let us get behind him and fight for him!' It was reported at the time that Guðjón himself had attended one such protest, brandishing a megaphone and calling the board 'fucking twats!' Nonetheless, Thórdarson's three-year spell at Stoke was over. The ill feeling between Guðjón and the board would last throughout the remaining years of the Icelandic era. John Acres, former sports reporter and commentator for BBC Radio Stoke (now working for the Radio Stoke breakfast show, as well as reporting for 5Live and Final Score), said, 'I invited Gudjón to be a guest summariser when the Icelanders were celebrating five years of ownership. The whole board came over from Iceland for a pitch presentation. They were absolutely fuming that Gudjón was in the ground and on the radio. They weren't happy, they thought it was disrespectful after the fallout. I didn't really know about the history between them, I thought it would be a good idea! It didn't go down well.' The Guðjón Thórdarson sacking was the first real moment of outward and outright resentment from Stoke supporters towards the Icelandic directors on a visible scale, the start of a downturn in the relationship between board and fans.

* * *

Looking back on Guðjón Thórdarson's time at the club, it is mostly seen as a positive period, underlined by the 2000 Auto Windscreens Shield and 2002 play-off victories. He was instrumental in bringing in some high-quality players from across the Continent, and he masterminded some memorable moments on the pitch. He was also popular, as well as entertaining, in the dressing room. Peter Thorne told *Duck Magazine*, 'Guðjón Thórdarson was a total nutter! In a good way, I mean! I loved him! He is the most passionate manager

I've ever played for. When he lost his temper, he went berserk. I remember at half-time of one match, when we were playing crap, he just randomly removed his watch from his wrist and launched it at full speed against the wall. It shattered into a thousand pieces. We were all in shock, completely silent. But on the flip side, he could have a right laugh. He would hug you and big you up. Those managers who can be tough but supportive as well are rare in my experience. He could be like your dad when he needed to be and like your best mate. If you worked hard for him, he loved you. In terms of man management, he reminds me of a modern-day top coach like Jurgen Klopp. Managers with smiles on their faces, but always getting the best out of their teams.' Potters fan Glenn Airey recounted the several occasions back in 2000 when Guðjón would show up at Siggi Gíslason's rented home in Trent Vale (next door to Glenn), where he would 'enter into noisy barking contests with Siggy's big German Shepherd on the front lawn!' I'm sure there is a potentially highly entertaining book on Guðjón's career in football; hopefully the man himself will write up his story one day.

* * *

Despite his popularity with fans and players, it was a mixed bag of a period for the Potters under Guðjón. For all the Brentford and Bristol City triumphs, there were the Gillingham and Walsall defeats. For the Peter Hoekstras and Sergei Shtanyuks that impressed, there were Rikki Daðasons and Jani Vianders that didn't make it. For the 5-0 home wins and occasional cup wins against the likes of Charlton, there were the heavy defeats to Wigan and Liverpool and the loss to Nuneaton. He was brought in to bring promotion; he did … but at the third time of asking. For every argument for or against him, there is a counter-argument, and a lot of 'what ifs'. What if we hadn't been screwed over by bad refereeing against Gillingham? What if Gavin Ward hadn't dropped that cross into his own net at Walsall? What if the referee didn't award the foul that led to the winner against Cardiff? I guess all we can do is look at what Guðjón *did* do for the football club, which was bring back the pride, the passion and, eventually, a respectable league status. He delivered silverware; how many Stoke managers can say the same? He also gave us one of the most unique and beloved cast of players to ever wear the red and white. In some ways, it was a prequel to Mark Hughes's 'Stokealona' team of Bojan, Affelay, Arnautovic, Shaqiri, etc., even if it was at a much lower level. Perhaps his lasting impression has been the relationship he forged with Stoke fans which still exists to this day. During his time at the club, he was a charming, very likeable man, a gentleman. There wasn't a Stoke fan who didn't want him to succeed, and not one that didn't wish him well. Tony Pulis would remark several years later at a 'Meet the Manager' evening that Thórdarson was one of the nicest men he'd met in football. This book wouldn't exist without Guðjón Thórdarson, so thank you for that! But mostly, thank you (*þakka þér*) for the good times that you brought to Stoke City.

Chapter 14

A New Hope

'I am very loyal to my players and very loyal to my club. I think it is important'
– Steve Cotterill

STOKE'S FIRST task back in Division One was to appoint a new manager amidst a financial slump after the collapse of ITV Digital. The most recent reported accounts up to May 2001 had posted club losses of £1.7m and debts of £13.4m, with £4.55m owed to the investors. Chairman Gunnar Gíslason described the predicament as 'not sustainable in the long run', a 'harsh reality' and 'a grave situation'. It was therefore likely that the managerial appointment would not be particularly high profile and would have to work under a strict budget. Several names had been floated about in the wake of Thórdarson's departure, including former Leicester manager Peter Taylor, ex-Stoke players Steve Bould and Adrian Heath, and former Port Vale manager and the Stoke director of football at the time, John Rudge. It was apparent that the board was looking for a British manager, perhaps suggesting a stronger role being played by Coates, Humphreys and

Rawlins and a waning of interest from some in the Icelandic consortium. Had the aims of utilising the club for profit and the development of Icelandic football failed already?

On 27 May 2002, Stoke opted for the Cheltenham Town manager Steve Cotterill as Thórdarson's replacement. The relatively inexperienced manager was a surprising but bold choice for the job (not dissimilar to the appointment of Chic Bates in 1997, or even Nathan Jones in January 2019). Cotterill had guided Cheltenham to Division Two, having joined the club in 1997 when they were a lowly Southern Football League Premier Division outfit. The 37-year-old Cotterill was Rawlins's choice for the hot seat, having followed his career from those early days at Cheltenham, where the young manager was christened 'the Messiah of Whaddon Road' by fans. Cotterill had been touted for several high-profile jobs at the time, including the Wimbledon job. Rawlins was an admirer of Cotterill's man management, his style of play and his hunger to prove himself. Gíslason also cited Cotterill's ambition as one of the driving factors behind the appointment. Gíslason commented, 'He is ambitious and wants to progress even further. That mirrors the philosophy of this club because we are ambitious, and we want to progress further too.' Chief executive Jonathan Fuller added that the former Cheltenham man was 'one of the most highly rated and sought-after young managers in the country', confirming that Cotterill's credentials stood out in a pool of several top-class candidates. Cotterill would say at the time, 'It's a big move for me and one I'm looking forward to. I spoke to Wimbledon last Thursday before I spoke to Stoke, but the minute I knew the Stoke job had come up I knew that was the job I wanted. The ground is nothing short of magnificent and the supporters here are fantastic.' The appointment was generally greeted with positivity from Stoke fans. Cotterill was a fresh-faced British manager with a big upside in how he had progressed through the footballing system, with a lot of personal drive.

The decision wasn't unanimously well received by all players though, as told by Chris Iwelumo: 'I remember Neil Cutler sent me a message when I was on holiday telling me about Steve Cotterill. I wasn't a big fan of Cotterill at all. Steve was manager at Cheltenham when I went there on loan. I scored against Mansfield in my first game and got injured, a six-week injury, but he made me travel to Cheltenham from Stoke every day to get treatment.' Iwelumo also said, 'When he became Stoke manager, my whole world nearly fell apart! He brought me in a week before training started and told me what I'd achieved the previous season was great. I was top goalscorer the season before. He said this was a clean slate, but he was very harsh. He tried to block me out from plans whenever he could, even when it wasn't justified. It was crazy times.' Big Chris stated, 'I thought Steve was a great coach, excellent on the grass. As a person, I thought he was very insecure and paranoid. We were sat having a chat in the dressing room, and he came over saying, "what are you talking about guys?", when we weren't even discussing him. He was very hard on me. I came to one of the preseason games, Birmingham at home, about 15 minutes before we were supposed to arrive. I was signing autographs for fans, I walked to the dressing room ten minutes before the meeting time and the door was locked. He then hammered me in front of all the lads. They started the meeting early; I wasn't even late! That was just the start of it.'

* * *

Chris Iwelumo's fears seemed to be ringing true immediately, as Cotterill's first notable action was to sign a striker. The new manager brought in the promising 24-year-old Chris Greenacre from Mansfield Town on a free transfer. The former Manchester City man had been prolific in Division Three, bagging 44 goals in 111 appearances for the Stags, drawing attention from the likes of Nottingham Forest and Sheffield Wednesday. Cotterill was delighted to get his man, boasting, 'Without doubt Chris was one of the most promising young strikers in the lower divisions and is a player very much on the up. He is an excellent signing and is the player we wanted.' Greenacre was also pleased with the transfer to the Potteries: 'I am delighted to sign for Stoke and can't wait for the new season.' He added, 'The set-up here and the stadium is impressive and Steve Cotterill's appointment in May was a big factor in my decision. I feel I can improve my game further and the manager has an excellent reputation as a coach and has a first-class coaching back-up team with him here.'

The move made a lot of sense. Not only was he a highly sought, young, prolific striker, available on a free, but Cotterill was tasked with rebuilding the squad following the departure of several short-term contracted players and those seeking regular first-team football. This included the inevitable departures of previously high-profile signings that had found themselves on the fringes of the first team, particularly in forward positions. Questions were raised about the future of the Icelanders at the club following Thórdarson's sacking, and whether Cotterill would work with them or try to move them on. Cotterill insisted, 'I don't care where players come from. If they are good players, then as far as I'm concerned, they are going to be Stoke City players. I certainly don't have any issues over whether players are the previous manager's or my players. There is no issue there. The priority is simply to find out if they are a good set of First Division players. We've got to take stock and see which ones can survive and possibly better themselves in the First. My message to the players will be if they work really hard, they won't have anyone who will look after them better than I will. I am very loyal to my players and very loyal to my club. I think it is important. They have got to be passionate, committed and dedicated.'

After his much-anticipated arrival, striker Rikki Daðason never really lived up to the expectation (or his impactful debut) and departed back to Norway in July to Lillestrøm. Though it never happened for him at Stoke, there was no ill feeling held against the big Icelander from fans or players, who appreciated his efforts but recognised the step up was too big for him. The English footballing culture was also very different to what he was used to in Scandinavia. Clive Clarke remarked, 'Rikki Daðason was funny – he couldn't believe we didn't have a winter break and was gutted he couldn't go skiing! We gathered that's where he got his bad knees from!' Fellow Icelandic forward Stefán Thórdarson also left, after contracting a serious virus which would leave him partially paralysed and keep him out of the game for 12 months. He made a full recovery and returned to Icelandic football in 2003, signing for ÍA Akranes. Loan signing Arnar Gunnlaugsson returned to his parent club Leicester. Elsewhere, Souleymane Oularé departed (after only two substitute appearances, his work here was done!), long-term keeper Gavin Ward left on a free to, of all places, Walsall, and right-back Mikael Hansson retired at the age of 34.

* * *

After a rather unimpressive preseason (the highlight of which was a Chris Greenacre hat-trick against Newcastle Town), Stoke kicked off their return to Division One on 10 August 2002 at Hillsborough against Sheffield Wednesday. It was a nervy walk down the hill to the old ground from the car in our red and white stripes, the colours of Wednesday's city rivals Sheffield United. Wednesday fans were amassed outside the pubs on this sunny day in Yorkshire, and they stared daggers through us as we schlepped past towards the ground. Stoke, sporting a new dazzling all-white away kit, would be backed by 5,000 supporters in the sold-out away end, as the fans were eager to be back in the second tier and to get behind the new manager. Due to the lack of available transfer funds, the team was close to the same side that had played a significant role in the 2001/02 promotion campaign. Greenacre would miss the opening game due to injury. There were starts for youth-team products Kris Commons and Karl Henry, with Brian Wilson appearing as a substitute. In the game, Sheffield Wednesday created several chances, drawing saves from Neil Cutler. For Stoke, Commons impressed with his pace and skill, as well as a couple of audacious efforts at goal – one from his own half, and one which rattled the crossbar. The game finished 0-0, a clean sheet and a solid point on the road for the newly promoted Potters.

Defeat at home to promotion-fancied Leicester City followed, before Stoke picked up their first three points of the season at home to Bradford City. The win came on 17 August 2002, with Andy Cooke and Pétur Marteinsson giving Stoke victory. Cooke's opener on four minutes was a bizarre one, after Bradford keeper Gary Walsh dawdled on the ball, allowing the childhood Stoke fan to charge him down, slotting into the empty net. After 31 minutes, a Commons free kick was flicked on by Gunnarsson, and fellow Icelander Marteinsson scored his first goal for the club from six yards out. The Bantams would grab a consolation to provide late pressure, but Stoke held on. The next four games were a struggle for Cotterill's men, only picking up one point from the 12 on offer. Striker Tommy Mooney arrived on loan from Birmingham but was sent off on his debut in a defeat to Burnley at Turf Moor. A late 4-3 defeat to Preston North End was particularly tough to take, having battled from 3-1 down to equalise in the 92nd minute, before Richard Cresswell scored six minutes into injury time to turn joy into despair for the Potters. Clive Clarke had assumed penalty duties, converting two at Deepdale, before Cooke levelled after Ricardo Fuller had put Preston 3-1 up. Cotterill had shown some clairvoyant tendencies before the game, as he was out on the pitch seemingly measuring the penalty area yardage by foot, but it was all to no avail. Form would improve from mid-September, as Stoke picked up two crucial 2-1 wins, first away at Brighton and then at home to Ipswich, thanks to late winners from Cooke. Stoke then produced three draws as autumn set in, and after a precarious start, things were starting to look steady under Cotterill. It was time to kick on and keep picking up points in the crucial run-up to the Christmas period. And then …

Chapter 15

Cotterill Quits

'That's probably the mistake I made – not leaving after two days. If you were to print that letter out to the Stoke City fans, they may well forgive me for leaving' – Steve Cotterill

MANY STOKE fans were in for a shock upon the morning of Thursday, 10 October 2002. If, like me and my brother, you started your day catching up on the latest football news on *Good Morning Sports Fans* on Sky Sports News, you may have choked a little on your cornflakes. News was breaking that Steve Cotterill had quit as Stoke City manager. What?! It would later break that Cotterill had walked to join up with Howard Wilkinson as his number two at Sunderland. *What?!*

With his departing words, Cotterill said, 'I just want the supporters to know it's one of those opportunities I just couldn't turn down and I hope they understand. The supporters at Stoke were absolutely magnificent for me and I haven't got a single bad word to say about them. But I have to go because another opportunity has come along which is just too big to turn down. At the end of the day, it's something I've just got to do.' He added, 'I've left Stoke with mixed emotions after just a short space of time but that has been eclipsed by getting the chance to join Sunderland. I would like to feel I have left Stoke after having guided them through a transitional period. I leave them level with Wolves and above clubs such as Crystal Palace, Millwall and Preston. I have also saved money on the playing side by showing the door to players, while my only signing, Chris Greenacre, will show how good a player he is by Christmas as long as he isn't rushed back from injury.' Gíslason, who appointed first-team coach Dave Kevan as caretaker manager after director of football John Rudge had refused the role, said, 'We are confident the club is in good hands while the search for the next manager goes ahead. We have already received a number of applications and we are looking at these immediately. We aim to resolve this issue as quickly as possible but we will avoid any panic or knee-jerk reaction.'

The fans were furious. To leave one club and join another as a manager is one thing, but to quit Stoke City to become assistant manager at Sunderland? That was unforgivable. Even Supporters Club spokesman Malcolm Clarke, often diplomatic in times of high emotions, would say, 'I'm outraged by Steve Cotterill going after a dozen games or so. I don't know how people in football can expect loyalty from players when managers walk away in this way. I'm gobsmacked. I think he's been an excellent manager for Stoke but I think it's outrageous that he hasn't shown loyalty.' The feeling was shared across the fan base. Cotterill was aptly dubbed 'Judas' and 'Quitterill' by the fans after his sudden walkout. There had to be more to the story than what was presented to us at the time. With hindsight, Cotterill's decision could perhaps be empathised with a little more now than back then. Boardroom disputes were rumbling on, and the new manager hadn't been backed financially at the start of the season. I asked Chris Iwelumo about his reaction to the news. He told me, 'I was dancing around my house! I used to stay behind in training with Dave Kevan to work on things, Dave was excellent. About four weeks in, Cotterill started watching, not saying anything. A couple of weeks after that, he started instructing, saying, "I want you to work on this, I want you to work on that." Another couple of weeks later, he was then taking the sessions! Then I got my first start against Palace, got my goal, then the day after, he left! I'd finally broken him, he got me back involved in the team, then he leaves!'

* * *

Beswicks Sports' Gary Mellor believes that Steve Cotterill resigned due to a fallout with the Icelanders, and that he walked out in anger, a decision that Cotterill would later regret. Looking back on the decision, the man himself thought that he made a mistake not walking out after *two days*. Cotterill would reflect, 'It's funny because when I went to Stoke – and I took a bit of grief for it, leaving after five months, and rightly so – but probably what I should have done is left after two days when I got a letter off the chairman explaining to me what he thought I should and shouldn't be doing. That's probably the mistake I made – not leaving after two days. If you were to print that letter out to the Stoke City fans, they may well forgive me for leaving. "You can't pick and choose who you sign, whether they are Icelandic or whether they're English", telling me there were some of the players there who you'd like to sign and put on new contracts were asking for too much money and they'd never even asked for a contract.'

Whether his decision to quit was driven by the disruption and lack of support from the board, or whether it was driven by a desire to join Sunderland under Howard Wilkinson, one thing was for certain. He left Stoke in deep excrement. Stoke were sitting relatively pretty in 15th place, but there was still a lot of football to be played in the season, with a tough run of fixtures coming up.

* * *

Dave Kevan took charge of the upcoming fixtures, as the Stoke board looked for a replacement for Cotterill. Since he had only been in the job for five months, a lot of the same names cropped up that had been linked to the position back in the summer – Peter Taylor, Adrian Heath, Denis Smith, as well as names such as Sammy McIlroy, Lee Sandford, Bryan Robson, Nicky Laws, Chris Turner, Steve Parkin and the popular former manager Lou Macari. There was even a link to Thórdarson … not Guðjón (although some fans were calling for his return), but compatriot Teitur, who was managing Norwegian club SK Brann. While the search for a new manager went on, the task awaiting the new man was to get more and more difficult, as Dave Kevan's brief stint in charge resulted in a slide down the table. First was a televised 2-0 home defeat to Midlands rivals Wolves, where the only positive was the return of summer signing Chris Greenacre to the bench following an injury-hit start to his Stoke career, followed by defeat to Sheffield United, a 4-0 thumping at Rotherham and a 2-1 home loss to Watford.

Despite a run of four straight defeats, and no wins in six, there was a shred of optimism from fans, as former Ipswich manager George Burley looked set to take over as manager. The Scot was a popular option for supporters. Burley had won the 2001 Manager of the Year award, after guiding the Tractor Boys to Premier League and UEFA Cup football, before leaving the club by mutual agreement after relegation to Division One. Burley was in attendance for the night match against Watford at the Brit, something that caretaker Kevan had let slip in his post-match interview. Kevan said, 'The players were made aware beforehand that someone was there. Hopefully they would have given the new manager a good impression and he has seen something that he can build on. I think that it was probably a help that the new manager was there. I am not sure if the details are finalised yet, but the players did know someone was in the stands.' Burley himself commented on the situation, insisting, 'I want to get back straight away because I've been involved in the game since the age of 15. Stoke spoke to me the day after I left Ipswich, but then I went away for a break. Now I am hungry to get back in again and don't want to be sitting around for six months waiting for another job to come along.' He added, 'Nothing is definite about me joining at the moment, there are still a few loose ends to tie up.'

The next day, on Halloween 2002, Stoke fans were in for a fright. George Burley had a change of heart and turned down the job. He cited that, 'The club wanted someone long term and I wasn't able to commit to that.' Worryingly, his decision came after speaking directly with chairman Gíslason, who was under the impression that negotiations had been successful. The Icelander said, 'We were given every indication that he would be willing to sign a contract, all terms and conditions had been covered, there was no area of dispute and he was keen to attend our home game against Watford on Wednesday evening. However, he informed us this morning that he would not be accepting the offer of the job.' Gíslason concluded, 'We recognise the fact that it is for the good of the club that an appointment is made as soon as is practically possible. As ever we remain determined to ensure that the appointment is the right one. As soon as we are in a position to make a definite announcement, we will do so.'

With Kevan unable to inspire the team to victory (or even a draw), and Burley pulling out, the task to find a new manager went from desperate to supercritical. By now, relationships in the boardroom had broken down completely, with the Icelanders closing ranks, cutting communications with the English board members and distancing themselves from making the big decisions. It fell to Peter Coates to step up and make the brave call for who should take the hot seat for the good of Stoke City. Once again, Coates had initially gone into bat for former Gillingham and Bristol City manager Tony Pulis. However, Coates knew that any suggestions coming from himself would not be looked upon favourably by the Icelanders, who were wary of the former chairman reassuming levels of control over football proceedings. Once Burley had said no, and with the support of chief executive Jonathan Fuller, Coates was able to resuggest his choice to the decision-makers. Coates said, 'I managed to get Tony onto the shortlist, but the Icelanders wanted Burley. I didn't think he was right for us at that time. He looked worn out and in need of a rest after the Ipswich job. Burley then turned them down and they didn't know what to do. Fortunately, I had some help. The chief executive at the time was Jonathan Fuller and he said to them exactly what I had said, although he didn't know it. I then told the board, "You can't leave things like this. You have to do something soon or we're going to get relegated. You like Tony – why don't you give him the job?" With me and Jonathan pulling for him, it made up their minds.'

So, the decision was made – on 1 November 2002, Tony Pulis was appointed as the new Stoke City boss.

Chapter 16

'You Don't Know What You're Doing'

'This is what I call a proper football club … Stoke City are capable of pulling in crowds of more than 20,000 and being competitive with the likes of the West Broms … it's a fantastic job. I am proud to be the new manager. I will work my socks off and I expect everyone around me to do the same, otherwise they will have to move on' – Tony Pulis

THE 1 November 2002 appointment of Tony Pulis wasn't exactly met with a great ovation from Stoke supporters. The fans had been conditioned to expect George Burley, so when he said no, the chances of finding a manager of similar calibre were slim. Perhaps the only affordable appointment that could have appeased supporters would have been crowd favourite Lou Macari or club legend Denis Smith. Forty-four-year-old Tony Pulis wasn't exactly a household name. Those who searched for the scoop on the Welshman from the online message boards and fanzines of his former clubs were not met with glowing reviews either. Following his time at Gillingham, Pulis was enveloped in an ongoing legal battle with Gills chairman Paul Scally, with some ugly allegations of gross misconduct, blackmail and misappropriated funds. In 2011, Scally would dub Pulis 'the most evil and despicable person I have ever worked with' … not the kind of reference you would want from your former employer. Pulis had also fallen out with Milan Mandarić at Portsmouth, a dispute that was only formally settled two days before he joined Stoke. Bristol City fans really disliked the man too, this time citing the style of football he promotes in his teams (on top of being a former Bristol Rovers player). The verdict was typically that Pulis was a 'dinosaur', favouring a dour, defensive, long-ball style of football. The main positive that Tony Pulis had on his CV was that he had never been relegated as a manager.

Despite fighting the tide of possible relegation, fan backlash, a lack of transfer funds and a squabbling boardroom, Pulis put on a positive show in his first press conference as manager. Pulis said, 'I can't tell you how delighted I am to be working at Stoke. I don't have a problem whatsoever with what happened yesterday [referring to the Burley U-turn]. It doesn't matter to me whether I am second, third, fourth or tenth choice. What matters is I want to come here, and this is what I call a proper football club. Others might say it's a difficult job and not a good career move, but I don't look at it like that at all. It's got a fantastic supporter base and tremendous potential. I liken it to West Bromwich Albion in that respect and what they have done has to be a long-term aim. Stoke City are capable of pulling in crowds of more than 20,000 and being competitive with the likes of the West Broms. But staying in this division is clearly the short-term aim and all I can ask for is time and everyone's support because it won't be easy at all. It is a very, very difficult job, I know, and the board have told me there is no money, but it's a job which can be done if everyone pulls in the right direction. It's a fantastic job. I am proud to be the new manager. I will work my socks off and I expect everyone around me to do the same, otherwise they will have to move on.'

Pulis clearly knew what he needed to say to win fans over and was also keen to bring key players onside. He talked up the importance of Sergei Shtanyuk, and much like his predecessor, stated that everyone would be given a chance to prove themselves, but was also concerned about the squad mentality. At a packed-out 'Meet the Manager' evening, Pulis told 300 supporters that he would fight tooth and nail to secure some funds from the board to strengthen the squad. He told fans, 'I'm desperate to get money off them. There are two or three young players I would love to bring in. It's vital Gunnar will hopefully back us. There's not enough there to keep us up. We need to bring a certain type of player into the football club to improve us. I want 11 winners. I do want people who can play, but they have got to be winners who don't cheat themselves, the football club, or the fans. There isn't a bad lad in our dressing room but, if anything, they are too nice, and we need one or two leaders to come in and lead from the front.'

* * *

Pulis's first job was to stop the rot, and preferably find an elusive win to get Stoke moving back up the table. Caretaker manager Dave Kevan's stint in charge had led to four straight defeats, meaning the pressure was on the new boss to deliver and do so quickly. His first chance to put points on the board came at fellow strugglers Walsall. The fans came out for this one, hoping there would be a new manager bounce to cheer for. In the end, there wouldn't be much to cheer for at all on a wet day in the Black Country. After a quiet first 45 minutes, the second half sprung into life five minutes in. Jorge Leitão opened the scoring for the home side after a mistake from Shtanyuk, before the Portuguese man claimed a second goal five minutes later. After 66 minutes, the game seemed dead and buried when Júnior made it 3-0 to the Saddlers … yet another second-half implosion from the Potters at the Bescot. With the game more or less over as a contest, Pulis decided to switch it up. On came Chris Greenacre and Andy Cooke, off went Chris Iwelumo and Bjarni Guðjónsson. The decision to take off two attacking options, particularly Guðjónsson, who would likely be the only player capable of creating chances for the forwards, wasn't popular with the fans. In fact, it was greeted with loud chants of 'You don't know what you're doing!' from the away end. Most managers get a honeymoon period when joining a new club. Others are given the benefit of the doubt until they can make their mark on the team. Tony Pulis was given 70 minutes before Stoke fans were audibly on his back!

Pulis would be somewhat justified, as Greenacre and Cooke dragged the game back to 3-2, before Wayne Thomas conceded a clumsy penalty and the home side ran out 4-2 winners (again). A disappointing start to life under the capped one. Pulis's first home game saw defeat to Grimsby, followed by a 3-0 loss at one of Pulis's former clubs, table-topping Portsmouth. Yet another defeat at home, this time to Millwall in late November, meant that Stoke had lost eight consecutive league games since Cotterill walked out; four under Kevan and now four under Pulis. Finally, on 30 November 2002, the Welshman would pick up his first point for the Potters, a 1-1 draw at former club Gillingham thanks to a free kick from Clive Clarke. The game saw a debut for Pulis's first signing for the club, goalkeeper Mark Crossley, on loan. The experienced keeper would only play the one game for the Potters during this particular loan spell (his mistake leading to the Gillingham goal), returning to parent club Middlesbrough soon after. He was replaced by another loan keeper, Steve Banks from Bolton.

* * *

Though Stoke would pick up a couple more draws in the Christmas period, including a hard-fought 1-1 draw at home to Portsmouth thanks to Brynjar Gunnarsson, form remained poor, predominantly due to an inability to keep clean sheets. In fact, Stoke hadn't kept a league clean sheet since the opening day of the season. In lieu of actual funds to make any permanent deals, Pulis once again made use of the loan market, bringing in left-back Marcus Hall from Coventry, as he slowly started to get a tune out of his inherited team. Another 1-1 draw came at Wimbledon, thanks to a last-gasp equaliser from Chris Iwelumo. It was an odd game at Selhurst Park for myself and my mate Sean in the away end, as the 'original' Wimbledon, under the club leadership of Pete Winkelman, were stepping up plans for their highly controversial move to Milton Keynes. This led to mass demonstrations at Wimbledon (eventually leading to the formation of AFC Wimbledon), and a crowd of only 1,697 fans for our pre-Christmas game in London (half of which were travelling Stokies). In some ways, it was a precursor to the 'behind closed doors' games that are taking place in 2020 amidst Covid-19. On the pitch, rescuing a late point provided some ray of light, but the win drought continued. A 4-2 Boxing Day defeat to Bradford City meant it was now 17 games without a win for the Potters, and 25 games without a clean sheet. Two days later, Stoke, firmly placed in the bottom three, hosted Sheffield Wednesday at home – the team bottom of the league but level on points with Stoke. It was a must-win game for Stoke's survival hopes, and for Pulis, who was now treading water with the fans.

The importance of the game, the festive period and a big away following made for a good atmosphere amongst the 16,042 in attendance at the Brit. Stoke started positive, with Peter Hoekstra and Chris Iwelumo taking the attack to the Owls. Guðjónsson was also posing a threat, and it was his cross and Gunnarsson's knock-down that led to the opening goal for Iwelumo on 16 minutes. Wednesday soon hit back through Dutchman Gerald Sibon. Into the second half and Stoke retook the lead after some skilful wing play from Hoekstra, crossing for Chris Greenacre to help the ball on for Iwelumo's and Stoke's second of the game. Sheffield Wednesday came back again, equalising through Adam Proudlock. As the game passed into injury time, it seemed that Stoke would lose further ground in the fight for survival but, this time, they would not be denied. In the fourth minute of injury time, with seconds remaining, Gunnarsson burst through the middle of the field and rifled home from 16 yards. Stoke won 3-2, Pulis's first victory as manager and Stoke's first league win in 17 matches.

The relief could be felt all around, not least from the manager. After the game, Pulis said, 'Hopefully the win will prove to be a weight off everyone's shoulders now and signal a better run. We've created lots of chances in every game since I came here and the players have given me everything. I still think we need a couple of new faces to help out and I'll keep plugging away in that direction.' The Welshman's words were initially ringing true, as Stoke picked up three more points in their next game, a 2-1 New Year's Day win at home to Preston thanks to Gunnarsson and Hoekstra. This was followed by a 0-0 draw at promotion-chasing Leicester City. The draw at the Walkers Stadium was Stoke's first clean sheet since the opening day, helped in part by new loan signing Frazer Richardson.

On 1 February 2003, the Potters showed their fighting spirit, battling from 2-0 down at Norwich to draw 2-2, on a day remembered by many Stokies for a snowball fight with the home fans, as well as a spectacular late equaliser. Gunnarsson, enjoying a prolific goalscoring season, pulled one back for Stoke midway through the second half, before former Port Vale striker Lee Mills, yet another loan signing, brought down a long ball from fellow Coventry City loanee Marcus Hall 20 yards from goal. Mills turned two Norwich defenders, and smashed the ball into the top corner with only two minutes left to play. The trip to Norwich was the final away game before the introduction of the controversial 'True Supporters Cards' scheme, brought in by the club to stop hooliganism at away games. Though the cards were cheap and simple enough to get (if you weren't a known hooligan at least), it rubbed many supporters the wrong way, and a great number of fans initially refused to sign up. It also meant that casual fans or friends of fans couldn't suddenly decide to attend an away game on a whim. I remember one time arriving at the official coaches for an away trip to Reading with my mates. About 15 minutes before leaving, I realised I'd forgotten my ID card! There was no way I would be able to get to the top end of Fenton and back to make the coach departure on time. I trudged off to the club shop to ask the staff to call me a taxi. While I was explaining the situation to the staff, a man tapped me on the shoulder and said he'd drive me home to pick up the card, then bring me back to the coach. I said, 'There is no way we can make it there and back in time', and he assured me, 'I'll ask the coach to wait for 15 minutes.' Turns out it was TJ, aka Anton Booth, the man who is well known amongst Stoke fans and is widely considered to be the instigator of Stoke fans singing 'Delilah' back in 1987! He darted me back to Fenpark estate, I grabbed my card and we returned to the Brit where all but one of the coaches had left. TJ had asked my coach to wait behind ... I hadn't realised he had that kind of stroke! I got on the coach and my mates all cheered at the back as the other waiting fans eyeballed me on my way past. I'm not sure what TJ was doing in the club shop on an away matchday – I guess he wasn't going to the game – but it was fortunate timing for me! All that for a 0-0 at Reading ...

The ID card scheme would eventually be scrapped in 2008 and it could be argued that it was successful in ridding the club of an undesirable part of the fan base. It would certainly have a pronounced effect on away attendances for several years for the Potters. The first game under the new scheme was an uninspired 2-0 defeat against fellow relegation strugglers Grimsby Town, and would put Stoke back into the bottom three, as inconsistency and a failure to keep clean sheets was costing Stoke valuable points.

Chapter 17

Hit for Six (Again)

'You could criticise our players or praise theirs, and Forest were outstanding today. They showed they are a class above us … they look a division better than us' – Tony Pulis

FEBRUARY 2003 started with some bizarre off-field news in the Potteries. Rumours were circulating that the Icelandic consortium were preparing a takeover bid for arch-rivals Port Vale, which could include the Valiants upping sticks and moving into a groundshare at the Britannia Stadium. Though an individual or group is not permitted to own shares in two clubs, the Burslem club's dire financial situation may have allowed for a loophole to be exploited. The intent would have been to buy the club, sell off Vale Park, and then sell the club on once the assets had been drained or even amalgamate the club into Stoke City. Around the time of the story, and while the Vale were up for sale, Stoke chairman Gunnar Gíslason had said, 'The financial merits of having only one football ground in Stoke-on-Trent are overwhelming and it makes perfect financial sense for any new owners of Port Vale to sell

Vale Park to a property developer and negotiate a ground-share agreement with Stoke City. People are forgetting that Port Vale is in administration and football is in crisis. Administration is being used in football not to pay creditors, which is bad business and ethically wrong. Ground-sharing makes financial sense and soon football will have to face reality.' Vale fans considered the idea crass and a calculated plan to merge the clubs, forcing them to take action to counter any forthcoming offer from the Icelanders. Thankfully for the people of Stoke-on-Trent, the takeover never happened, and Port Vale went on to many happy years under the steady leadership of Valiant 2001 …

* * *

On the pitch, Stoke were looking forward to a break from the stresses of the relegation battle by welcoming Premier League big boys Chelsea to the Brit in the FA Cup fifth round. Stoke had previously seen off Wigan and Bournemouth in rounds three and four respectively (both 3-0 victories), giving Stoke their furthest progression in the FA Cup since 1987. In front of a packed stadium, Stoke battled hard against Claudio Ranieri's star-studded line-up, which included John Terry, Frank Lampard, Emmanuel Petit and Jimmy Floyd Hasselbaink. There was also a start for Icelander Eiður Guðjohnsen, and future Stoke favourite Robert Huth made an appearance from the bench. Second-half goals from Hasselbaink and substitute Jesper Grønkjær gave Chelsea a 2-0 win, with Pulis reflecting, 'Chelsea punished us like the very good side they are.'

Next up in the league for the Potters was a trip down the A50 to face Nottingham Forest on 22 February 2003. While Stoke were looking to secure vital points to claw their way out of the bottom three, Forest were chasing promotion and were about to bring in Darren Huckerby on loan to bolster their goalscoring threat. On this day, they wouldn't need him. Marlon Harewood's scuffed shot on 13 minutes somehow beat the hapless Steve Banks in the Stoke goal to give Forest an early lead. Eleven minutes later, Harewood got his second of the game, a much crisper finish this time, volleying home following neat interplay with David Johnson. The big striker completed his hat-trick before half-time, side-footing home after some delightful wing play (if you're a Forest fan at least) from the dangerous Andrew Reid; 3-0 became 4-0 before half-time, and it was Harewood again, this time from the penalty spot after the referee punished Pétur Marteinsson for handball. The Icelander received a red card for the incident, adding to Stoke's ongoing suspension issues, as key players Sergei Shtanyuk and Brynjar Gunnarsson were already suspended. Johnson and Reid combined in the second half to make it five, before Eoin Jess completed the rout for the home team. Stoke didn't even muster a shot on target.

Much like the Wigan game back in November 2001, a combination of an inspired home performance with an abject display from the Potters led to a grim day on the road. Manager Pulis made no excuses but fell short of throwing his players under the bus in public. He praised Forest, saying, 'You could criticise our players or praise theirs, and Forest were outstanding today. They showed they are a class above us, and when you think they have got Huckerby to come in, they look a division better than us.' The 6-1 defeat at Wigan ultimately drew a reaction from Stoke, bouncing back to recover their form and march on to promotion. Pulis was hoping for a similar reaction in the fight for survival, but games were running out, and Stoke were now rooted to the bottom of the table.

* * *

Stoke's immediate reaction to the 6-0 defeat at the City Ground would come against Walsall, the team that had put four past the Potters in Tony Pulis's first game in charge. One suspects that following the Forest calamity, Pulis had the players running extra defensive drills and putting in the hours on the training ground. Whatever he did in the four days between the two fixtures paid off, as Stoke kept a clean sheet and ran out 1-0 winners thanks to a goal from Lee Mills. Stoke were off the bottom and had pulled back ground on the clustered clubs directly above them, providing a mentality boost in the crucial stage of the season. A defeat to Burnley at home in the next fixture meant the pressure was back on. Next up was a massive six-pointer against fellow strugglers and the team that had come up from Division Two as champions, Brighton & Hove Albion.

The game drew the biggest crowd of the season to date, 21,023. Stoke were tense and tentative in the first half, as Brighton looked more threatening in front of goal. Their main threat was Bobby Zamora, the prolific goalscorer who had helped them secure promotion the previous season, finishing as the league top scorer, and who was hitting double figures again this season. His Division Two goalscoring prowess had even seen him booed by Stoke fans during an England under-21 game at the Britannia Stadium 11 months earlier. In the second half, Stoke were much livelier, inspired by positive forward play by Bjarni Guðjónsson and Lewis Neal. Gunnarsson was also posing a threat to the Brighton goal, showing just how much the team missed him during his suspension. The all-important goal came just seven minutes before time. It was the goal-shy but hard-working Chris Greenacre who earned Stoke a massive three points following good build-up play by Neal down the left. Greenacre, who arrived at the Potters with a reputation as a goal-getter, had only mustered two league goals prior to the Brighton win, but his team efforts and attitude meant he was still well liked by fans and manager alike. This would prove to be his most important goal for the club.

* * *

The win took Stoke out of the bottom three, and Pulis now looked to further sure up his leaky defence which was showing signs of improvement since the Forest game. Middlesbrough goalkeeper Mark Crossley was brought back for a second loan spell, finding himself straight into the side the day after signing for the fixture at Ipswich, who were chasing a play-off place. His second 'debut' of the season for the Potters went much better than his first, helping the team secure an unlikely 0-0 on the road. Stoke would grind out another goalless draw in their next game against Sheffield United. Mark Wilson (not that one) was brought in to bolster the midfield options, as was experienced Northern Irish defender Mark Williams, as Pulis looked to fill the dressing room with battle-hardened leaders. Williams would form part of the next fixture, a trip down the road to Molineux to face Wolverhampton Wanderers. This would be a vintage Tony Pulis display. His starting line-up gave a strong indication as to what the manager was looking to get out of the game, starting with six defenders (seven if you include Gunnarsson as a defender), including four centre-halves across the back, Marcus Hall and Clive Clarke in midfield (at a push) alongside industrious Gunnarsson, O'Connor and Wilson, with Andy Cooke leading the line (or defending from the front). The tactic worked, as Stoke managed their third 0-0 in a row, picking up another unlikely point away from home. In some ways, the game was so bad that it was good, although I don't think Wolves fans saw it that way.

Stoke managed to secure their second away win of the season, their first since September, thanks to an inspired performance from Peter Hoekstra at Watford. Hoekstra gave Stoke the lead from the penalty spot in the first half, but his second goal shortly after the restart was an absolute cracker. Crossley's long ball forward was chested by Cooke into the path of the Dutchman 25 yards in front of goal. The fan favourite pivoted and hit the ball first time on the half-volley, sending it flying over the Watford goalkeeper and into the top corner in front of the travelling Stoke fans. Icelander Heiðar Helguson reduced the deficit for the home side but Stoke held on to take the points. It was a crucial win for Pulis's men, but we were still struggling in the bottom three, and we couldn't rely on Hoekstra to produce performances like that every week. Goals were still hard to come by, and with the defence showing improvements, the Potters would need to start turning draws into wins if we were to avoid an immediate return to Division Two. Pulis would revisit the loan market one more time, as he looked to mastermind the great escape.

Chapter 18

Power Ade

'I've just got this sneaking feeling about this season. I still think it will go to the last game'
– Steve Coppell

AT THE end of March 2003 and with seven games remaining, Tony Pulis made his final squad improvements, once again utilising the loan market to his advantage. Experienced and versatile defender-cum-midfielder Paul Warhurst joined from Bolton Wanderers, and high-profile striker Ade Akinbiyi arrived after a poor spell at Crystal Palace. Akinbiyi, who had played for Pulis during their time together at Gillingham, had become something of a figure of ridicule following big-money moves to Leicester and Palace. His £5.5m switch from Wolves to Leicester only produced 11 goals in 58 appearances, while his £2.2m move to the Eagles was even more disappointing, mustering one goal in 14 league and cup appearances. His recent failures had led to a few derogatory nicknames, including 'Shockinbiyi' and 'Ade Akinbadbuy'. Despite his recent record, Akinbiyi had previously been a prolific striker, including during his time at the Gills under Pulis. He was also another big personality in the dressing room and could provide a lift for the players and fans.

Warhurst and Akinbiyi made their Stoke debuts at the start of April 2003 in an uninspiring 0-0 draw at home to Gillingham. Akinbiyi would miss the next game, Rotherham at home, through injury, but Warhurst would start and score in a 2-0 win which saw Stoke move out of the bottom three. Andy Cooke's 30-yard lob in the first half secured the victory for the Potters, while Mark Crossley was once again inspired in goal to keep the Millers out. Pulis would remain grounded after the win and the climb out of the relegation zone, insisting, 'We are in with a fighting chance but there is still a hell of a lot of work to do.' The manager's scepticism was proven right, as Stoke fell to a disappointing 3-1 defeat to Millwall at the Den, ending the Potters' seven-match unbeaten run. Away fans were banned for the trip to Millwall, meaning the defeat would be endured on a beam-back at the Brit. Once again though, Pulis's men bounced back from defeat to win at home, this time seeing off Wimbledon 2-1 thanks to Gunnarsson and Akinbiyi, his first goal for the club, providing a shred of breathing space above Brighton, Grimsby and Sheffield Wednesday. Another brilliant save from Mark Crossley in the dying minutes had ensured victory for Stoke.

* * *

Stoke's next game was away at Coventry City and it was a huge day for Pulis's men. Gary McAllister's Coventry were still not mathematically safe from relegation, while rivals Sheffield Wednesday and Brighton were facing off against each other that same afternoon. Elsewhere, Grimsby and Walsall met. It was must win for the Mariners, while Walsall were hoping to secure their own Division One status with a win. With only three games to go, it was time to start doing the maths again. Grimsby were bottom on 38 points, looking doomed. Sheffield Wednesday were second from bottom on 39 points, desperately needing a win against the Seagulls. Brighton themselves were occupying the final relegation spot on 40 points, with a similar goal difference to Wednesday but a superior difference to Stoke, who were sitting just above the bottom three on 44 points. A win for Stoke and a draw between the Owls and the Seagulls would put safety into Stoke's hands with two games left. However, a draw or a defeat for Stoke and any winner at Hillsborough would throw it wide open. It was going to be one of those days. Tensions had already started in our family car, as my dad went in search of an elusive car-parking space. He ended up falling out with my brother on the A444 dual carriageway, slamming the brakes on in the outside lane and getting out of the car in the middle of traffic, shouting 'well you drive then!' at him. Like we weren't all nervous enough already!

Pulis went cautious once again with his starting line-up but found room for Peter Hoekstra to provide support for former Coventry man Lee Mills up front. The first half went the same way as many would under Pulis's reign – a tight, rigid affair as Stoke's first thought was to not concede … after all, can't lose if you don't concede. The tactics of sit and defend were there to frustrate the home side, with the possibility of a break or a set piece at the other end to provide a rare goalscoring opportunity. An opportunity for Stoke presented itself after a strong run by Gunnarsson was illegally checked by Gary Caldwell in the box, giving Stoke a chance to take the lead and double down on the defensive duties. Chris Iwelumo, who had only been on the pitch for two minutes, stepped up to take the all-important penalty. The big Scot missed, as the ball ricocheted off the inside of the post but, thankfully for Stoke, the ball hit the backside of Sky Blues keeper Gary

Montgomery and crossed the line for an unlikely own goal. The home side pushed for an equaliser, led on by John Eustace in midfield, but Stoke looked relatively comfortable overall. Mark Crossley was once again the hero at the back, keeping out a number of long-range efforts, commanding his defenders and masterfully running down the clock without drawing the ire of the referee. A hearts-in-mouths moment came ten minutes from the end as Mo Konjić rattled the outside stanchion of post and bar, but once again the defence stood strong to earn a priceless three points.

The away end was bouncing at the final whistle. As the tannoy announcer read out the final scores from elsewhere, the feeling got even better. Grimsby had lost at home to Walsall, meaning they were officially relegated and one of the bottom three spots was taken. At Hillsborough, the game finished 1-1 thanks to a Bobby Zamora equaliser for Brighton. The perfect result for the Potters (and for Coventry, as they were now mathematically safe). Sheffield Wednesday were also officially down, meaning that only Brighton could catch Stoke now. The cheers and chants of 'We are staying up!' were now being belted out with gusto from the Stoke fans making their way out of Highfield Road. With two games remaining, Stoke were six points clear of Albion, but with an inferior goal difference. Stoke only needed a point to secure safety; Brighton needed to win both games and hope Stoke lost both of theirs.

* * *

The stage was set for Tony Pulis to lead his patched-together team of five months to secure safety with one game left to play. The opportunity came on 26 April 2003, a tricky away game at Selhurst Park against caretaker manager Steve Kember's Crystal Palace. The Eagles should have been the very definition of 'on the beach', stranded in mid-table with no chance of making the play-offs and mathematically safe. One would also suspect that Palace fans would not want to see their rivals Brighton avoid relegation, although there may still have been some lingering affection for Albion manager Steve Coppell from his former club. Coppell, Brentford manager during the 2002 Millennium Stadium play-off final, would talk up his own team's chances, as well as putting faith in Palace to help them out. He said, 'We've got to keep our part of the deal and that is to win and see what happens elsewhere. I've just got this sneaking feeling about this season. I still think it will go to the last game. Steve Kember is trying to make a claim for the job. He doesn't do that by being beaten every week. It's a difficult place for anyone to go to, as we found out earlier in the season, and I am sure Stoke will find that.'

Tony Pulis was in typically grounded form in the week leading up to the Palace fixture. He said, 'It would be wrong to think we are safe. We still need a point to be sure and this is no time to be stepping off the gas and thinking we have done it. I've been in the game too long to take anything for granted. We've just come off the back of two great wins and there's nothing to say Brighton can't do the same at home to Watford and at Grimsby. We've got two difficult games to come at Palace then at home to Reading and we all know what a great season they've had.' The manager had a point. Reading, promoted with Stoke the previous season, were sitting pretty in the play-offs, looking to build momentum and give themselves the best possible chance by aiming for third place. The Potters would hope they could get the job done at Palace or look to Watford to do them a favour. It was a day that brought out the Stoke fans in numbers, including a lot who were boasting at the service station about not having an ID card but were planning to get into the ground anyway, by whatever means!

Considering Pulis would usually set Stoke out to play for at least a point away from home in normal circumstances, the guarantee of safety with a point here meant the tactics were even more defensive than usual. Stoke would again line up with seven defenders behind the hard-working James O'Connor and industrious duo of Andy Cooke and Chris Greenacre. Their plan was working too, barely threatening in the first half but keeping the Eagles out, with Mark Crossley called into action to deny Danny Butterfield and Noel Whelan. Stoke's negative tactics had an adverse effect on stupefying the game, drawing the annoyance of the home fans who suddenly decided they would rather not help seal Brighton's relegation after all. News from the South Coast wasn't good for the travelling Stoke fans, as Brighton were romping to victory against Watford. It wouldn't matter if Stoke could hold on to the draw in South London though, and the game seemed to be petering out into an end-of-season nothing contest. On 82 minutes, Stoke made the unforgivable mistake of losing concentration, or as Pulis himself put it, 'We switched off for a second.' Indeed, we did, as Tommy Black's quick free kick and Dougie Freedman's pass were not picked up, and substitute Dele Adebola took advantage to put the Eagles 1-0 up. With the game plan out of the window, the Potters tried to mount a comeback, but it was too little too late, as their approach came back to cost them and opened the door for Brighton to take it to the last game of the season.

* * *

So, after 45 games, three managers, last-minute U-turns, boardroom disputes, an influx of loanees, heavy defeats and last-minute winners, it all came down to one Sunday afternoon on 4 May 2003. Stoke City vs. Reading and Grimsby Town vs. Brighton & Hove Albion. The maths hadn't changed. Stoke needed to avoid defeat or hope that Brighton failed to win at Grimsby. Brighton needed to win and hope that Stoke lost to Reading. It was set to be a nail-biting day.

Tony Pulis would line up with a more ambitious team in the home fixture compared to the previous week at Palace, as he backed up his midweek statement, 'We'll go for the throat'. This was the team selected on that all-important day:

Mark Crossley, Wayne Thomas, Peter Handyside, Sergei Shtanyuk, Marcus Hall, Peter Hoekstra, Brynjar Gunnarsson, James O'Connor, Lewis Neal, Ade Akinbiyi, Chris Greenacre.

Substitutes: Steve Banks, Clive Clarke, Mark Williams, Andy Cooke, Chris Iwelumo.

Akinbiyi was back in the side after a few niggling injuries. Hoekstra and Neal came in to add some more creativity. James O'Connor and Brynjar Gunnarsson were now the only survivors from both the Wembley and Millennium Stadium heroics to be starting the game. Reading were to play their part in the drama, going full strength despite play-offs already being assured. A win would secure third place for the Royals, but the day was all about Stoke City. You could feel the nerves amongst the fans. It would also be a nail-biting afternoon ahead for the Stoke City hierarchy. Director of football John Rudge commented, 'I am OK, but I'm sweating a bit. It is good that our destiny is in our own hands, but the fact that Brighton have to go for a win should be an advantage to them.'

Stoke started the game confidently, testing Reading keeper Marcus Hahnemann within the first five minutes, before Reading gained their composure to control possession for the rest of the first half. Nerves were certainly not helped by the travelling Reading fans, who were revelling in their lofty league position and the woes of the home fans, singing 'We can smell your fear from here' and '1-0 to the Albion', despite the score being goalless at Blundell Park. As Stoke fans were scrambling to check their phones, radios, executive box TVs, whatever way possible to keep up to date with the Brighton score, news was finally coming through of an opening goal at Grimsby. It was the already-relegated home side that had actually taken the lead, much to the delight of the Stoke fans in a packed-out Brit. Celebrations started as if we'd scored a goal, followed by a loud roar of 'Come oooooon!' and chants of 'We are staying up!' Just before half-time, with the score still 0-0 at the Brit, Bobby Zamora equalised for Brighton at Grimsby, with Reading fans leading the cheers, enjoying their role as antagonists for the afternoon. Two minutes after the restart, Danny Cullip put the Seagulls 2-1 ahead, and now nerves were *really* jangling at the Brit.

For five minutes, Stoke fans were sweating buckets under the May sunshine. A goal for Reading would have seen Stoke slip into the relegation zone, and Nicky Forster went close for the visitors, drawing a parried save out of Crossley. On 55 minutes, a dinked ball forward towards the left was misjudged by Reading right-back Graeme Murty. Lewis Neal gambled on the defender missing the ball, steaming on to make a first-time delivery into the penalty area. Akinbiyi darted to the front post, getting his head to the ball ahead of John Mackie and powering past Hahnemann to give Stoke the lead in front of the Boothen End. Three sides of the stadium erupted with delight, as Ade removed his shirt and laid it on the pitch in front of the Stoke fans. The white-vested powerhouse pointed to his name, as Chris Greenacre bowed to the shirt and the rest of the team swamped the striker. Akinbiyi had been the subject of torment amongst the footballing community, particularly in Leicester and Croydon, but had just made himself a cult hero in ST4. Lewis Neal should not be forgotten for his role in the goal either, alert to the hesitation of the Reading defence, before putting the cross perfectly on to Ade's head with enough pace on it to be steered home. Akinbiyi had struggled to make the fixture due to fitness and would be subsequently substituted soon after his goal. His departure was met with the familiar chants of his first name, along with a loud chorus of 'Sign him up!' from the Stoke fans. The worry that had encapsulated the stadium following Brighton's second had now disappeared, as Stoke put themselves in pole position for securing safety.

The rest of the second half would be game management from the Potters. Cooke and Clarke were introduced from the bench to sure up the defensive duties. Nicky Shorey and Steve Sidwell went close for Reading, who were looking to build momentum going into the play-offs. While Reading pushed forward, news got better for Stoke from Blundell Park, as Grimsby had equalised against Brighton. From then on, the Potters would hold on to the 1-0 victory, while Brighton could only draw, meaning safety was secured. Four victories in the last six and a glut of clean sheets after the Nottingham Forest defeat would prove crucial for the Potters. Tony Pulis, the survival expert and escape artist, had done it again. There was no question now about whether the capped Welshman knew what he was doing … he was 'Triffic Tone'! The signings of Mark Crossley and Ade Akinbiyi were shrewd and opportunistic from the manager, who had brought in several experienced dressing-room leaders in the second half of the season to steer the team towards safety. Chris Iwelumo spoke of what Pulis did to change Stoke's fortunes that season, commenting, 'Tony Pulis was just very thorough. As boring as his training sessions were, everyone knew what their responsibilities and jobs were. He broke things down, simplified them and made you concentrate on your defensive responsibility for the team before anything else. He made us solid, and that's exactly what kept us up. We had players that could nick a goal for us. I wouldn't say it was the most attractive football, something he's been labelled with throughout his career, but he knew how to win games, and he didn't care about the brand of football. That's come more into the game today, the responsibility now is to entertain the fans as well as win games, but he just came in and made us a solid unit. He knew the strengths and weaknesses, and he'd work on them day in day out.' Speaking about Pulis's management style, Iwelumo said, 'I really liked TP. He was ruthless when he had to be, but he was honest. You could chat or argue with him, and the next day he would be back on terms again. He wanted that desire and ambition to play no matter what. To argue and fight for your place. That's what made him different to Guðjón, who wanted you to go out and enjoy yourself. TP could be really hard on the players, but then come in the next day and hold your hand. He had the respect of all the players, and he had the contacts and scouting networks to bring in the players that he wanted.'

* * *

After the celebrations, Pulis knew that he would have to significantly strengthen the squad to push on. The first question was whether Akinbiyi could be signed on a permanent deal. 'Without knowing what league we were going to be playing in, we couldn't negotiate,' Pulis said. 'He had a tough time at Leicester and they're giving him some stick at Palace, but I've got terrific respect for the kid.' Ten years on from the final-day win, Pulis would reflect on the importance of the win and the role of Akinbiyi. He reminisced, 'Had that game not gone our way, we wouldn't be here [at the time in the Premier League] today. I think the Icelandic owners would have cut back and all sorts of things could have happened, all sorts. Staying in the Championship gave them the life to carry on and push the club on. But if we had gone down to the third tier and they walked away, we could have been in all sorts of trouble. They invested a lot of money and I was their third manager that year, as Guðjón Thórdarson and Steve Cotterill had both left. It would have been very difficult for them to stay. It's one of the defining moments in the club's history and it was a very important game, one I'll never forget. For that reason alone, Ade Akinbiyi is the best loan signing I ever made.'

Chapter 19

All Change at Stoke

'If Ade comes here, he knows how good the fans are and the sort of welcome he would get from them. They would love him … if he wants something outside our wage structure, then we will have to look elsewhere. It's now up to Ade to decide on his destination … he knows the club, he knows me, and we can only offer what we have done' – Tony Pulis

THE DAWN of the 2003/04 season had a feeling of a new chapter for Stoke City FC. For the first time since the mid-90s and for the first time under the rule of the Icelanders, there was a feeling of security about Stoke's footballing position. We were under the steady management of the experienced Tony Pulis, who now had an entire preseason to build his own squad and instigate his own regiments and philosophies. For Pulis to bring in his own men, some would inevitably have to leave. Short-term contracted players like Steve Banks, Lee Mills and Mark Williams departed. Surprisingly, midfield mainstay and the hero of Ninian Park James O'Connor left for Gary Megson's West Bromwich Albion. Super James's contract was up, and he turned down Stoke's offer in favour of a move to the Hawthorns. The move wasn't looked upon kindly by Stoke fans at the time, but once again, with hindsight, he was likely the victim of behind-the-scenes actions out of his control. He would later confirm that manager Pulis wanted to keep him, expecting a new contract to be offered. It was, but not until June 2003, and it was for less money than he was earning at the time. The powers that be in Iceland wanted to cash in on O'Connor in a tribunal, leaving the player and the manager disappointed. Pulis remarked, 'He's been terrific in the short time I've been here, but West Brom are a million miles in front of where Stoke are at the moment so it's a great move for him.'

Four other high-profile departures were crowd favourites Sergei Shtanyuk, Peter Handyside, Brynjar Gunnarsson and Bjarni Guðjónsson. The quadrant left under different circumstances. Pulis had wanted to keep Shtanyuk, trying to tie him down to a new contract as his previous deal had some stipulations in that would allow him to leave for little compensation. The Belarussian was feeling homesick and missing his family after two years in England, which led to a move to the Russian Premier League to Shinnik Yaroslavl. It was quite a low-key transfer for such an important member of the first team, one who many saw as a potential Premier League centre-half. Former captain Peter Handyside left after his contract expired and he wasn't offered a new one. Icelander Brynjar Gunnarsson departed on a free transfer to Nottingham Forest. The Stoke record signing at the time, much like James O'Connor, was pivotal in the team's success since his arrival, playing a key role in the Auto Windscreens Shield victory, the promotion campaign and in securing survival the previous season. His Icelandic compatriot, Bjarni Guðjónsson, also left the club having found himself out of the manager's plans as the 2002/03 season progressed. Bjarni joined up with his brother Thórdur at VfL Bochum. After the departures of Guðjónsson and Gunnarsson, Pétur Marteinsson was now the only remaining Icelander on the playing books at Stoke.

With space and limited funds available, Tony Pulis went shopping to rebuild Stoke's squad. His first port of call was an experienced goalkeeper to replace Mark Crossley, who had finished his loan spell at the club. Former Manchester United keeper Raimond van der Gouw joined the club on trial, but it was another former Premier League Dutch keeper who would end up joining, 36-year-old ex-Chelsea man Ed de Goey. The moustachioed goalkeeper was a familiar face to Stoke fans thanks to his long spell in the Premier League, and his unique looks and accent led to the newly coined chant of 'I want a 'tash like Ed de Goey, Super Dutch Porn Star!' He joined new signings Gifton Noel-Williams, Clint Hill and John Eustace, who all joined in early preseason. Striker Noel-Williams, a long-term target for Pulis, joined from Watford, scouse defender Clint Hill joined from Oldham, and former Coventry midfielder John Eustace signed as a replacement for Gunnarsson. As preseason rolled on, the squad would be bolstered even more with the signings of full-back John Halls, midfielders Darel Russell and Keith Andrews and forward Carl Asaba. Notable absentee from the glut of new signings was the hero of the previous end of season, Ade Akinbiyi, as the club battled hard to bring him in from Crystal Palace without breaking the bank. Regarding the potential signing of Akinbiyi, Pulis said, 'It's no secret that we've been chasing Ade, and it's also common knowledge that Gillingham and Walsall are keen. If Ade comes here, he knows how good the fans are and the sort of welcome he would get from them. They would love him. But one of those clubs has made a better financial offer than us, and if he wants something outside our wage structure, then we will have to look elsewhere. It's now up to Ade to decide on his destination, he knows the club, he knows me, and we can only offer what we have done.'

* * *

The new-look squad would have their work cut out in preseason, as Pulis took them to Austria for a week of running up hills, cycling and tireless training. John Acres is full of praise for Pulis's management style and methods. John said, 'He was a real leader of men and an interesting bloke, he used to study Napoleon. I remember going on a preseason tour of Austria and it was fascinating. The year I went, they used to have a 7am circuits gym session. On the first morning I came down for breakfast at about 9am before they trained outside, he asked me, "Where were you this morning? Why weren't you in the gym?" I'm not going down to the gym at 7am! I'm up until midnight writing the bulletins and website articles for the next morning. I thought he was joking, but he wasn't! He wanted me to be in the gym … Spinksy [Martin Spinks from *The Sentinel*] was hitting the gym! The next year, any media that went were told "If we're doing it, you're doing it, we're all in this together and doing the sessions!" When I was there, we were all supposed to go white water rafting, including the media. We were waiting in the library in this big hotel, like a big Austrian castle. He told us all that the area had seen record rainfalls in April and May, with record snow melting in June and July, so the water is as deep and quick as it has ever been. The instructors told us that it was so dangerous that they couldn't insure us. Tony said, "I'm still happy for you to go, you're all fit lads and you'll be alright. Anyone who wants to go, stand on that side of the room, anyone who doesn't fancy it, and that's fine with me too, stand on this side of the room."

So obviously I stood on the side of the room where there was not a chance I was going! He looked at the lads that said they would go, then looked at the ones who said they wouldn't go, and he said, "Of course we can't go fucking white water rafting if we can't get you insured!" He did it to see who had the minerals and the fight to do it. The lads that were on the other side of the room were basically the ones who played every week for him. His soldiers, the cavalry that would run up and down for him every week. That's why he picked them even when fans disagreed. Tony was so interested in your attitude, how far you'd run and what you could do without the ball. He wanted the best players in the league without a football in his team.'

The two friendlies ended in defeat against Germinal Beerschot and Westerlo, before a draw with Notts County and losses to Macclesfield and Rhyl. The 4-2 defeat in North Wales was the final friendly before the season opener at Derby County; the full-strength team losing so comfortably to a Welsh Premier League side didn't fill fans with optimism, albeit only in a friendly. Stoke would play one more friendly match, surprisingly a midweek fixture between the first and second games of the Division One season. The reason for the date decision was that it would be a high-profile home clash with Premier League champions Manchester United. Over 21,000 came out to see Stoke beat Sir Alex Ferguson's United 3-1, as Marc Goodfellow lobbed World Cup-winner Fabien Barthez from the halfway line.

The season started with a tricky opener at Pride Park against Midlands rivals Derby. To add a little extra spice to the fixture, the Rams were being managed by George Burley, the man who had turned down the Stoke job at the last minute nine months earlier. Only Chris Greenacre, Marcus Hall and Wayne Thomas remained from the team that ended the previous season against Reading, as Pulis handed debuts to no fewer than seven players. This, combined with the erratic preseason, meant the outcome of this opening match would be difficult to predict. And indeed, few would have predicted the final score. Two of the debutants, Keith Andrews and Gifton Noel-Williams, combined in the 14th minute to give Stoke the lead, Noel-Williams shinning home from close range. Five minutes later, Carl Asaba played in Chris Greenacre to double the Potters lead, as the travelling Stoke fans broke into 'We are top of the league!' Asaba was having a fine debut, as were Eustace and Russell, but unfortunately Ed de Goey left the field injured early in the second half. It would still be Stoke's day though, as substitute Lewis Neal completed the scoring late on to give Stoke a 3-0 opening-day away victory. Pulis, not the type to normally line up with a three-pronged attack, stated, 'I had watched Derby a couple of times preseason and I decided to go with all three strikers. It was a plan which worked. Asaba and Noel-Williams are quick and powerful and will cause problems, while Greenacre is a clever player.'

Following the win at Derby and the friendly victory against Manchester United, Stoke beat Wimbledon at home to go top thanks to Asaba and a last-minute winner from Wayne Thomas. This was followed by a couple of draws and a string of defeats to bring the fans crashing back down to earth. Despite inconsistent form, Asaba and Noel-Williams were forming a decent partnership up front. In mid-September, the long-awaited signing of Ade Akinbiyi was confirmed. Pleasingly, Ade was signed permanently on a free transfer and three-year deal. The deal would lead to the eventual transfer of Chris Iwelumo. Reflecting on the move, Iwelumo said, 'The club did offer me a two-year contract but with the signings of Gifton Noel-Williams, Carl Asaba and Ade Akinbiyi, it was probably the right time for me to move on to play football.

When it was my time to leave, Stoke made a CD with all my goals and attributes to send around to all clubs to entice them into making an offer. Tony Pulis was watching it with John Rudge, and Tony turned to Rudgie and said, "This is exactly what we're looking for!" I was in the building all along! John Rudge goes to the same gym as me and always reminds me of that.'

* * *

Stoke's form fell off a cliff from mid-September up towards Christmas, managing only three wins as the old habit of a lack of clean sheets kicked in. The Potters were suddenly pondering another relegation battle. Notable defeats included losing 1-0 at West Brom after being reduced to nine men after the sending offs of John Eustace and Marcus Hall, and a 3-2 home defeat to newly promoted Cardiff, thanks to a hat-trick from Peter Thorne. The former Stoke favourite didn't celebrate any of his goals and was even applauded by the home fans after his third. Stoke also managed to scrape a last-minute draw against Crewe thanks to Chris Greenacre.

The beginning of the poor run coincided with the departure of Stoke's last remaining Icelander – Pétur Marteinsson. John Rudge called it a 'mutual decision', insisting that the Icelander wanted to return to Scandinavia to be with his family, although there were also rumours surrounding his standing with the manager, his potential high wages and a possible play-related contract status. The defender-cum-occasional central midfielder was a bit of an enigma throughout his sparsely spaced 18 appearances for the club between 2001 and 2003. On some occasions, he appeared to be a highly cultured defensive option for the club, the kind that many a modern manager would love to have in their team. Despite impressing on the occasions that he was afforded a chance, he often found himself back out of the team when everyone was fully fit, or new signings were brought in to play in his position. It's fair to say that he was popular with Stoke fans, which was only exacerbated when a run of defensive frailties showed up and he was no longer an option. There was also a feeling that he represented an era that was quickly evaporating – the Icelandic hoard which had once defined us, initiated by Guðjón Thórdarson. There was a sense, rightly or wrongly, that Pulis wasn't a big fan of foreign players due to them not being his own signings, their perceived lack of fitness and physical prowess, or their lack of integration into the squad. Whether that was true or not, we will probably never know, and Pulis has always stated that if you're good enough and your attitude is right, you'll be a part of his plans. The Welshman had kept faith with the likes of Peter Hoekstra, although he was not a regular starter (and let's face it, it would be difficult to ostracise such a special player), and he even brought Brynjar Gunnarsson back to the club for a short, unremarkable loan spell later in the season.

As well as the impact the Marteinsson transfer had on the squad and the fans, there were also questions as to how the board would react. Exploiting the Nordic market and developing Icelandic football had been a big part of their ethos and execution in the initial days of their reign and had continued every season up to the dismissal of Thórdarson. Would the lack of Icelanders in the squad anger the board? Or were they happy for Pulis to continue to dictate transfer policy his own way if it was producing results? Only time would tell.

* * *

The run of poor form led Tony Pulis to make a couple of additions to the squad. Frazer Richardson was back in on loan, and veteran Northern Irish centre-half Gerry Taggart joined on loan from Leicester. Taggart's debut led to an immediate upturn for the Potters, winning 1-0 at West Ham, who had come down from the Premier League the previous season. Richardson scored the winning goal with a fine first-half strike, ending a run of eight straight defeats on the road for City. The win would spark Stoke's season back into life, initiating a run of nine games without defeat, including seven wins. During the run, Peter Hoekstra bagged a superb hat-trick against Reading. For his first, the big Dutchman rounded the keeper to open the scoring, before smashing home the goal of the season with a sweet strike from the corner edge of the penalty area. The popular winger rounded off his hat-trick in style with a Panenka penalty that he himself had won through a mazy run down the right that the Reading defence couldn't handle (at least within the laws of the game).

In true Stoke style, the unbeaten run came to a spectacular end, losing 6-3 at Crystal Palace in a game which saw Palace forward Andrew Johnson score two penalties on his way to a first-half hat-trick. Stoke's form ebbed and flowed after that for the remainder of the season, including a defeat to Crewe at Gresty Road, an evening which I remember well after my dad drew the attention of Kris Commons. The winger, whose contract was coming to an end, was a substitute, and while warming up at half-time, my dad took it on himself to offer him some advice (shouting 'Sign a contract!' at him as he collected a ball from the net). Commons wasn't best pleased with the suggestion, smirking at my dad and muttering something under his breath. Although maybe it did inspire him to make his name more known when presented a chance from the start, inspiring a stunning 4-1 win against West Brom in the last home game of the season. The Baggies had already secured promotion but were well trounced thanks to a match-winning performance from Commons. The result, which led to a chant of '4-1, get used to it' from the Stoke fans towards the visiting Baggies, was a pleasing end to a fairly positive season for the Potters, which was officially signed off with a 0-0 draw at Gillingham. Stoke finished the season in 11th position, a very respectable return after battling relegation the season before. Noel-Williams and Akinbiyi both notched up ten goals apiece, as the manager had firmly put his stamp on the team. All in all, things were positive at the club. A season without play-off or relegation drama is something we hadn't had since 1999, and back then it was only thanks to a disappointing slump down the Division Two table from the top under Brian Little. Having inherited an inexperienced, relatively weak squad from Thórdarson and Cotterill, Tony Pulis had built solid foundations, mixed with a bit of quality and goalscoring potential, and the hopes for the 2004/05 season were high.

Chapter 20

The Binary Season

'The final outcome should come as no surprise to those students of form noting that Stoke's last 17 Championship fixtures have now contained 15 1-0s and two 0-0s'
– Martin Spinks

BY PRESEASON of 2004/05, Stoke were starting to look stable and competent both off and on the pitch. Chief executive Jonathan Fuller left the club to join West Brom and was succeeded by former Preston chief executive Tony Scholes. The newly appointed Scholes wanted to revive interest in the club from the roots of the area. Simon Lowe, who at this point was involved in both the Stoke City Southern Supporters Club and the Friends of Stoke Supporters Trust, recalled, 'In one conversation, Tony Scholes told me that he was fed up of driving around the city and seeing youngsters wearing "big club" shirts of the likes of Manchester United and Liverpool. So, he instituted the new well-established City 7's programme, in which Stoke's outreach team focused on seven-year-olds, getting them to games, becoming members and then keeping hold of them. It was a really good initiative which bore fruit as the club revived towards the end of the decade.' On the pitch, Tony Pulis had built Stoke into a tough-to-beat, mid-table side with a coherent game plan – try to get through our two banks of four, and we'll try to hit you with a set piece, capitalise on a mistake or show an occasional display of individual skill. It was simple, but it was effective. After the flurry of summer transfer activity in the previous season, the manager and board saw fit that less would be required this time round. Former Port Vale and Crewe Alexandra midfielder Dave Brammer was brought in, as was one-time British record transfer fee-setting goalkeeper Steve Simonsen. Both would go on to become regulars under Pulis. John Acres recounts a time that Dave Brammer's relationship with the manager took a turn for the worse, despite being a much-loved first choice for the manager: 'Pulis liked Brammer, he was one of his favourites in the team every week. He did what he was told and kept it simple. Pass the ball, run about, intercept things, stuff like that. Tony used to train him and the others to play in the cage system, drawing rectangles from the edge of your own penalty area up to the halfway line, about ten yards in from each touchline. He used to say to the central midfielders, "You stay in the fucking cage, I don't want to see you leave there." In one game, Brammer was on the halfway line when he picked up the ball. He didn't have a ball on, so he decided to knock it round his man and try to run onto it, trying a bit of a trick. He didn't have any pace, so he lost the ball, the team went up the other end, forced a corner and almost scored from it. Brammer said, "As I was running back, I could feel Tony's eyes just daggering into me. I was his favourite player, I was his captain and he would speak to me all the time. He didn't speak to me for two weeks!" and they both knew why … because he tried to take someone on at the halfway line!'

Such stories of headmaster-like strictness from Tony Pulis weren't rare from the time. Simon Lowe recalled the manager giving centre-half Paul Williams a firm but friendly rollicking for arriving just about on time for a training session. Not late, but not early, and that was enough to face the wrath of the capped one! There was now a real feeling of Pulis firmly planting his flag at the centre of the football club, with more players signed under previous managerial regimes moving on over the summer. Fan favourite Peter Hoekstra retired at the end of the prior season after being given a big send-off by supporters. The big Dutchman had become a firm favourite and is still fondly remembered. Rob Doolan, 90s football blogger said, 'My favourite player of the age is, by some distance, the great Peter Hoekstra, a fabulous Rudge gamble. I'd remembered him playing for Ajax and Holland and it was marvellous to see he still had his bag of tricks – the hat-trick against Reading in his last season was just sublime.' Hugo Hemlin, member of the Swedish Stokies Official Supporters Branch, also waxed lyrical about the winger: 'A prime highlight of that time was Reading at home 2003. The Peter Hoekstra show. The game was televised here in Sweden and I had a few non-Stoke-supporting friends over to watch the game. I almost converted a few of them after the game. Hoekstra was extremely skilful, and he could send a defender down the Trent four times in one move.'

Long-term squad members Neil Cutler, Andy Cooke and Chris Iwelumo also departed in search of regular first-team football. The highest profile departure was promising 20-year-old talent Kris Commons, who had snubbed contract offers from Stoke in favour of joining his (supposed) childhood team Nottingham Forest. John Rudge had said prior to Commons's departure, 'He has refused the terms his agent requested – terms we not only met but actually went above in a bid to get his signature. He had a meeting with manager Tony Pulis a week ago and we emphasised how strongly we wanted him to stay.' Naturally, he was labelled a greedy bastard by Stoke fans for his decision. My dad wasn't happy! John Acres commented on the move, saying, 'He had an agent in his ear, but I think it was probably the right move. He was being asked to bomb up and down under Tony. The manager didn't think he worked hard enough or was big enough for him. For Tony it was work hard first, football ability second.'

After running up a few more Austrian hills, Stoke had a more productive preseason results-wise, including home wins against Valencia and West Brom (we were now back into 'we always beat West Brom' mode). The Potters got off to an excellent start to the season once again, beating Wolves at home 2-1 thanks to goals from Darel Russell and Clive Clarke. A couple of draws in Yorkshire against Sheffield United and Rotherham were followed by three straight wins and three clean sheets, thanks in part to the second arrival of Gerry Taggart, this time on a permanent deal. The run included satisfying wins against Graham Kavanagh's Cardiff and George Burley's Derby. Stoke only lost one of their first 11 games, as Akinbiyi notched up five goals in an impressive start for the Potters. Two of his goals came in a trip to Burnley, now managed by Steve Cotterill. The former Stoke manager, not helped by the Turf Moor tunnel leading straight out in front of the away fans, received torrents of abuse from the visiting Stoke fans. The fans were on his back for 90 minutes after he had walked out on the club to join Sunderland as assistant manager in 2003. The draw at Turf Moor kept the points ticking over for the Potters, who dared to dream about a promotion push. One point from the first four games of October brought the fans and expectations back down.

* * *

The defeat against QPR at home was a particularly memorable match, in a game that could have seen Stoke go top of the league. After a bright start for Stoke, which should have seen a penalty awarded after Akinbiyi was barged to the ground with a clear sight at goal, the game was marred by the 36th-minute decision to award Gerry Taggart a red card for a clash with Marc Bircham. The decision not to award a penalty angered the fans and the manager on the touchline, and 90 seconds after the incident, Taggart picked up the ball to protest the awarding of a foul to QPR. Bircham tried to wrestle the ball from the grasps of the big Irishman, who responded by swatting the blue and white-spiked-haired midfielder away. It was nothing more than a gentle shove to the Rangers man, who went down like he had been shot, holding his face theatrically. The referee brandished a red card, to which Taggart responded by trying to confront Bircham, who had *miraculously* recovered from his near career-ending injury. Skirmishes ensued for a few minutes, before carrying on in the tunnel at half-time.

Ian Holloway's side offered very little in the first half but snatched the lead halfway through the second with their first shot on target. As Bircham was substituted late on, Akinbiyi got right up in his face, screaming all sorts of expletives but showing enough restraint not to physically touch him. Let's face it, Bircham probably would have exploded at the slightest of contact. The QPR man was escorted away by stewards to the dressing room, as tempers flared in the stands and objects were thrown. Pulis reacted to the defeat by criticising Bircham. 'The kid went down as though he was hit by a sledgehammer and my players were incredibly upset at half-time,' he said. 'They say we were cheated and after seeing the video I can see their point. Taggart is a tough warrior who has been around the block a few times. He's absolutely incensed.' The comments were quite uncharacteristic for Pulis, who normally stuck to his usual script of 'the lads worked 'ard Nige, triffic bunch of kiddies, we're a million miles behind the opposition', etc. It was an ugly encounter at the Brit with QPR to say the least, not the last one to occur in this fixture either.

* * *

This wasn't Taggart's only memorable moment in the month of October 2004. Stoke ended a run of seven games without a win by beating Millwall 1-0 at home thanks to a late Chris Greenacre goal. The game saw the reunion of Taggart with his former Leicester team-mate Dennis Wise. The Millwall man had been sacked from Leicester for allegedly punching Callum Davidson while the youngster was in bed during a club trip to Finland. However, it was an incident during the match that had Taggart all riled up with Wise. While Taggart was shielding the ball out for a Stoke goal kick, the notorious midfielder took an opportunity to leave one on the Northern Irishman, scraping his studs down the back of the big defender's calf. Taggart would recall on Jon Parkin's Undr The Cosh podcast, 'Anyone will tell you, that doesn't tickle. It's not a sensation where you turn around and say, "Oooh, thanks very much." So, I thought, "Here we go, Mr Wise is at it again." It would have been easy to turn around and run after him, but I thought, "Leave it, something will happen …"' Something did happen. Close to the halfway line, Taggart clattered Wise with a high tackle (although it was more accurately described by Taggart as a 'karate kick'), leaving Wise rolling around in agony. Wise then showed Marc Bircham-levels of recovery to grab Taggart, who responded by pinning his much-smaller former colleague to the pitch, hands around his throat. After the tackle and the reaction, surely Taggart would be seeing red yet again this month? Not on this day. Instead, referee Uriah Rennie simply watched on with a wry smile on his face, before brandishing a yellow card! Taggart recalled, 'As he's [Rennie] dragging me over, all the melee is going off and he drags me into no man's land, he starts winking at me as if to say, "Don't worry, I'm not going to send you off." Then he says to me, "I've got to give you a card … but it's only a yellow." I've thought, "Cheers Uriah, next time I see you at the dogs, the first drinks are on me!" It was probably two red cards! Top man Uriah.' Top man indeed, and a very funny moment! Judo black belt Uriah Rennie is part of a long list of 'very good friends' of Stoke fan and former kit man Neil 'Nello' Baldwin BEM, the inspiration for the exceptional BBC television film *Marvellous*. Perhaps Nello's significant influence meant Stoke had some support from Rennie!

* * *

Greenacre's only league goal of the entire season, in the Millwall game, marked the start of an astonishing run of results for Pulis's side, as Stoke went 17 matches where one or fewer goals were scored in each game. The run of scores 0-0, 1-0 or 0-1 lasted from 30 October 2004 up to 22 February 2005. Coincidentally, the final consecutive binary score in the run also came against Millwall. There were some notable results during the run, including a win against Crewe at home and away wins at Watford, Brighton and Millwall, but it truly was a dour time to be a paying follower of Stoke City Football Club. The period between 28 November 2004 and 22 January 2005 saw five consecutive 1-0 league defeats, which led to a sizeable section of the fan base turning on manager Pulis. Not everyone was unhappy with the spell of results. John Acres recounts, 'I loved it because every week I had a bet on under 2.5 goals! For 17 weeks, I made a fortune!' There was an FA Cup Sunday day out to the soon-to-be closed Highbury for

Tony Pulis to face off with Arsène Wenger's Arsenal for the first time, which saw Stoke take an unlikely lead against the Premier League giants through Wayne Thomas. The Potters would succumb to the full-strength Gunners in the second half, as goals from José Antonio Reyes and Robin van Persie resulted in a 2-1 defeat to the soon-to-be Arsenal Invincibles. After the game, police had cordoned off the roads to keep Arsenal fans and the 5,000 Stoke fans separate. This wasn't good news for me and my family, who had once again parked a considerable distance away from Highbury (somehow my dad had found a free place to park in London on a slip road leading on to a dual carriageway!). While most had already departed by sensible means such as official coaches or tubes and trains from Finsbury Park, we ended up hopelessly lost in North London for over an hour. Everyone we stopped to ask for directions was from out of town, including the police officers. In the end, it was a little old Chinese lady who knew exactly where we meant and pointed us in the right direction! Never drive and try to park in London for an away day …

* * *

The run of defeats was ended by a win at Wigan, but even then, the performance was so soul-destroying that fans were audible in their derision of both Pulis and the Icelandic board. At first, the songs from the away end were more self-deprecating and tongue in cheek, but soon became the more direct 'Iceland Out' and 'We're shit, and we're sick of it' chants. Noel-Williams's winning goal tempered emotions to some degree, but the mood walking away from the JJB Stadium was very much a sense of 'we've won, but it doesn't feel like it'. There was also a sense of division in the stands on that day too, which would seep into both home and away games for the rest of the season. Many fans were now audibly unhappy with Pulis, while others saw his merits and achievements to date under difficult circumstances. I remember waiting at the Brit for the coaches before an away game at Coventry, and the players' coach was still parked up outside the away end. Pulis was walking over from the car park towards the coach, and my mate Nathan Edwards decided to approach him. 'Are we going to try and win today?' the teenage Nathan boldly asked him. 'We always try to win son, today will be no different!' The game finished 0-0, thanks to a penalty save from Steve Simonsen. Pulis would say after the game, 'We were poor and didn't have any spirit. I've got no excuses for the first half. Coventry were just much, much better than us.' Friday night radio phone-ins and post-match *Praise and Grumble* shows were full of fans with strong opinions on Pulis, one way or the other. Though our lives were not yet blessed with the wonders of Twitter for expressing opinions, *The Oatcake* online fanzine message board was the one-stop shop for Stoke City news, opinions, gossip and hot takes. Between rumours of Lee Trundle buying a house in Trentham and sightings of Wayne Thomas buying a Greggs pasty, there was the creation of the two sides of the Pulis coin – Pulis supporters were poetically known as 'Pulis Rimmers', while Pulis cynics were the equally elegiac 'Pulis Hating Wankstains'. Not only were the board and manager seemingly divided, the supporters were now divided too. These were dark days indeed.

Things weren't about to get any cheerier either. Despite the lack of goals or transfer activity to resolve the issue (the only incomings were defenders Lewis Buxton and Michael Duberry), attacking talisman Ade Akinbiyi was bizarrely sold for £600,000 to Steve Cotterill's Burnley. The Clarets and Sheffield United had both shown interest in the 2003/04 Fan's Player of the Season, who chose Turf Moor over Bramall Lane. Akinbiyi had been quite unhappy with his contract situation at Stoke following his permanent move, at one point demanding an audience with chairman Gunnar Gíslason and even staging a sit-in protest in John Rudge's club office. John Rudge said, 'Both clubs had offers accepted by us and it was down to Ade to make his choice. He has agreed terms with Burnley after speaking to Sheffield United. We are obviously disappointed to lose Ade, but everybody has a price. The board of directors put that price on his head and two clubs met it. Ade has been a crowd favourite here and done exceptionally well for us. He signed for us after a lull in his career at Leicester and Crystal Palace but got back to his best here and we wish him all the best for the future.' The comment about the board of directors suggested that the Icelanders were looking for a quick cash-in on any asset with notable valuation – first James O'Connor, now Ade Akinbiyi. Stoke would bring in attacking midfielder Kevin Harper and striker Kenwyne Jones to try to change our fortunes in front of goal. Akinbiyi would debut for Burnley shortly after the move as a substitute, receiving a red card on debut after only a couple of minutes after grabbing Sunderland's George McCartney by the throat!

The final result of the depressing binary run was a 1-0 win at the Den. The *Sentinel* correspondent Martin Spinks reported on the game, writing, 'The final outcome should come as no surprise to those students of form noting that Stoke's last 17 Championship fixtures have now contained 15 1-0s and two 0-0s. It is an astonishing sequence, but all the more laudable this time as half-a-dozen absentees not only cleared the path for [Kevin] Harper and [Kenwyne] Jones to make their debuts, but also prompted a makeshift defence growing all the more makeshift as the game wore on. Stoke were also armed with sufficient know-how and composure in other areas to prevent either the opposition or their frustrated followers raising the temperature.' The binary run ended with an unexpected 3-2 home win against Leicester, a shock to the system for many Stokies in attendance. Goals from Brammer, Noel-Williams and former Fox favourite Taggart gave Stoke the victory. After the game, Pulis had some interesting comments to make regarding the off-field situation. He said, 'There is a meeting with the chairman in the morning when we hope a lot of the nonsense behind the scenes will be sorted out.' The manager and chairman seemed to be in a dispute over numerous issues, most notably, transfer dealings.

* * *

The issue between Pulis and Gíslason had been publicly recognised at the end of January 2005 after a curious double signing. Icelanders Thórdur 'Toddy' Guðjónsson (brother of Bjarni and son of former manager Guðjón Thórdarson) and Tryggvi Guðmundsson joined the club, seemingly out of nowhere, after Pulis had been unsuccessfully chasing long-term target Rob Hulse to soothe the Stoke's goalscoring woes. There was no doubt that the transfers had been fully instigated by the Icelandic board. Their motives may have been that they felt the duo could provide some more goals and entertainment to on-field proceedings. It may have also been a power move, to show the manager where the power truly lay at the club. Perhaps the board were simply losing interest in a side void of their fellow countrymen. Whatever the true reasons for the transfer, manager Pulis would remain defiant in the face of the obvious suggestion from the higher-ups. Toddy Guðjónsson only made two substitute appearances, while Tryggvi Guðmundsson, a prolific goalscorer in his home country, didn't manage a single appearance. The manager and the board were now in direct opposition to each other, which spelt disaster for Stoke City.

To make matters worse, the season was petering out to another mid-table finish, including seven defeats in the final ten games. The final-day defeat to Sunderland at the Stadium of Light was a particularly dull affair. Stoke arrived to try to spoil the party for the already-crowned champions by trying to hold out for a 0-0. This was nothing new for the Potters, but after falling 1-0 behind, Pulis seemed to switch to even more defensive to try to hold out for the one-goal defeat. This was perplexing considering neither team had absolutely anything to play for in the game. In total, over 60 per cent of games in the 2004/05 season ended with scores totalling one goal or less, as Stoke finished the season with 36 goals for and 38 against from 46 games. Thank God the season was finally over! Author Neil James reflected on that season, saying, 'It was painful to watch. Watching the team go out with the intention of drawing 0-0 every week made it difficult to keep attending when there were other things to be doing with your time (like watching paint dry).' John Acres recalled the binary season and the possible reasons for the extreme levels of dull football that were served up. John said, 'When I was interviewing him during that binary season, I wish he had been just a bit more honest with me. I wish he had said to me, "John, they are not giving me the money we need to compete, the budget we have is probably about 18th in the league, and I'm getting us to mid-table. They won't back me with the players I want to sign." Tony had Damien Francis at Stoke, in a Stoke tracksuit, eating his lunch, he wanted a fair wage, but they wouldn't sign it off. Francis then went on to do really well for Norwich. Tony was great at spotting players, but the board just wouldn't back him and give him the money to go and have a go.' Acres continued, 'Tony had been embarrassed by the 6-0 defeat at Forest in 2002, and he was so scarred by it that he didn't want it to happen again. He knew he was a 3-0 or 4-0 defeat away from getting the sack during that binary season. They didn't trust him, so they were reluctant to give him the cash. They thought the football was boring. If I knew then what I knew now, I wouldn't have given him such a hard time about the football. He was just trying not to get hammered and was so close to getting binned, he just kept it tight.'

Pulis was in typically upbeat mood in the face of criticism after the Sunderland game, saying, 'We now begin to look to next season – in fact, we have already started. I'm off to look at some games this week and other members of the management team are abroad this weekend. We want to get cracking as quickly as possible. There are players who have contract offers on the table and now it's up to them to get back in touch with us. Looking at our season overall, there's no doubt it went a bit flat at the end. But we have finished in the top half of the table and I think the players put in a lot of effort to get there.' One wonders if the comment of 'other members of the management team are abroad this weekend' was a last-ditch attempt to appease the board after the Toddy Guðjónsson–Tryggvi Guðmundsson debacle, but it's unlikely. Perhaps the reasoning for a change in Pulis's attitude towards the Icelanders in the hope of keeping his job would be that there was now the real possibility of change on the horizon at the top of the club.

Chapter 21

Sale on in Iceland

'Despite all the good work he [Pulis] has done, he has failed to implement the strategy of exploiting foreign markets. It is felt we will again fail to exploit those markets this summer with him in control' – Gunnar Gíslason

TONY PULIS'S reluctance to give game time to Toddy Guðjónsson and Tryggvi Guðmundsson was the final straw for the beyond-frustrated Icelandic consortium. At the end of April 2005, as the season drew to a close, the Icelanders of Stoke Holding, club owners since November 1999, put the club up for sale. Chairman Gunnar Gíslason would declare, 'Part of the original idea was to improve the opportunities of Icelandic footballers to play professionally in England. All team managers in the last five years have been aware of this.' Pulis, having had prior issues with former chairmen at his past clubs, was savvy enough to insist on a one-year rolling contract when he joined the club, and had re-signed on another 12 months prior to the club being put up for sale. However, the relationship between the manager and Stoke Holding had completely broken down. Stoke Holding, who were already out of communications with the English board representatives by this point, were in no mood to give Pulis any more funds for transfers. Consortium chairman Magnús Kristinsson had been thought to have said that they would not give the club any money while Tony Pulis was still in charge. To further add to the confusion surrounding the club, Gíslason would say, 'Tony will continue to have the full support of directors. Stoke Holding have indicated that potential buyers must exhibit the financial strength to continue to improve the club. Stoke Holding will continue to financially support the club until a sale has been completed, a process which will take a number of months and even go beyond the end of next season.' It seemed like the club was being pulled in different directions, with Gíslason stuck between the day-to-day personnel and UK-based board, and the Icelandic consortium who had the majority control of the club. Something had to give.

* * *

With Peter Coates, Keith Humphreys and Phil Rawlins the only real prospects of purchasing the club from the Icelandic consortium and any bids to date not meeting the Icelanders' valuation, it seemed like the power would remain in Iceland for the time being. Rawlins had tried on several occasions to purchase the club from the Icelanders (with Gary Mellor likely to become chief executive if successful) to no avail. His latest bid of $10m (approximately £6m, the same as the initial purchase the Icelanders had paid to take over the club in 1999) was turned down, as the Icelanders wanted closer to £10m. Rawlins knew that paying that much would mean he wouldn't have sufficient funds to invest in the squad, so did not return to the table. Peter Coates also launched his own takeover bid, with the condition that Pulis be kept in charge. This was also rebuffed, meaning Gíslason and Co would continue to run the club. For the board it was time, as they say in Iceland, to lay their heads in water (*leggja höfuðið í bleyti*) and figure it out. They decided, since no bids in their price range were forthcoming, that they would roll the dice one more time in a bid to gain promotion to the Premier League and reap the financial benefits that would follow. As Pulis was clearly not getting any more funds from Kristinsson, and Coates wasn't stumping up the cash that the Icelanders wanted to secure the club and Pulis's position, the decision was made – on 28 June 2005, Tony Pulis was sacked as Stoke City manager.

Gary Mellor recounted his discussions with Pulis that led up to his dismissal: 'He called me as I was at a cricket match at Durham and he read out a letter from the chairman. I told him that, in my legal opinion, they were setting him up to fire him, which proved to be the case.' The official reason given for Pulis's dismissal was that he had 'failed to implement the strategy of exploiting foreign markets'. Gíslason said, 'Despite all the good work he has done, he has failed to implement the strategy of exploiting foreign markets. It is felt we will again fail to exploit those markets this summer with him in control.' No doubt this was a key reason in the dismissal of Pulis, but the style of football in the previous season must have played a part in the decision too. The Welshman had lost a lot of support from the fans, softening the blow of his sacking for those who were ready for a change. There could be no doubt that Pulis had done a remarkable job in stabilising the club on the pitch in the space of two and a half seasons, after taking over with Stoke looking destined for relegation straight back down to Division Two (rebranded as League One for the 2004/05 season). Despite the obvious issues between the board and Pulis, the sacking was still a surprise considering Pulis had signed a new contract towards the end of the previous season and was talking up the new season in his interview after the Sunderland game. He had also been publicly backed by Gíslason (in hindsight, receiving the dreaded vote of confidence), and had been allowed to make the signing of striker Mamady Sidibé from Gillingham. Ultimately, it was a decision that was always going to be made once the consortium decided to gamble on one last attempt at reaching the promised land.

* * *

A week is a long time in football. Before fans could speculate on who the next manager would be, the decision was made the day after Pulis was sacked. The Icelandic board had already moved swiftly, appointing Eiður Guðjohnsen's dad, Arnor, to find a new manager. Arnor suggested Dutchman Jan de Koning, a former Ajax youth coach. Jan de Koning did not fancy the role as manager, so suggested his friend and compatriot for the job, with De Koning happier to take an assistant's role. And so, it was former Holland international Johan Boskamp who was named as Pulis's replacement as manager of Stoke City. The 56-year-old former manager of Anderlecht and Genk was unknown to the vast majority of Stoke fans, and indeed English football fans in general. The move was reminiscent of Gary Megson's dismissal for the unknown Guðjón Thórdarson, who arrived with a reputation built overseas. Boskamp had played in the famous Holland team of the 1970s that featured Johan Cruyff, and had a good managerial pedigree in Belgian football, winning three titles with Anderlecht, as well as coaching the Georgian and Qatari national teams.

Gíslason was happy with his appointment, stating, 'In the past two or three years we have not been able to attract foreign players as much as we would have liked. We are hoping that

Mr Boskamp, with his experience and knowledge of foreign markets, especially in Holland and Belgium, can bring players to this club that can be something for the supporters to look forward to seeing.' Suddenly, the words coming out of Iceland seemed positive again, almost as if there was a change of heart. Gíslason said, 'We have a shareholders agreement – Stoke Holding, Peter Coates, Phil Rawlins and Keith Humphreys – it was in jeopardy at the end of last season, but I expect that to be on track now. There's no reason why that shouldn't be honoured in full – so we should have the money that was here before and then some more.' Magnús Kristinsson didn't mince his words when he told BBC Radio Stoke, 'I'm very happy that Tony Pulis has left. I support chairman Gunnar Gíslason's decision to appoint Dutchman Johan Boskamp in his place.' It was clear that Boskamp was the Icelanders' choice. There was no way Coates, Humphreys and Rawlins would have even known who he was, let alone champion him for manager. Rawlins would later confirm that despite being promised to be kept in the loop by the Icelanders, the consortium had gone ahead and appointed Boskamp after a face-to-face meeting in Amsterdam, before informing the English board members by email.

* * *

New manager Boskamp arrived to a mixture of excitement and apprehension. The burly Dutchman had ignited the optimism of the Stoke fans by declaring, in his thick Dutch accent, 'I like to play attacking, attractive football and I like fast football.' He would later say, 'I had to be interested. This is a real football country. I'm crazy about the football of Spain, Portugal, Argentina. But my favourites were the Busby Babes, the Manchester United side who had the air crash at Munich in 1958. I met the directors in Amsterdam. They didn't tell me to bring in foreign players, only to get the right players. If I believed the bookies, we're on our way to the Third Division [League One]. Me, I'm hoping we can make the play-offs.'

It wasn't long before the promises of new transfers would be fulfilled, as a glut of new players arrived, domestically and from the Continent. In came Belgian defender Carl Hoefkens, compatriot midfielder Junior and Czech winger Martin Kolar, as well as experienced domestic players Bruce Dyer, Marlon Broomes, Peter Sweeney and Luke Chadwick. The British-based players were no doubt brought in under the guidance of John Rudge, who was working closely with Boskamp in order to build the Dutchman's familiarity with the English game. The Rudge signings were a reaction to a poor preseason, during which Boskamp even considered stepping down. Rudge would recall, 'On our preseason tour, Johan Boskamp talked of phoning the chairman and quitting the job. I had gladly worked night and day to help him get a team together that could compete in the Championship.'

Boskamp talked up his relationship with Rudge at the time and his role in bringing in targeted players. Shortly after his appointment, Boskamp said of Rudge, 'He knows the game here in a way that I don't. Also, I don't have the patience to sit in an office. John spoke for seven hours to the agent of Carl Hoefkens. I was saying, "Stop it, let him go", but he went on. We got him.' New signing Carl Hoefkens, brought in from Germinal Beerschot, was a football-playing centre-half turned right-back, with prototypical good looks and style. It was his wife, Vanessa, who attracted more attention from the fans than the defender upon their arrival. She was a stunning model with a WAG-style personality, which had led the couple to be something of a Belgian version of Posh and Becks. Junior and Kolar arrived with high expectations, thanks to their new manager. Boskamp said, 'Junior is one of the most talented players in Belgium, and I think the people will be as crazy about Kolar as they were about Peter Hoekstra, he has the same magic.' The latter statement was an audacious one indeed.

Towards the end of the summer, Boskamp would make his boldest signing yet, splashing out a record fee of £950,000 for Guinea international striker Sambegou Bangoura. Twenty-three-year-old Sambegou, or Sammy as he was referred to by fans, was a prolific goalscorer in the Belgian league for Lokeren and Standard Liège. New chief executive Tony Scholes said, 'Sambegou was Johan Boskamp's number one target over the summer. We're delighted that with the backing of the board, we have been able to bring him to the club, and we look forward to seeing him in action for Stoke.' Stoke weren't done in the summer transfer window either, bringing in Scottish forward Paul Gallagher on loan from Blackburn, before returning to the Icelandic market, capturing international forward Hannes Sigurðsson from Viking Stavanger. Stoke's new-look squad was steadily being put in place throughout the summer, as the Potters entered their most unpredictable season in years.

August 1999: Stoke fans demanding change in the boardroom following years of failure on the pitch

November 1999: The Icelandic consortium take over the club, including consortium chief Magnus Kristinsson (far left) and club chairman Gunnar Gíslason (third from left)

April 2000: Manager Guðjón Thórdarson (middle, with Peter Thorne, left, and Graham Kavanagh, right) brought silverware to the Potteries in his first season with the Auto Windscreens Shield triumph at Wembley

October 2000: Icelandic forward Ríkharður Daðason would eventually join the club after a long pursuit

May 2000: Clive Clarke (left) and Grahan Kavanagh (right) on the receiving end of some shocking refereeing from Rob Styles or a dismal night in the play-offs at Priestfiela

November 2000: Robbie Fowler (right) and Liverpool run riot at the Brit in the League Cup

May 2001: Walsall's Pedro Matías (left) beats Gavin Ward to inflict more play-off heartache on Stoke

October 2001: Stoke fans being carefully monitored by the police during the Potteries Derby at Vale Park

May 2002: Stoke face a familiar foe in the play-off semi-final, former club captain Graham Kavanagh

May 2002: Clive Clarke and James O'Connor celebrate a famous win in the play-off semi-final at Ninian Park

May 2002: Guðjón Thórdarson overjoyed on the pitch after the 2-0 victory over Cardiff

May 2002: Stoke finally triumph in the play-offs at the third attempt, beating Brentford 2-0 at the Millennium Stadium

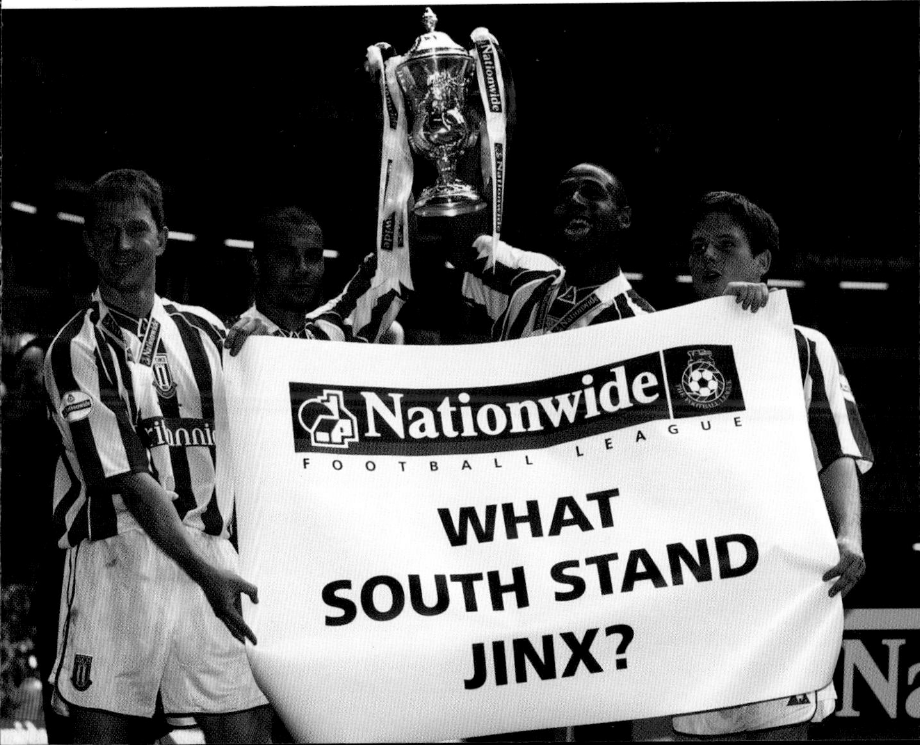

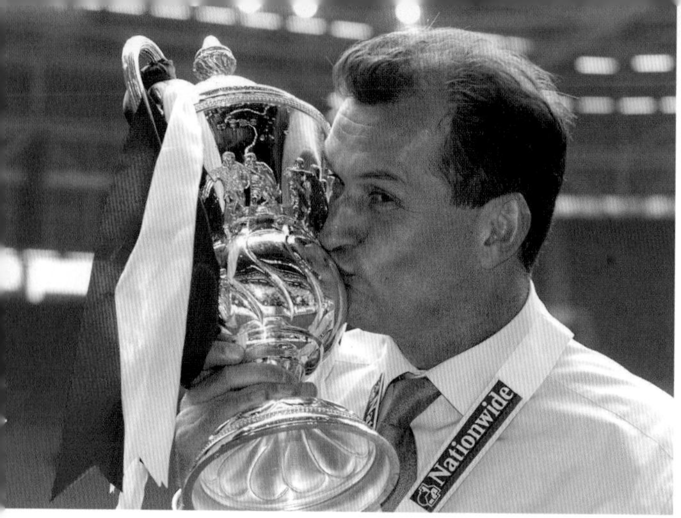

May 2002: Guðjón Thórdarson kisses the play-off trophy, days before he was sacked by the club

September 2002: Steve Cotterill, who took charge of 13 games before walking out on the club to join Sunderland as Howard Wilkinson's number two

November 2002: Gunnar Gíslason (left) welcomes Tony Pulis (right) to Stoke. His challenge was to save the club from an immediate return to Division Two

May 2003: Ade Akinbiyi (centre) secures Stoke's Division One status with the only goal in the final game of the season against Reading at the Brit

May 2003: Tony Pulis (left) with Mark Crossley (right), who was pivotal in keeping Stoke up during his short loan period

Top left: December 2003: Dutch winger Peter Hoekstra was a fan favourite thanks to his silky skills and stunning goals

Top right: September 2005: Manager Johan Boskamp cuts a frustrated figure during a bonkers season in charge

Right: April 2006: Peter Coates (right) returns as club chairman and reinstates Tony Pulis (left) as manager. The rest is history …

Chapter 22

One Night in Coventry

'I'm not Adolf Hitler. But [Jan] knows I will never work with him again. We work only for one thing: for Stoke' – Johan Boskamp

BOSKAMP'S STOKE started the 2005/06 season with a repeat of the 2002 opener against Sheffield Wednesday. This time round, the Potters were at home and Sheffield Wednesday were the newly promoted side. Stoke fielded six debutants, but the side wasn't helped by the 13th-minute dismissal of Gerry Taggart. Despite playing the majority of the game with ten men, it was Stoke who should have taken the three points. Scottish winger Kevin Harper, signed during the previous season by Pulis, blazed over a late penalty after Carl Hoefkens was fouled in the box. The game finished 0-0, as fans were made to wait for the adventurous football we were anticipating. We wouldn't have to wait long. The next game was a trip to the Walkers Stadium to face Leicester City. It didn't exactly go the way we were hoping though, as Leicester ran out convincing 4-2 winners in a defensive nightmare for the Potters which also saw new signing Junior see red.

Still, at least we saw a couple of Stoke goals! The result and performance were perhaps a foreboding omen of what was to come unless Boskamp could find the right balance between attack and defence. The manager and team bounced back with two straight wins, and Boskamp was underway. His first league win came at Millwall thanks to a goal from Johnny Halls, after which the manager would proclaim, 'We like to play good football and to work hard, and that was what earned us the three points today.'

More away wins would follow at Hull and Preston, mainly inspired by loan signing Paul Gallagher. Fans had warmed to the jolly Dutch giant in the dugout, mainly due to his wonderful mixture of confidence and lack of English during his interviews. He described a would-have-been Polish signing as a 'shit guy' after a last-minute U-turn and would often proclaim his affection for a good chip shop. There was another time during the January transfer window where Nigel Johnson asked Boskamp, 'Are there any new signings coming?' His response was, 'We will see. Asians are coming, and we will talk with them about what they have for us, but I don't really trust the Asians.' Nigel responded with surprise, 'The Asians are coming??' Johan pondered his surprise, before replying, 'Eh? … oh, no! Agents, not Asians!' He also misinterpreted a chant from the fans of 'Boskamp, give us a wave' as a declaration that they wanted him to leave, before being informed that it was an affectionate chant and waving wildly in response after a bit of a delay. John Acres described interviewing Boskamp as 'brilliant' and 'hilarious', and described some of their interactions: 'I love Tony Pulis, I really rate him as a manager and he's a bit of a God for Stoke fans for what he did for the club, but when Boskamp came in, it was so different. He was the opposite of Tony Pulis. The press would go into the reception where they had these big leather sofas in the corner next to where you would do interviews, next to a door for the club shop that would constantly bang during interviews. Johan Boskamp used to sprawl out on the leather sofas in his Adidas shorts with his blond highlights, making jokes to everyone who walked through. He would sit there with you drinking coffee for ages, being really honest with you. Interviewing him was hilarious. We did a player profile with him and I asked him to tell us something about you that might surprise us. Most players would say things like "I'm a really good cook" or "I played cricket for my county", something like that. Boskamp said, "I'm not really a man" and then he just burst into hysterics! He found it hilarious!'

His antics and interviews were humorous, but it was the team's form on the pitch that had really won the fans over in those early days. Popular long-lived fanzine *The Oatcake* stated that 'the magic of the match-day experience has been reignited after last season's effective but mind-numbingly boring football [under Tony Pulis]'. The Boskamp entertainment dynamic even led to the birth of the (short-lived) 'Stoke City Amigos' group, as a section of fans gathered in Mexican sombreros and ponchos to celebrate the new-found fun factor around the club. While the early experiences were enjoyable, a worrying trend in home form started to develop in the autumn. Stoke lost home games to Watford, Wolves and Cardiff by scores of 3-0, 3-1 and 3-0 respectively. Under Pulis, home fans were conditioned to see the Britannia Stadium as a fortress, typically backed up by wins. At the very least, teams would have to work incredibly hard to take something away from the Potteries and seldom scored more than one goal.

A run of four defeats was broken by a 2-0 win at home to Crewe, thanks to a first goal for Stoke for record signing Sammy Bangoura. Another red card for the Potters, this time for defender Michael Duberry, meant the squad was looking thin at the back. Assistant manager Jan de Koning confirmed, 'I've phoned Gerry Taggart and he's coming back – we want him on the [training] pitch on Thursday. Gerry is on a training course in Holland with Feyenoord. I told him he had to come back because we don't know what happened to Dube.' Taggart was to take on more coaching responsibilities for Stoke. The plan was to ease him into the role, but things don't always go to plan, as fans were about to find out.

* * *

Stoke travelled to Coventry's new Ricoh Arena for a night match on 2 November 2005, looking to move back up towards the play-offs. After Coventry took an early lead, Stoke drew level thanks to a long-range effort from Taggart, back in the side to cover for Duberry. A wonderful curling second-half finish from Paul Gallagher would give Stoke all three points, and things were looking rosy for the Potters heading towards Christmas. However, unbeknownst to the travelling away fans who were enjoying the on-field performance, something was rumbling on the touchline and in the stands that would affect Stoke's entire season.

During the game at the Ricoh, and with Boskamp on the touchline instructing his team, director of football John Rudge had come down from the directors' box to get the attention of Jan de Koning. Rudge passed a note to De Koning, presumably containing some tactical advice. Boskamp was unaware of the interaction between the two until a player on the bench brought his attention to the incident. The manager was incensed. He felt like actions were being taken behind his back, that his integrity was being called into question and that he may lose the respect of the players if he did not act upon the situation. His anger was mostly directed towards Rudge, but De Koning would also feel his wrath for not informing his compatriot (not to mention friend of 30 years) about Rudge's efforts to communicate with the players.

There was very little to witness on the night from the away end to suggest that there were any issues amongst the management team. The public fallout of that night would start in the days following the match and rumble on for the rest of the season. Rudge and De Koning were immediately sent home and put on gardening leave. Noel Blake and Gerry Taggart were promoted to first-team coaching duties to assist Boskamp, who was ready to walk out of the club over the row. The manager issued an ultimatum, they go or I go, and said, 'My contract ends on 30 June. Everyone knows the problems and I won't change my mind. I have my principles.' The decision to send Rudge and De Koning home appeased the manager until the end of the season but he was not willing to stay any longer if the duo were to remain at the club. Fans, who weren't particularly pleased with former Vale man Rudge anyway since his refusal to take the caretaker position back in 2003, were pleased with Boskamp's decision to stay on. The team were up to fourth in the league and new signing Bangoura was approaching top goalscoring form. Boskamp also expressed his desire to stay, stating, 'I have a meeting with the chairman to discuss what's happening. I don't want to go because I feel we're building something good here. I don't want to lose that, but we will see after the meeting.' John Acres spoke about the Coventry incident, saying, 'What a shambles! Boskamp was a proud man, and he just couldn't handle the fact that Rudgie had gone down to pass a message on about the tactics. Before that, Rudge was able to give Johan and Jan information on the opposition teams. Johan and Jan were good coaches and knew about the foreign markets, but they wouldn't have known anything about the opposition's threat from set pieces, their danger men, and so on. Rudgie had all that information. It's interesting to think what would have happened had they not had that blow-up. It would have been interesting to see.'

* * *

Though the situation had seemed to have been partially resolved in the weeks following the Coventry game, the effects and bad feeling would continue well into the new year. By January 2006, Boskamp was still threatening to walk, prompting chief executive Tony Scholes to speak out. He said, 'The objective of the Stoke City Board of Directors when the managerial issue first arose last November was to avoid any further upheaval. That position has not changed, and any further decisions made by the board will be made as and when they feel appropriate. Johan Boskamp is an honourable man and we are confident he will remain at the club until the summer at least. The players have been aware of the managerial issues since they first became public. They are professionals and have continued to do their job.' It is also thought that Stoke Holding chairman Magnús Kristinsson, who had only stuck around after ousting Tony Pulis in favour of Boskamp, told the Dutchman, 'You will finish what you have started.' The message was simply 'just get on with it', or as they say in Iceland … *áfram með smjörið* ('on with the butter!').

Boskamp's words made it clear that he still harboured a lot of ill feeling about the incident. In February 2006, he said, 'If the players hadn't told me that John Rudge had come downstairs to tell a player what to do I wouldn't have known anything. If Jesus Christ came downstairs to say, "do this", I wouldn't care. I knew then that it was over. If I had said nothing, I would have lost all the respect of my players. Everybody says forgive; I can forgive, that is no problem. But I can't forget. Some people are disappointed, but it's got nothing to do with the club. It's between me, John and Jan. I said, "if you want John to stay with me or Jan to stay then it's not possible". If the club say John Rudge is more important than me then I really have no problem.' Boskamp confirmed that himself and De Koning were back on speaking terms, but their working relationship was broken: 'It is total nonsense that Jan and I do not talk. I'm not Adolf Hitler. But [Jan] knows I will never work with him again. We work only for one thing: for Stoke.'

Chapter 23

Bangoura Goes Bye-Bye

'I seem to be the only one who's still mad with him. I'm so surprised that my players say, "OK Sami, it's the last time." If I was on the pitch with him, I would kill him. If he had the ball my sole purpose would be to go and deal with him. Of course, in time I'll forgive him, but I won't forget it' – Johan Boskamp

THE IMMEDIATE worry following the Coventry incident was whether all the off-field shenanigans and rumours of managerial walkouts would affect the team's performances on the pitch. The worries were eased after Stoke won their next two games, including a 2-1 win at Crewe to complete the double over the Cheshire side. Paul Gallagher was continuing to impress during his loan spell, while Sammy Bangoura was starting to show the form that had led to his record signing. The Guinean bagged a brace against Brighton before netting against Crewe. John Acres reminisced about the Brighton performance: 'The 3-0 win at home against Brighton was really great, Stoke played some lovely stuff. Bangoura scored twice and Darel Russell. Gunnar Gíslason used to listen to commentary of the games. He phoned me up and told me he really liked the commentary, and that the team sounded brilliant based on what I was saying. Bangoura, the record signing, scored two and everything was looking good. That's when optimism was quite high, that was my favourite game under Boskamp.'

The goals against Brighton were the start of an incredible run that saw Bangoura net in six consecutive games. The run saw Stoke keep pace with the play-off contenders and kept up our impressive away form. Boskamp would comment, 'You need deep strikers who can hold the ball up and you need players who can score, and we have that in Paul Gallagher and Sam Bangoura. But our secret away from home is that we just keep scoring one more goal than the other team.' Home form was still proving to be a problem for the Potters, and defeat to QPR at the start of December after another bad-tempered game with the London side led to ugly scenes when a Stoke fan ran on to the pitch to attack Rangers goalkeeper Simon Royce.

Stoke bounced back at home to beat Leicester 3-2 thanks to a winner from Bangoura, but the Potters would soon be without the in-form striker, who departed on international duty for the Africa Cup of Nations. Stoke would not miss the striker in their next game, a memorable trip to Kenilworth Road just before Christmas to face Luton Town. The old-fashioned ground in amongst the terraced houses of Luton is a unique away-day experience. You are basically required to walk through someone's back garden to enter the tight away end behind the goal. To the left, there is a stand which is comprised totally of executive boxes and, to the right, the noisy home fans are gathered to provide an intimate atmosphere with the away section. There isn't much pitchside room either, meaning home fans can really get into the ear of the visiting team on the touchline. The Hatters took the lead in the game after 20 minutes thanks to Ahmet Brković, leading to a chant of 'Shit ground, 1-0' from the home section. The travelling Stoke fans hadn't even initiated the familiar chant of 'Shit ground, no fans' at any time up to that point, suggesting it was some Pavlovian reaction to a goal for the Luton fans. Of course, when Stoke equalised through Gallagher before half-time, the response was a predictable rendition of 'Shit ground, 1-1'. Gallagher once again showed his quality to make it 2-1 after 83 minutes, as the Potters looked to hold out for three points. Luton seemed to have grabbed a late point, scoring a penalty after 88 minutes. However, a late free kick on halfway for Stoke was thrown deep into the Luton box and, under pressure from Michael Duberry, Luton's Chris Coyne put through his own net to hand Stoke a 93rd-minute winner in front of the away fans. There were wild celebrations from the travelling Stokies, as the team moved up to fifth in the league for Christmas Day.

* * *

Unfortunately, this would be as good as it got for Stoke under Boskamp, as the absence of Bangoura would start to be felt in the new year. In the eight games that Bangoura missed between Boxing Day 2005 and Valentine's Day 2006, Stoke failed to score in six. The team also failed to register a win during that period, losing six, including another 3-0 defeat at home, this time to Hull, slumping back down to mid-table. Simon Lowe, who was writing fan columns for *The Sentinel* by the time of the Hull result, said, 'After the woeful home defeat by Hull, I wrote a piece condemning the actions of some hooligans who had started fights in the stands as the team subsided not only to defeat, but contrived to miss three penalties in the one game just to compound the embarrassment. The day after my column was published, I received a phone call from Chief Executive Tony Scholes to thank me for what I had written in my column. These were quite dark days and he felt the shame of hooligans raising their ugly head quite personally.' The run also included a home draw with Ipswich, Stoke's first draw since the opening day of the season. To make matters worse, Bangoura had gone AWOL after the Africa Cup of Nations. He was expected to return before the 4 February home fixture against Preston (which finished 0-0) but wouldn't be seen until the 14 February clash with Plymouth Argyle. The Pilgrims had been struggling with the threat of relegation in the first half of the season, leading them to turn to former Stoke manager Tony Pulis to do what he does best and steer the club to safety. Pulis was greeted with a warm reception from the Stoke fans, which the Welshman was pleased about after the game. The game itself was a typical Pulis masterclass, grinding out an away point in a dreadfully boring 0-0 draw.

Bangoura was back in the team for the game, but his relationship with the manager, club and fans had soured following his delayed return. Tony Scholes confirmed, 'We'll discipline him, as he's let everyone down.' Boskamp was equally frustrated, stating, 'He's apologised to the players but I don't understand. I seem to be the only one who's still mad with him. I'm so surprised that my players say, "OK Sami, it's the last time." If I was on the pitch with him, I would kill him. If he had the ball my sole purpose would be to go and deal with him. Of course, in time I'll forgive him, but I won't forget it.' The club had rejected a bid of £2.5m for the striker a week before his return (i.e. when he was expected back at the club), something the board and management no doubt regretted very soon after.

The Guinean would only net one more goal before the end of the season, although that did come in a surprise 4-1 win away at Ipswich. His final tally of nine goals in 25 games was more than respectable for a first season in English football, especially having missed the start of the season and a large chunk of it over the winter. His red-hot form in November and December had fans dreaming of promotion, having seemingly finally found that '20 goals a season man' that every team strives to locate. But his lack of discipline and respect for the club is what ultimately spelt his departure from the Potteries. Indeed, after showing so much promise prior to his arrival and during his first few months at the club, he seemed to be destined for bigger things, but they never came. Bangoura went missing again, this time for the entirety of preseason after the 2005/06 season had finished. Amidst one of his mysterious disappearances, John Acres went in search of the missing Guinean, recounting, 'When Sammy disappeared and didn't come back, we just couldn't score. When he was missing, I went to his house to try and find him! Someone tipped me off for his address in Newcastle, so I went to the door. "Hi, is Sammy around?"; it was full of all his mates and family from Guinea! There must have been at least 12 in his house, but not him! They were speaking to me in pigeon-English and a bit of French, but I established very quickly that he wasn't there, and they didn't know where he was! It was like some sort of comedy sketch. "Where's Sammy?"'

Bangoura returned a day before the new season and would receive very limited playing time before moving back to Belgium. From there, he bounced around Portugal, Spain and Greece, where goals were a rarity, before returning to African football. The whole tale had highlighted the importance of appropriate background checks and screening of player attitudes when delving into big money transfers for reputable players, particularly from the Continent. Unfortunately, Stoke would repeat the errors they had made with the Bangoura saga in our final Premier League seasons under Mark Hughes, with the likes of Jesé Rodríguez, Saido Berahino, Kevin Wimmer and Giannelli Imbula. At least Bangoura had that six-game run which will be remembered!

Chapter 24

Going Dutch

'You cannot discuss every week about selling the club. You cannot work with two groups. Either the Icelandics stay, or the English buy the club. Otherwise you destroy the club'
– Johan Boskamp

BOSKAMP VENTURED into the transfer market again in January and February 2006, bringing in winger Peter Kopteff and midfielders Josip Skoko and Luke Chadwick. So far, Stoke's 2005/06 transfer activity had seen mixed results. Bangoura had obviously made a big impact upon his arrival, but soon fizzled out. Junior and Kolar had done little to impress (the latter was certainly not the second coming of Peter Hoekstra!), and Hannes Sigurðsson had done little to impress in his limited appearances, although he was played out of position on more than a few occasions. Carl Hoefkens was by far the best signing that could be directly attributed to Boskamp, impressing at right-back after being switched from central defence on his way to being named player of the season. The domestic signings that Rudge had a key role in bringing in had been more consistent, with Paul Gallagher impressing with his creativity and ability to score some lovely long-range goals.

While Chadwick would prove to be another steady signing, Kopteff joined the list of disappointments that plagued Boskamp's time at Stoke, as the season dwindled out to another mid-table finish. There was still time for another 3-1 home defeat, Crystal Palace the benefactors in mid-March, as well as away wins at QPR and Ipswich. The season ended with a stunning 5-1 win at Brighton, with youth product Adam Rooney bagging a hat-trick at the Withdean Stadium. By this point, it was already common knowledge that Boskamp would likely be leaving the club, and it was confirmed following the final-day win. As well as the Rudge–De Koning incident, Boskamp had been at odds with the Icelandic board about a potential new deal that was not forthcoming. The decision by the club came amidst circulating rumours of a new bid being tabled by Peter Coates, as the Icelanders were once again ready to sell. Chairman Gunnar Gíslason had sparked discussions of board and managerial departures a week before the season ended, declaring, 'If an agreement can't be made to buy our shares, we'll have to make decisions.'

After his final game, Boskamp said, 'I'm not sad, but disappointed to leave, but football goes on and I think Stoke have a great future. It's not bad to finish with a 5-1 win, and I hope our good following of fans enjoyed it. We've made progress, winning ten games away from home. I believe if the team is kept together things will develop well.' The Dutchman also stated, 'I'm now available to talk to other clubs and will probably end up in Belgium or Holland. I don't regret asking for two years. I have no contract and you can't work with two groups.' Once again, the Icelanders were under the spotlight after another failed relationship with the team manager.

Boskamp had some parting words for his former employers, saying, 'You cannot discuss every week about selling the club. You cannot work with two groups. Either the Icelanders stay, or the English buy the club. Otherwise you destroy the club.'

* * *

In the years that followed his departure, Johan Boskamp admitted that he wished he had stayed at Stoke City. In an interview with *Voetbal International*, he said, 'If I'm honest, I've regretted every day that I did not see out my contract. Stoke is a really great club. But I can't work with people who don't like me. If this happens, I just give back my contract.' Boskamp's short but dramatic reign was, and still is, polarising for fans. Season-ticket holders would be glad to see the back of him, after so many three-goal defeats at home and a poor season record at the Britannia Stadium in general. His signings of Junior, Kolar, Kopteff, Sigurðsson and ultimately Bangoura were poor decisions, and his high-profile bust-up with Jan de Koning and John Rudge was embarrassing for the club. However, there were bright moments throughout the season too, particularly away from home where the 600–800 committed fans who travelled every other week to see Stoke play saw some high-scoring wins that are still an unfamiliar sight today. His signing of Carl Hoefkens should also be applauded, as the popular defender later went on to help West Brom seal promotion. This was also Boskamp's one and only season in England, and he did keep us comfortably away from the bottom three, even threatening the play-offs for the first half of the season. Given the time (and possibly a stronger board presence), he *may* have improved and pushed the club forward. That's a lot of ifs and buts though, and in hindsight, much of his reign undid the stability that Tony Pulis had built in his first spell as manager, while his departure definitely preceded the start of a highly successful period in Stoke City's history.

Ultimately, the Boskamp experiment was a failure, and the Icelanders' one last try for promotion had ended with his long-foreseen departure. His initial selection for the job was not well thought out and seemed to be an appointment to spite both the former manager and Peter Coates. In some ways, his overall performance was comparable to Chris Kamara's in the 1997/98 relegation season, the main differences being that Boskamp was afforded far more transfer funds and had inherited a much stronger squad. Both managers made wholesale changes in just a few weeks, rather than working with the players we had or trying to get more out of an underperforming team that was low on self-belief and in desperate need of organisation. Boskamp's stint was nowhere near as disastrous as Kamara's, but he was the incorrect man for the time at Stoke. An Icelander might say *Hann er á rangri hillu í lífinu* ('He is on the wrong shelf in life'), indicating that Boskamp was simply in the wrong job. But he wasn't the only one. The question now was, how long could the Icelanders hold on to their position of power? They were now desperately looking for a way out; the only interested party was Peter Coates. A final decision was forthcoming.

Chapter 25

The End of the Icelanders

'I'm 68 years old and have all the money I need. I don't need to be making a £10m-plus investment into a football club which is losing money. It's clearly not a sensible financial investment. I passionately want this football club to succeed and this overrides other considerations' – Peter Coates

WITH JOHAN Boskamp departed, there was only one other exit that Stoke fans were anticipating – the Icelandic owners. The club was put up for sale as far back as April 2005 prior to Tony Pulis's sacking, but Stoke Holding were reluctant to sell to the only interested parties at the time – Phil Rawlins and Peter Coates. The sacking of Pulis and subsequent appointment of Boskamp were portrayed as a last-ditch attempt to make it to the Premier League, although some saw it as a way of forcing Peter Coates's hand and getting him to stump up the money to their own valuation. Coates was an outspoken supporter of Pulis, sharing his philosophies and trusting him with transfer money. By ousting Pulis in favour of the polar opposite in

Boskamp, some thought it was a way of sparking Coates into action to save his beloved Stoke City. Peter Coates is a savvy businessman, and wasn't prone to quick, emotionally driven decisions, be it as Stoke City chairman, or as a director of the vast bet365 gambling empire that made him a billionaire. His smart-minded approach had seen him amass a much larger personal fortune than he had held when he was previously at the helm of Stoke City in the late 90s, so money was not the issue for him. He waited until the time was right – for him, for the club, and for the city of Stoke-on-Trent. Simon Lowe had spoken to Coates at the time, recalling, 'Just after the season drew to a particularly unimpressive close, I received a phone call from Peter Coates's PA. Mr. Coates, I was told, wanted to meet with me and would appreciate an hour of my time. He would come to me, so I arranged a meeting for the bar of a hotel near where I was working at the BBC's Elstree Studios. Mr Coates arrived exactly on time and greeted me warmly. He read my column, he said, and was on an exercise to speak with people who could help him. I sat forward, this sounded interesting. The two revelations he dropped on me at that point – after swearing me to secrecy until they became public – were that he was leading a buy-back of the club to take control back from the Icelanders, which would give him 100% control of the club, and that once completed, he would be appointing Tony Pulis as manager again.'

The sale of the club rumbled on as the 2005/06 season ended but, with only one interested party, there would need to be an agreement between the Icelanders and Coates. In March 2006, Gunnar Gíslason stated, 'It is safe to assume that Icelandic ownership of the majority shareholding in the club will not be eternal. Stoke Holding SA will continue to be willing to speak to potential buyers. I don't know if at some stage in the future, Peter Coates and Stoke Holding SA will be able to agree on a fair valuation of the club. I am sure that with his financial clout and passion for the club, his aim would be to get the club promoted to the Premier League.' After several rejected bids, and with Gíslason stating in April that the negotiations were 'getting further apart and not closer', it seemed like the two parties had reached a stalemate. Coates's informal package offer totalling £7m was deemed not enough by the Icelanders. However, on Monday, 22 May 2006, Stoke chairman Gunnar Gíslason officially announced that he was resigning from the club, effective immediately and bringing an end to the Icelandic era of Stoke City FC.

Outgoing chairman Gíslason was typically bullish about how the consortium had handled the running of the club. In his departure statement, he said, 'Later on Monday I will step down as chairman of this great club. The time has come for others to continue our work of preparing Stoke for promotion back to the top flight of English football. The Icelandic involvement at Stoke City FC has overall been very good for the club. Of course, some mistakes have been made along the way and with the benefit of hindsight some are easy to spot, but to expect to go through any venture without making mistakes is naive. The main thing to keep in mind is that the club has improved dramatically over the past seven years, and strong foundations for future success have been laid.' He defended the way that he and his compatriots had handled managerial appointments, saying, 'We have had our share of criticism for the managers we have employed. Although he is not perfect, I think Johan [Boskamp] did a decent job last season and that he would have done an even better job next season if he'd had the chance to work with his team for another year.' Chair of the Norwegian supporters' branch Runar Kvernen has spoken of the forthcoming Icelandic banking collapse as a potentially disastrous time for the club had the Icelanders remained in power: 'Gíslason and his fellows were a little unprepared for English club football, but for sure they tried. The whole country of Iceland almost went broke during the finance crisis a few years later, and former Stoke City owners were affected by that. The Icelanders and the whole country were stretched economically, and a couple of years later everything went down for them … It would have been a horror scenario if they had owned the club in 2008/09 … what would have happened if Peter the Great had not taken over …?'

* * *

The day after Gíslason's statement, Peter Coates was officially confirmed as the new owner of the football club. He acquired the majority shares from Stoke Holding for £1.7m, with the total package adding up to £8.3m for fixing the club's finances and clearing existing debts. Phil Rawlins described the deal as 'a really good price' for Coates, stating that it was 'virtually what they [Stoke Holding] had paid for the club'. Returning chairman Coates stated, 'It's a return to local ownership and with local decision-making and I am excited at working with everybody at the club. The investment will transform the club's finances, clearing all shareholder loans and stabilising what is a precarious position. The club will be largely debt-free and have a fresh start with a unified board of directors and a senior management team. Our first task is to build a side capable of challenging for the play-offs with the ultimate dream being making it to the Premier League.' Simon Lowe believes that Coates retaining a golden share in the club in 1999 would prove to be crucial in his subsequent takeover in 2006: 'I had often been critical of Mr Coates, both in print and with other fans, as I had felt that keeping hold of his "golden share" had held back the Icelanders in many ways. But Peter Coates was clever. We'll never know if it was a plan all along, but he retained his place on the board despite selling a large proportion of the club to the Icelanders, which meant he kept hold of an interest in the club as well. The Icelanders didn't own the club lock, stock and barrel. Coates's friend and director Keith Humphreys had a golden share too. They were an immovable, if non-controlling presence throughout the Icelanders' time at Stoke.'

For Coates, this was a do-over, a chance to set the record straight after his first spell as chairman. He saw that the club was in turmoil and heading in the wrong direction and stepped in to make things right. This time round, he had the financial clout to invest both on and off the pitch, with his sights set on building a squad under a trustworthy manager, purchasing and improving the stadium, upgrading the training facilities and cementing the club in the heart of the local community. With the golden shares rights of outvoting and vetoing removed, he would again be working with Keith Humphreys and Phil Rawlins, and his son, John, would also assume more responsibilities in the club. Peter Coates would admit in 2011 that his family weren't 100 per cent sure that his decision to buy back the club was right at the time, saying, 'I bought it back again against my better judgment, in some ways, and my family's, who all thought I was daft to do it. The club was in a mess at the time and I thought I could help it and do things for it, and I was a bit disappointed with my previous time, and there was a little bit of unfinished business about it and all that sort of thing. But I thought it would be important for the area if the football club were doing well. Stoke was having a difficult time. It has lost the pot banks and the mining industry. I thought that if Stoke could get in the Premier League it would give the place a lift and would be good for it.'

* * *

Stoke City was a mess on and off the pitch, but the severity of the financial plight that the club was in would only become apparent to Coates after his takeover. Shortly after reassuming control of the club, Coates stated, 'It is difficult to describe the financial performance during the 2005/06 season as anything other than dire. The former owners, Stoke Holding, took the decision in the summer of 2005 to increase the budgeted football management and player wage bill significantly in "one last push for promotion" and the rewards it would bring. This gamble did not pay off. Not only that, it was compounded by poor results and performances at the Britannia Stadium which saw the team win only seven of 26 home matches. Not surprisingly, this led to a reduction in attendances and a very challenging commercial environment. By the end of the season, the club's debt had risen to £9m and the company was technically insolvent. We had reached a watershed in the club's history and drastic action was required.'

Fortunately for the club, Coates's improved financial status thanks to the success of bet365 meant that he could bear the brunt of the debts and costs, rather than relying on loans, fan-funding schemes or outside interest from anyone not associated with Stoke City or the local area. If anyone was going to work alongside the Coates family, they had to be trustworthy and with the club's best interests at heart. Coates said, 'There is a great deal of work to be done to create a football club that all of its supporters and all of the people of Stoke-on-Trent can be proud of. I am putting together a team of people who I believe can deliver success, while at the same time making economically viable long-term. I have not invested a significant amount of money in Stoke City for the good of my health. I have done it because I am a passionate supporter of this football club and I want Stoke City to be a successful club both on and off the pitch. This will not be done overnight but the process has already begun. I'm 68 years old and have all the money I need. I don't need to be making a £10m-plus investment into a football club which is losing money. It's clearly not a sensible financial investment. I passionately want this football club to succeed and this overrides other considerations.'

* * *

The rebuilding of the club may not have been an overnight job, but there was the immediate task at hand to appoint a new manager. Well, not exactly a *new* manager. There was only one man for the task for Peter Coates – Tony Pulis. The Welshman was still at Plymouth Argyle after steering them from relegation-threatened to comfortable mid-table. This wasn't going to stop Coates from approaching his first choice, and compensation was agreed with the Pilgrims to bring Pulis back to the Potteries in mid-June 2006, after just 12 months away. Though Pulis was hugely popular with the new owner, he wasn't exactly the most popular choice with the fans, many of whom were still recovering after the turgid performances and results in the binary season. Coates admitted, 'I am fully aware some supporters have been publicly voicing their opposition to the return of Tony, who was our manager for two-and-a-half years before being sacked by the club's previous owners in June. It is difficult to make an appointment which will be universally accepted. The board have discussed and enquired about several managers over the past few weeks, and we are all agreed that the best candidate is Tony Pulis. Tony has a reputation for playing a direct style of football. But in our league, is a direct style of play necessarily such a bad thing? As we saw in the season just ended, Watford and Sheffield United were promoted playing direct football. Tony wants to come back because he truly believes he can bring the club success, and I am absolutely convinced he can. I did not make a recent £10m investment in the club for us to remain a mid-table Championship side.'

Former striker Chris Iwelumo returned to the club on several occasions as a visiting player. The changes that the Coates–Pulis partnership were instilling were noticeable to the Scot, who commented, 'I came back with Colchester and Wolves and had some good times. I scored for Colchester, I didn't celebrate, and the fans actually applauded me scoring, it was crazy! Things had changed for sure. The Coates family and TP looked at the foundations around the club, how it was run and what was best for the squad. The investment in the training facilities was a big one. When I was at Stoke, we used to get changed at the Britannia Stadium and drive down to the Michelin. Those days had gone, TP wanted everything down at the training ground. The club bought all the portacabins from Aston Villa to start it all up. That was the way forward and had to be done.'

The move may not have been universally popular at the time, and after an underwhelming start, it seemed that the club may still be stagnant in the middle of the Championship table yet again. There were even rumours of a forthcoming 'red card protest' organised by an outspoken critic of Pulis on *The Oatcake* message board (sorry, I mean a 'Pulis Hating Wankstain'). However, once Pulis had made progress trimming the squad (moving on a number of Boskamp's signings), Coates was able to provide the funding for the manager to bring in his own men, including Lee Hendrie, Rory Delap, Liam Lawrence, Danny Higginbotham, Andy Griffin, Salif Diao and Ricardo Fuller. The signing of Hendrie was a big statement at the time (resulting in the cancellation of the red card protest), a real 'rock the city' signing. Stoke would just miss out on the play-offs on the last game of the season. After another injection of transfer funds, it would only take Coates and Pulis one more season to meet their objective, achieving automatic promotion to the Premier League for the first time in the club's history. It wasn't just a flying visit either. Stoke City would stay in the league for ten years, including the rest of Tony Pulis's tenure in charge. The club would reach its first FA Cup Final after a 5-0 semi-final win at the renovated Wembley Stadium, make it to the knockout stages of the Europa League, continually upset the Premier League big boys and provide plenty of memorable matches and moments for the fans. For that, we Stoke City fans will always be grateful and thankful to the Coates family and to Tony Pulis.

Chapter 26

The Icelandic Era – Retrospective

'I think they didn't know anything about running a football club. Definitely'
– Hannes Sigurðsson

STOKE FANS are still divided on whether the Icelandic era was a successful one for the club. Peter Coates did a good job of summarising the spell in a 2015 interview: 'I had sold to an Icelandic group and they came in and had a go. They spent some money and thought they would take the club into the Premier League, make some money and have some fun. But it didn't work out because it's much harder than people think. So, they ran out of money and began to sell assets off – a player or whatever – and I could see another downward spiral for Stoke. By then I had the money so I thought I would come back and have one last go. I wanted to see if I could achieve what I had always wanted. I thought it would take five years to get into the Premier League. We did it in three.'

In a way, to make a sound judgement on the Icelanders' time in ST4, there needs to be some objectives to measure against. The most obvious measuring stick to go against is the Icelanders' own objectives, as laid out by the chairman Gunnar Gíslason, which were (broadly speaking):

- Achieve Premier League football for Stoke City – 'Our main target is to do well in the Premier League [...] We have to take it one division at a time. Our plan was to reach the Premier League in five years [...] We are here to make Stoke City great again.'
- Make a profit from the purchase – 'We never made it a secret that we intended to make money.'
- Use the club to develop Icelandic footballers in English football – 'Part of the original idea was to improve the opportunities of Icelandic footballers to play professionally in England.'

Let's break that down then.

Premier League football

Did we achieve Premier League football under the Icelanders? No. Big fat no, in fact. We didn't even come close. It's also difficult to defend this failure, as Peter Coates was able to achieve it in three years after taking over, through sensible managerial selection and communications, and money spent in the right areas on the right types of players, all for the benefit of the team and the team only. No appointments made out of spite and no picking up managers from distant lands with no Football League experience. The appointment under Coates was clearly communicated to all interested parties, with a unanimous decision to go ahead with it. Players were not brought in for the benefit of developing football from elsewhere or keeping the interest of any board members. No distant or close relations (well, apart from Anthony Pulis!), no unproven players, none that carried a flight risk. It is entirely possible, though not probable, that the club could have achieved promotion in another season or two under the Icelanders, had the investment been right and the managerial selection been right. But it didn't happen, and their track record suggested it wasn't forthcoming, so that's a definite cross against that objective.

Financial performance

Icelanders have a strong passion for English football and there was an abundance of money in Iceland in the days before the Icelandic banking collapse. The consortium seized an opportunity to buy into the English game, sniffing out a moneymaking opportunity. But, did the Icelanders make money out of the purchase? We can't say with any certainty that they did or did not, but everything suggests that the acquisition was a financial failure. It turned out that way for the club at least, and the numerous fallouts between directors and management over money emphasised the financial failings.

This is something that would repeat itself in English football when Icelandic businessman Eggert Magnússon led a doomed Icelandic consortium at West Ham. In the final days of the Stoke Holding consortium, Peter Coates made it absolutely clear that the club was losing money, the financial performance was dire, and the club's debt had risen to £9m. Cost-cutting measures had been in place prior to promotion to Division One back in 2001/02, with key players being sold off, managers not being given funds to spend and discussions held to close the academy down to save some cash. Beswicks Sports' Gary Mellor said that the club was 'undoubtedly heading for administration as ownership splintered'. When Coates bought the club back from Stoke Holding, it was for around the same price as they had originally purchased it for, suggesting no money was made on the sale. Making money in a football club is a near impossible task under any circumstances, so the idea that this venture would have made the Icelanders much or any money is questionable at best. Think about the money that could have been made in any other business venture between 1999 and 2006 with the capital that they put into the club, particularly a sector that they may be more familiar with. Again, I think it's fair to say that this objective was not met – another cross.

When posed the question as to whether he felt the period was a success, BBC Radio Stoke's John Acres said, 'I spoke to Gunnar after Tony Pulis took Stoke to the Premier League, and he was basically like "Whoops! We had the manager to take us to the Premier League and we just didn't give him quite enough money. Instead we gave it all to Boskamp." While Boskamp went out and bought Bangoura for nearly a million quid and big wages, while Tony just wanted about four £10k loan players and two decent signings. The Icelanders probably know in hindsight that they were probably a £4–5m investment with Tony away from Premier League and the massive windfall that comes with it. They had picked the right manager initially!' Acres continued, 'They were the peak years of Praise & Grumble, everybody would have a moan! I think you have to look at it as a failure really. They got the appointment of Tony Pulis right, and then for some reason they didn't back him properly. That is a massive fail to then watch that man take Stoke into the Premier League and Europe, and watch the Coates family essentially earn your money, that must have made them sick. They almost made a brilliant success of it. A missed opportunity. If they had given Tony Pulis the money that they gave Johan Boskamp then I think he would have taken them up.'

Development of Icelandic football

Finally, was there a significant development of Icelandic footballers associated with Stoke City between 1999 and 2006? It is perhaps a little more open to interpretation, but I would say – no. With one or two exceptions anyway. Think about how many Icelanders came through the doors during that time – I count at least 14. Were they all failures? No, not all of them … Brynjar Gunnarsson had a very successful stint at the club and was an integral part of the initial success under Guðjón Thórdarson. He was also a highly dependable part of Tony Pulis's team that survived in Division One in 2003. Gunnarsson went on to play for Nottingham Forest, Watford and Reading. He helped Reading win the title in 2005/06, making 163 appearances between 2005 and 2013. Apart from Gunnarsson, I'd say that Bjarni Guðjónsson had a largely successful time at Stoke City and improved as a player throughout. Beyond these two, perhaps we got a few decent performances out of Pétur Marteinsson, Arnar Gunnlaugsson (although he was already established in English football with Leicester, so not really due to our transfer policy) and Stefán Thórdarson, but nothing to really write home about, apart from a few memorable goals from the latter two. If you were to ask a neutral to name five Icelandic players from English football between 1999 and 2006, many would probably point to Eiður Guðjohnsen, Hermann Hreiðarsson, Heiðar Helguson, Joey Guðjónsson and Guðni Bergsson before maybe reaching Brynjar Gunnarsson or any other Stoke-affiliated players of the time. Even many Stoke fans would put Toddy Örlygsson and Lárus Sigurðsson as our numbers one and two above any Icelanders that signed during the Icelandic era. Many of the Icelanders that came to Stoke were unsuccessful in making the step up to English football, struggling with the pace of the game and the levels of fitness required. Even the likes of Ríkharður Daðason and Pétur Marteinsson, who both arrived with glowing CVs, couldn't sustain a prolonged spell in the team.

Speaking of Icelander performances at Stoke during the period, author Vidar Halldórsson said, 'In general, Icelandic players are not greatly skilled players. Not many go from club-to-club and succeed. But they are hardworking, team players that thrive in the right environment. This is why they perform well for the national team.' Vidar added, 'We had always been a country of amateur football isolated in the mid-Atlantic. It put Icelandic football in the global game. This was a statement of Icelandic football, but nothing dramatic. Maybe one or two Icelanders stayed as fans, and some people have fond memories and Stoke are their second or third team, but I don't think it created any fan base that still exists now.' The period did not move the needle much for Icelandic football, and that is another failure for the takeover.

* * *

Since their departure, the Icelandic consortium hasn't exactly received much praise from those associated with Stoke City, including from players who played during the regime, and even their own compatriots. Clive Clarke, who was sold by Stoke in August 2005, admitted that the Icelandic owners were an important reason for him leaving the club he had been at since a teenager: 'We never really met the Icelandic board much, but everything was run on a shoestring and they didn't invest enough in the team, so none of the players had any time for them. Before I left, Stoke offered to make me the highest-paid player, but I'd had enough of the poor management by the owners. I had a lot of chances to leave Stoke every season and felt it was the right time. I felt sorry for the management team then and got on well with them, but felt it was time to leave. If Peter Coates had become chairman before I left, I don't think I would have done so, as I loved being captain of the club that I had been part of since I was 14.' Former Stoke midfielder Toddy Örlygsson had long left Stoke before the takeover but kept an eye on his former club under Icelandic stewardship. Speaking to *Duck Magazine*, Toddy said, 'I was surprised that they took over Stoke. I think the main reason it did not work was lack of knowledge of Stoke City and the community.' Hannes Sigurðsson was the last Icelandic signing of the era. In 2017, he discussed life at Stoke under his compatriots and, perhaps surprisingly, was anything but complimentary: 'I didn't really know them. I had very little contact with them. But I think they didn't know anything about running a football club. Definitely. And they weren't exactly honest in anything they did.' By their own objectives, the Icelandic takeover can probably be viewed as a failure. Perhaps this is more a product of their unrealistic plans rather than a true reflection on their time here. Let's look at their list of successes …

Silverware and promotion

Overall, they got the club moving in the right direction after we'd been relegated under the Coates and Humphreys original reign and a failed promotion attempt under Brian Little. The Auto Windscreens Shield win in 2000 was a wonderful day out, and promotion via the play-offs in 2002, albeit at the third time of trying, was crucial for the club in starting what would eventually come under Coates and Pulis. But rather than attribute this to the Icelanders of Stoke Holding, I would much rather attribute this success to another Icelander – Guðjón Thórdarson. He came in with the board, and the whole thing was his idea, so perhaps he's as culpable as the rest for what transpired. But as a manager and a man, he was liked and respected by the fans, who took to him and kept with him through tough times, more than his own compatriots in the boardroom did. Soon after the Icelandic takeover, and certainly by the end, Thórdarson felt more like one of us than one of them, having fallen out with the board long before his eventual dismissal. It took Thórdarson three goes at it, but he did take us up, giving us that special win at Ninian Park along the way.

Exploiting the foreign market

Would I consider the Icelanders' (or more specifically, Guðjón Thórdarson's) reign to have been a successful one in terms of foreign signings? In the end, yes, I would. Thórdarson and John Rudge were also able to bring in a number of exciting players from the much-sought and lucrative 'foreign market', including across Scandinavia and the rest of Europe. While many of the Icelandic players had failed to make an impact, the likes of Hansson, Shtanyuk and Hoekstra are still lauded for their efforts by fans to this day. Even Oularé made himself a cult hero who would be welcome back for the half-time raffle draw at any time he desires. Chris Iwelumo was full of praise for his former team-mates from overseas too, saying, 'I thought the dressing room complemented each other very well. I am still in contact with them, good characters. Bjarni Guðjónsson probably spoke the best English. With Brynjar Gunnarsson, you knew what you were going to get – he trained hard, he tackled hard. Arnar Gunnlaugsson made a big difference when he came in, he was just a level above everyone. He was outstanding and one of the real reasons why we went up. The squad just blended. You look at James O'Connor and Brynjar, doing what they do, with Peter Hoekstra on the flank. Peter Hoekstra was a very fiery character. Great personality, loves football, and as a player, he made so many goals for me. Stefán

Thórdarson and Rikki Daðason came in and scored goals. Sergei Shtanyuk, the big man, used to come around my house most nights. He would take his English lessons everywhere we went, he would write in English, read in English. We used to call him Ivan Drago! He didn't mess around, he would go on the treadmill and never break a sweat, he was such a strong and physically athletic player. I think he was in the Army, so it wasn't a surprise he was the machine that he was.'

Stabilising the club

By the time the Icelanders left the club, we had finished comfortably mid-table in the Championship for three consecutive seasons, showing that the club had progressed from where they started, a promising Division Two position under Gary Megson, to where we had ended. The reason for this success was, of course, Tony Pulis. Cotterill had quit early on, and Boskamp took the team backwards, but Pulis kept us up and built a solid foundation that he would eventually be able to capitalise on the second time round. Pulis was first appointed by the Icelanders after Cotterill walked out, but only after (1) George Burley had turned us down, and (2) Peter Coates and Phil Rawlins had pushed hard for the Welshman's selection. Nonetheless, it happened under the stewardship of Gunnar Gíslason, so you have to give them some credit for that too.

Expanding the fan base

It may sound cheesy, but maybe the biggest success story during the Icelandic era was the friends we made along the way! Trips to Wembley and the Millennium Stadium brought back lost fans after feeling disillusioned under Coates and Humphreys. I am not sure how popular Stoke City were in Scandinavia prior to the takeover (although we were massive in Norway in the 70s according to Anders Jacobsen!). It's likely that our global name value diminished during our years in the wilderness in the 80s and 90s, so the takeover played its role in reaching out to our overseas fans, as well as introducing us to new fans. We still have strong representation across Sweden, Norway, Denmark and, of course, Iceland. The years under the consortium could have only helped in that aspect! Hugo Hemlin, of the Swedish Stokies, explained, 'The Icelandic era coincided with the rise of the internet, which made it far more accessible and easier to follow Stoke for us fans overseas. Before the late 90s, the only information we could find were the tables and results. All other info was hard to get a hold of and when the news reached us it was often at least a week old. My own Stoke interest grew from a small interest to a full-on obsession.' Fredrikke Wongraven of the Norwegian Stoke City Supporters Branch said the takeover made Stoke 'seem like a Scandinavian club at the time', adding, 'It made me even more interested in the club because it kind of felt closer to home. It was an adventure! I have understood in later years that the business part of the Icelandic years was completely bonkers, but this did not affect me as much since I was so young when it happened. I can imagine for the older Stoke fans back then it was a more stressful time. The Icelandic years did a lot for my interest in football, even though I probably did not understand it at the time. Although I was quite young when the Icelandic years happened, I can still remember a few things, especially the Norwegian players Frode Kippe and Anders Jacobsen. Those years not only feel like an Icelandic revolution within football, but also a Scandinavian one. It was a crazy time!'

Entertainment!

There is perhaps one more unintentional victory for the Icelanders that they achieved during their reign. They provided a highly emotional, exciting, agitating and chaotic journey for the fans, season after season. It isn't something that had happened much prior to their arrival, and truthfully, isn't something that has been repeated much since they left. As well as the pure joy of the Wembley 2000 win, the rollercoaster of emotions in both legs against Gillingham in the play-offs are still something that fans remember to this day. The heartbreak after the second leg at Priestfield was perhaps more felt than the relegation from the Premier League for some fans. The feeling of frustration is also still there for the night at the Bescot Stadium where it all went wrong in the second leg of the play-offs against Walsall. I can still hear fans asking, 'Why didn't he pick Thorne?' and declaring 'if Ward had just caught that cross, we'd have won that game'. Then there's *that* night at Ninian Park, which could rival all the victories against Arsenal, the wins in the Europa League and perhaps even the FA Cup run. Oularé's backside could be the most famous arse in football (except for Arsène Wenger perhaps – interpret that however you like). The whole situation surrounding the Cardiff game, coupled with the way that we won the game … it's genuinely tough to beat the feeling from that night. Winning at the Millennium Stadium, surviving on the last game of the season thanks to Ade, even the whole Boskamp experience – these seasons provided some wonderful moments and absurd stories that fans of other teams could never even comprehend. I don't recall Pep Guardiola ever calling anyone a 'shit guy'! Has any other manager had such a public spat with his director of football and his assistant (someone who recommended him for the job in the first place and has been his friend for decades!)? Did Barcelona ever break a dressing-room curse? Nah. Only at Stoke during the Icelandic era.

Angela Smith, presenter on KnotFM and member of Stoke City Fans Council, sums up the time suitably: 'The

Icelandic years promised much. Like any new era, expectations go through the roof. We had some thrills and some mad, crazy times. We sacked an Icelandic manager straight after his successful promotion season. The owners ditched TP for "failing to exploit the foreign market". I think that in reality meant not playing those players that the board wanted to play. We had 14 Icelandic players who pulled on the shirt in that period. A manager who "quit" to become an assistant and then we had Boskamp. It became clear after a couple of seasons that the owners were not experienced enough to run an English club. I guess the highlights were the class of Lárus Sigurdsson and the waving of Iceland flags for a few years. Promotion too. The promise of Rikki Daðason, a goalscoring machine which came to nothing. The silky skills of Peter Hoekstra … Whilst we got a promotion, it was clear that without the return of Peter Coates, the club would have struggled in the lower tiers of English football. The Icelandic board did not appear to have the means to take Stoke higher, nor the inclination. It was quite a ride though.'

To conclude the overall impact of the Icelandic era at Stoke City, I would have to say it was an overall success in spite of them, rather than because of them. They stepped in at a time when any change was necessary, shifting the mood of the club which had been in despair since Lou Macari left. The progress and achievements of the club between 1999 and 2006 happened around the Icelanders, mainly driven by Guðjón Thórdarson and Tony Pulis, neither of whom the board wanted when they were pushing the club upwards. To a degree, the Icelanders accidentally initiated the success of Stoke City that followed 2006 through their own inept decisions, paving the way for the triumphant return of Peter Coates and Tony Pulis. Had they left in 2005 with Pulis remaining in charge, many would look back on their reign much more favourably, but the 2005/06 Boskamp season damaged their reputation and the club's finances, almost beyond repair. Conversely, if Peter Coates had decided that he wanted nothing more to do with the club after he was hounded out in his initial reign, who knows where we would be today? His own family didn't see the merit in him returning to the hot seat! Fortunately, Coates stepped up when we needed him to, and Stoke went from strength to strength. Even if we've ended up back where we started under Coates at time of writing, the Premier League journey and the club's growth off the pitch put us light years ahead of where we were back in 2006. We even signed another Icelander! Eiður Guðjohnsen too, arguably the best that English football has seen! Unfortunately, Eiður's spell was about as good as his dad's taste in managers back in 2005. Whether you agree or disagree that the Icelandic era was an accidental success is a debate that will go on and on. Plenty of personal experiences, hearsay and 'what ifs' to mull over. Still, at least it was better than West Ham's spell under Icelandic ownership …

* * *

In the end, we can merely reflect 'I can't believe that it happened' … or *Það eru margar undur í höfuðkúpu* ('There are many wonders in a cow's head').

Takk Fyrir Síðast.

The Icelanders

What Happened Next?

WHILE SOME of our Icelandic representatives left both football and the public eye following the 2006 departure (specifically Gunnar Gíslason and Magnús Kristinsson), those on the pitch and in the dugout continued in the game. Here is a quick 'where are they now?' recap of some of the more well-known Stoke City-affiliated Icelanders.

Guðjón Thórdarson – The former Stoke manager has moved around England and Iceland quite a lot since leaving the Potteries. After his dismissal in 2002, Thórdarson briefly moved to Norwegian football to manage relegation-doomed IK Start, before returning to English football in 2003 to manage Barnsley. Thórdarson was dismissed after Peter Ridsdale took over the Yorkshire club in 2004, returning to Iceland to manage Keflavík. However, he left three days before the start of the season to take charge of Notts County, where he stayed until May 2006 as the club's first non-British manager. After an initial good start, the team declined to their lowest-ever league position at the time, 21st in League Two, leading to Thórdarson's resignation. He was then appointed manager of ÍA Akranes. During a disappointing spell, he was linked with the Hearts job in Scotland, but ended up back in the North Staffs-South Cheshire region in Christmas 2008, taking charge of Crewe. Guðjón was sacked after relegation to League Two and again returned to Icelandic football. Thórdarson was unemployed for quite a while after his managerial stint at Grindavik (2012). Amazingly, he then turned to a different trade in 2016, when he started a new job as a bus driver, taking tourists to the beauty spots around Iceland! He was given a chance to return to football in 2019 in the Faroe Islands with NSÍ Runavík. He applied for the vacant Faroe's national team managerial position but was unsuccessful. NSÍ Runavík finished third in the Úrvalsdeild. In recent times, 64-year-old Guðjón has decided to head back home to Iceland, living in Kópavogur, but hasn't ruled out a return to football. He told Icelandic media outfit RUV, 'The Faroe Islands suited me well. I lived in a small community and there was really nothing about it. I missed not getting a chance to play golf, but the football was fun. The football filled up completely in the empty space ... I just decided that now I wanted something different. There are hooks out there, but it's like fishing in turbid water, you never know if something will happen.'

Brynjar Gunnarsson – After spells at Nottingham Forest and Watford, Gunnarsson enjoyed a highly successful time at Reading, achieving promotion in 2006 and surviving in the Premier League in 2007. He left the Royals in 2013, returning to KR Reykjavík to see out his playing career. Gunnarsson helped the Icelandic side to the title before his retirement, and went on to be assistant manager at Stjarnan. At time of writing, Brynjar is the head coach of HK Kópavogur, the surprise 2019 newcomers of the Úrvalsdeild. He is currently starting his third season with the club.

Bjarni Guðjónsson – Bjarni had playing spells at VfL Bochum, Coventry and Plymouth, before returning to Iceland in 2006. He played for ÍA and KR Reykjavík before his retirement in 2013. Guðjónsson followed in his father's footsteps by going into management, with spells at KR Reykjavík and Fram between 2013 and 2016. Bjarni is now working in a different type of management outside of football, as a key account manager at VÍS Insurance Ltd in the Vátryggingafélag Íslands. Bjarni's son, and Guðjón Thórdarson's grandson, 15-year-old Jóhannes Kristinn Bjarnason, is now making a name for himself in Icelandic football, having made his first senior appearance for KR Reykjavík in a friendly against Keflavík in the run-up to the return of the Icelandic Super Cup. Jóhannes is a midfielder and was briefly on the books as an under-17 at Rangers. He also trained with FC Copenhagen and Genk, as well as captaining Iceland under-15s. Who knows, perhaps one day he will follow in his father's footsteps and don the red and white of Stoke City – three generations of Icelander to wear the badge!

Lárus Sigurðsson – Following a successful five-year stint at West Brom, Sigurðsson finished his playing career in Iceland with Þór Akureyri and ÍA. Despite his move to Albion, Lárus stayed local to Stoke and followed the club progress closely, saying, 'It was nice to have so many fellow countrymen in the neighbourhood!' Lárus went on to have spells in the hot seat at Þór Akureyri and KF, presumably still making players run several laps of the pitch. Lárus recently told me, 'For the first time in years, I'm not involved in football. I stopped in autumn 2018. I have no plans to go back, but you never know.'

Þorvaldur Örlygsson – Toddy left Oldham in 1999 after sustaining an injury, eventually retiring in 2003 at KA in the north of Iceland. He managed six Icelandic teams between

2000 and 2016, including his old club KA in 2001 as a player-manager. He is now in charge of the Iceland under 19s and under 18s, as well as assisting with the under 17s. Toddy is doing a great job for the under 19s, guiding them to the elite round of the (currently postponed) European Championships in Italy.

Rikki Daðason – The once highly promised striker returned to Norway after his disappointing Stoke spell, but limited appearances for Lillestrøm and Fredrikstad meant he was unable to capture the goalscoring form that had built his reputation in the late 90s. He returned to his original club Fram Reykjavík to finish his career in 2005, managing the same club in 2013. He will be best remembered in Iceland for his legendary goal for the national team against World Cup champions France in 1998.

Arnar Gunnlaugsson – The two-time Stoke loanee left Leicester in 2003 for a brief spell in Scotland for Dundee United, before returning to Iceland where he played out his career until 2011. He is currently managing Víkingur in the Úrvalsdeild.

Tryggvi Guðmundsson – Tryggvi is the all-time top scorer in Icelandic football, with 192 goals scored during his career for club and country. It is a record that is unlikely to ever be broken, as promising Icelandic youngsters are typically scooped up by bigger professional teams across Europe. After failing to make a single appearance for Stoke under Tony Pulis, Tryggvi returned to Iceland, where he was once again a prolific goalscorer. Tryggvi went into management in 2018 at the wonderfully named Vaengir Jupiters, a third division Icelandic club which recently just missed out on promotion.

Thordur Gudjonsson – The second Icelandic 'Toddy' to appear for Stoke, Gudjonsson only made two appearances for the Potters from 2005 to 2006, before seeing out his career at ÍA Akranes. In 2008, Toddy switched from football to politics, standing for election for the western province in Icelandic parliament. Toddy's family, famed for their footballing achievements, also had links to politics, as father Guðjón Thórdarson's brother-in-law was previously the prime minister of Iceland. Toddy would also move into business, specifically key account management and corporate sales, and is currently the chief sales officer of fuel and lubricants distributors Skeljungur HF.

Acknowledgements

FIRST AND foremost, I'd like to thank my wife Cris for her love and patience while I spent hour after hour writing this book from the small desk in our bedroom *¡Muchas gracias mi amor!* This book is dedicated to you, a newly appointed Spanish Stokie, and to my mother Kathleen, who sadly passed away just before our promotion to the Premier League. She was a committed Stokie all her life. I would also like to thank all the contributors who took the time to speak with me, particularly Simon Lowe, Chris Iwelumo, Denis Smith, John Acres, Clive Clarke, Lárus Sigurdsson, Gary Mellor, Pete Smith, Marc Boal, Vidar Halldórsson and Víðir Sigurðsson. Also, many thanks to Angela Smith, Anthony Bunn, Rob Doolan, Neil James, Fredrikke Wongraven, Hugo Hemlin and Runar Kvernen for their contributions and personal recounts. Shout out to away days mates – Rob Holmes, Sean Allen, Nathan Edwards, Adam Brannigan and Mark Dobson … we've put up with some dreadful performances together! Thanks to Thomas Cooper (despite being a Wolves fan) for his inputs on the first manuscript, and Dave Coxon for his help setting up contacts. Many thanks to Paul and Jane Camillin at Pitch Publishing, Pete Gentry of Pete Gentry Editorial and Andrea Dunn Professional Proofreading and Editing Services for helping to make this book possible. Finally, to my dad Dave and my brother David, I wouldn't be such a passionate Stoke City fan without the two of you, which I suppose is a good thing! Thanks for dragging me to games at the Vic that I was completely uninterested in as a child.

Be Loyal, Be Proud, Be Stoke.

Bibliography

The Sentinel articles

'Stoke City waited four months for new striker – and he delivered in four minutes', Peter Smith, 1 November 2017, https://www.stokesentinel.co.uk/sport/football/football-news/stoke-city-waited-four-months-712611

'The inside story behind what Stoke City did after George Burley's disappearing act', Peter Smith, 1 November 2017, https://www.stokesentinel.co.uk/sport/football/football-news/inside-story-behind-what-stoke-714831

'Wycombe 0 Stoke City 4 revisited: 18 years on from THAT chant by 500 away fans', Peter Smith, 23 November 2017, https://www.stokesentinel.co.uk/sport/football/football-news/stoke-city-wycombe-icelandic-thordarson-818624

'Toddy Orlygsson picks out his favourite Stoke goal (from one amazing month of contenders)', Peter Smith, 9 February 2018, https://www.stokesentinel.co.uk/sport/football/football-news/stoke-city-Toddy-orlygsson-macari-1194419

'Major transfer target or sorting out unhappy star? The number one priority for last five Stoke City managers', Peter Smith, 14 June 2018, https://www.stokesentinel.co.uk/sport/football/transfer-news/stoke-city-manager-transfer-news-1675515

'"You don't know what you're doing!"The story behind Stoke fans and an infamous chant', David Lee and Peter Smith, 23 August 2018, https://www.stokesentinel.co.uk/sport/football/football-news/stoke-fans-gary-rowett-pulis-1932503

'The full story of the Stoke City striker who came back from near-death to play key role in one of club's greatest nights – with his backside!', Peter Smith, 22 February 2019, https://www.stokesentinel.co.uk/sport/football/football-news/stoke-city-cardiff-souleymane-oulare-1522536

'Steve Cotterill: My mistake at Stoke City was not walking out after two days', Peter Smith, 28 March 2019, https://www.stokesentinel.co.uk/sport/football/football-news/stoke-city-steve-cotterill-manager-2695976

'Was this the weirdest season in Stoke City history? The story of Johan Boskamp's year in charge', Peter Smith, 30 April 2019, https://www.stokesentinel.co.uk/sport/football/football-news/johan-boskamp-stoke-city-manager-2817075

'The Rob Styles anniversary: Assessor "gave Styles 10 out of 10" for THAT play-off nightmare for Stoke City at Gillingham', Peter Smith, 17 May 2019, https://www.stokesentinel.co.uk/sport/football/football-news/stoke-gillingham-playoff-rob-styles-1580355

'This is the mess that Peter Coates walked into when he took charge of Stoke City again on this day in 2006', Peter Smith, 23 May 2019, https://www.stokesentinel.co.uk/sport/football/football-news/peter-coates-stoke-city-takeover-2897973

'The story of Steve Cotterill and the shock resignation which left Stoke City in chaos', Peter Smith, 10 October 2019, https://www.stokesentinel.co.uk/sport/football/football-news/steve-cotterill-stoke-city-manager-2096188

'The inside story of the curse, the backside and Stoke City manager's final flourish', Peter Smith, 25 October 2019,

https://www.stokesentinel.co.uk/sport/football/football-news/stoke-city-curse-gudjon-thordarson-1556495
'"Momentous" – The inside story of the day Stoke City was taken over by Icelandic consortium', Peter Smith, 2 November 2019, https://www.stokesentinel.co.uk/sport/football/football-news/stoke-city-icelandic-consortium-takeover-3490207
'"I saw my chance and thought bingo!" – Gerry Taggart on THAT Dennis Wise throttle', Peter Smith, 24 January 2020, https://www.stokesentinel.co.uk/sport/football/football-news/gerry-taggart-dennis-wise-stoke-3776759
'"Astonishing" – 17 Stoke City games that will never be repeated', Peter Smith, 19 February 2002, https://www.stokesentinel.co.uk/sport/football/football-news/stoke-city-binary-season-pulis-3864061
'Son of ex-Stoke City star Bjarni Gudjonsson has trial at Rangers, makes senior debut at 15', Peter Smith, 6 June 2020, https://www.stokesentinel.co.uk/sport/football/transfer-news/stoke-city-johannes-bjarnason-gudjonson-4199668

BBC articles

'Fighting mars Matthews tribute', 26 February 2000, http://news.bbc.co.uk/2/hi/sport/658258.stm
'Stoke secure slim lead over Gills', 13 May 2000, http://news.bbc.co.uk/2/hi/sport/football/747442.stm
'Gills crush nine-man Stoke', 17 May 2000, http://news.bbc.co.uk/2/hi/sport/football/752886.stm
'Wembley glory for Stoke City', 29 June 2000, http://news.bbc.co.uk/sport2/hi/football/teams/s/stoke_city/791104.stm
'Stoke 3-2 Barnsley', 1 November 2000, http://news.bbc.co.uk/sport2/hi/football/worthington_cup/1000411.stm
'Stoke 0-0 Nuneaton', 18 November 2000, http://news.bbc.co.uk/sport2/hi/football/fa_cup/1028146.stm

'Nuneaton 1-0 Stoke', 21 November 2000, http://news.bbc.co.uk/sport2/hi/football/fa_cup/1032732.stm
'Liverpool blast eight at Stoke', 29 November 2000, http://news.bbc.co.uk/sport2/hi/football/worthington_cup/1045418.stm
'Port Vale 2-1 Stoke', 5 March 2001, http://news.bbc.co.uk/sport2/hi/football/1204202.stm
'Oldham 1-2 Stoke', 28 April 2001, http://news.bbc.co.uk/sport2/hi/football/eng_div_2/1297967.stm
'Stoke 0-0 Walsall', 13 May 2001, http://news.bbc.co.uk/sport2/hi/football/eng_div_2/1325152.stm
'Thorne joins Bluebirds', 13 September 2001, http://news.bbc.co.uk/sport2/hi/football/teams/c/cardiff_city/1540166.stm
'Wigan 6-1 Stoke', 13 November 2001, http://news.bbc.co.uk/sport2/hi/football/eng_div_2/1652115.stm
'Kavanagh relishing Stoke return', 26 April 2002, http://news.bbc.co.uk/sport2/hi/football/teams/c/cardiff_city/1952505.stm
'Stoke 1-2 Cardiff', 28 April 2002, http://news.bbc.co.uk/sport2/hi/football/eng_div_2/1951111.stm
'Stoke break Cardiff hearts', 1 May 2002, http://news.bbc.co.uk/sport2/hi/football/eng_div_2/1959318.stm
'Stadium jinx finally ends', 11 May 2002, http://news.bbc.co.uk/2/hi/uk_news/wales/1981703.stm
'Stoke seal promotion', 11 May 2002, http://news.bbc.co.uk/sport2/hi/football/eng_div_2/1979286.stm
'Stoke sack Thordarson', 16 May 2002, http://news.bbc.co.uk/sport2/hi/football/teams/s/stoke_city/1987271.stm
'Fans campaign for manager's recall', 21 May 2002, http://news.bbc.co.uk/2/hi/uk_news/england/1999889.stm
'Sheff Wed 0-0 Stoke', 10 August 2002, http://news.bbc.co.uk/sport2/hi/football/eng_div_1/2181130.stm
'Stoke 2-1 Bradford', 17 August 2002, http://news.bbc.co.uk/sport2/hi/football/eng_div_1/2195409.stm

'Preston 4-3 Stoke', 24 August 2002, http://news.bbc.co.uk/sport2/hi/football/eng_div_1/2198205.stm

'Walsall 4-2 Stoke', 2 November 2002, http://news.bbc.co.uk/sport2/hi/football/eng_div_1/2363901.stm

'Stoke 3-2 Sheff Wed', 28 December 2002, http://news.bbc.co.uk/sport2/hi/football/eng_div_1/2597071.stm

'ID scheme "big success"', 22 January 2003, http://news.bbc.co.uk/sport2/hi/football/teams/s/stoke_city/2682885.stm

'Norwich 2-2 Stoke', 13 February 2003, http://news.bbc.co.uk/sport2/hi/football/eng_div_1/2693875.stm

'Chelsea sink brave Stoke', 18 February 2003, http://news.bbc.co.uk/sport2/hi/football/fa_cup/2740045.stm

'Nottm Forest 6-0 Stoke', 22 February 2003, http://news.bbc.co.uk/sport2/hi/football/eng_div_1/2762253.stm

'Stoke 1-0 Brighton', 5 March 2003, http://news.bbc.co.uk/sport2/hi/football/eng_div_1/2803959.stm

'Wolves 0-0 Stoke', 18 March 2003, http://news.bbc.co.uk/sport2/hi/football/eng_div_1/2851169.stm

'Watford 1-2 Stoke', 22 March 2003, http://news.bbc.co.uk/sport2/hi/football/eng_div_1/2852721.stm

'Stoke 2-0 Rotherham', 9 April 2003, http://news.bbc.co.uk/sport2/hi/football/eng_div_1/2932813.stm

'Coventry 0-1 Stoke', 21 April 2003, http://news.bbc.co.uk/sport2/hi/football/eng_div_1/2950501.stm

'Crystal Palace 1-0 Stoke', 26 April 2003, http://news.bbc.co.uk/sport2/hi/football/eng_div_1/2950727.stm

'Akinbiyi keeps Stoke up', 4 May 2003, http://news.bbc.co.uk/sport2/hi/football/eng_div_1/2967967.stm

'Baggies bag duo', 11 July 2003, http://news.bbc.co.uk/sport2/hi/football/teams/w/west_bromwich_albion/3055657.stm

'Stoke sign De Goey', 1 August 2003, http://news.bbc.co.uk/sport2/hi/football/teams/s/stoke_city/3116041.stm

'Marteinsson leaves Stoke', 3 September 2003, http://news.bbc.co.uk/sport2/hi/football/teams/s/stoke_city/3077916.stm
'Stoke pin hopes on Akinbiyi', 5 September 2003, http://news.bbc.co.uk/sport2/hi/football/teams/c/crystal_palace/3081108.stm
'Commons snubs Stoke offer', 16 June 2004, http://news.bbc.co.uk/sport2/hi/football/teams/s/stoke_city/3793851.stm
'Stoke 0-1 QPR', 2 October 2004, http://news.bbc.co.uk/sport2/hi/football/eng_div_1/3689234.stm
'Stoke 3-2 Leicester', 22 February 2005, http://news.bbc.co.uk/sport2/hi/football/eng_div_1/4279711.stm
'Stoke owners put club for sale', 28 April 2005, http://news.bbc.co.uk/sport2/hi/football/teams/s/stoke_city/4494161.stm
'Sunderland 1-0 Stoke', 8 May 2005, http://news.bbc.co.uk/sport2/hi/football/eng_div_1/4500825.stm
'Manager Pulis is sacked by Stoke', 28 June 2005, http://news.bbc.co.uk/sport2/hi/football/teams/s/stoke_city/4630755.stm
'Boskamp named as new Stoke boss', 29 June 2005, http://news.bbc.co.uk/sport2/hi/football/teams/s/stoke_city/4633511.stm
'Kristinsson cash to boost Potters', 5 July 2005, http://news.bbc.co.uk/sport2/hi/football/teams/s/stoke_city/4652413.stm
'Stoke sign Anderlecht midfielders', 30 July 2005, http://news.bbc.co.uk/sport2/hi/football/teams/s/stoke_city/4731063.stm
'Stoke complete Bangoura signing', 30 August 2005, http://news.bbc.co.uk/sport2/hi/football/teams/s/stoke_city/4181162.stm
'Boskamp keen to resolve future', 20 November 2005, http://news.bbc.co.uk/sport2/hi/football/teams/s/stoke_city/4454324.stm
'Luton 2-3 Stoke', 17 December 2005, http://news.bbc.co.uk/sport2/hi/football/eng_div_1/4516210.stm

'Boskamp may quit over Rudge row', 5 January 2006, http://news.bbc.co.uk/sport2/hi/football/teams/s/stoke_city/4584396.stm

'Quotes of the week', 17 January 2006, http://news.bbc.co.uk/sport2/hi/funny_old_game/4619946.stm

'Goalkeeper attacker is jailed', 31 January 2006, http://news.bbc.co.uk/2/hi/uk_news/england/staffordshire/4666016.stm

'Stoke anger at no-show Bangoura', 10 February 2006, http://news.bbc.co.uk/sport2/hi/football/teams/s/stoke_city/4701094.stm

'Stoke chief still open to offers', 31 March 2006, http://news.bbc.co.uk/sport2/hi/football/teams/s/stoke_city/4864606.stm

'Stoke takeover bid is turned down', 13 April 2006, http://news.bbc.co.uk/sport2/hi/football/teams/s/stoke_city/4905990.stm

'Brighton 1-5 Stoke', 30 April 2006, http://news.bbc.co.uk/sport2/hi/football/eng_div_1/4933554.stm

'Boskamp confirms exit from Stoke', 30 April 2006, http://news.bbc.co.uk/sport2/hi/football/teams/s/stoke_city/4960852.stm

'Chairman Gislason departs Stoke', 22 May 2006, http://news.bbc.co.uk/sport2/hi/football/teams/s/stoke_city/5004658.stm

'Coates takes over as Stoke owner', 23 May 2006, http://news.bbc.co.uk/sport2/hi/football/teams/s/stoke_city/5007780.stm

'Rudge reveals Boskamp bombshell', 7 June 2006, http://news.bbc.co.uk/sport2/hi/football/teams/s/stoke_city/5056130.stm

'Pulis confirmed as Stoke manager', 14 June 2006, http://news.bbc.co.uk/sport2/hi/football/teams/s/stoke_city/5075140.stm

The Independent articles

'Football: Megson takes over at Stoke', Phil Shaw, 15 July 1999, https://www.independent.co.uk/sport/football-megson-takes-over-at-stoke-1106557.html

'Football: Megson is victim of Stoke takeover', Phil Shaw, 16 November 1999, https://www.independent.co.uk/sport/football-megson-is-victim-of-stoke-takeover-1126541.html

'Icelandic influence takes root in Stoke', 11 August 2000, https://www.independent.co.uk/sport/football/football-league/icelandic-influence-takes-root-in-stoke-696532.html

'Lightbourne to Stoke's rescue', Phil Shaw, 18 September 2000, https://www.independent.co.uk/sport/football/football-league/lightbourne-to-stokes-rescue-700926.html

'Taylor in line to succeed Thordarson at Stoke', Phil Shaw and Alan Nixon, 17 May 2002, https://www.independent.co.uk/sport/football/football-league/taylor-in-line-to-succeed-thordarson-at-stoke-9130192.html

'Stoke owners in bid for Port Vale', Phil Shaw, 1 February 2003, https://www.independent.co.uk/sport/football/football-league/stoke-owners-in-bid-for-port-vale-117569.html

'Icelanders draw veil over Stoke groundshare', David Conn, 8 February 2003, https://www.independent.co.uk/sport/football/news-and-comment/david-conn-icelanders-draw-veil-over-stoke-groundshare-118345.html

'Boskamp the cosmopolitan adventurer brings "total football" cool to Britannia', Phil Shaw, 24 September 2005, https://www.independent.co.uk/sport/football/football-league/boskamp-the-cosmopolitan-adventurer-brings-total-football-cool-to-britannia-314797.html

The Telegraph articles

'White extremists blamed for race riots', Paul Stokes, 29 May

2001, https://www.telegraph.co.uk/news/uknews/1332047/White-extremists-blamed-for-race-riots.html
'Free-spending Cardiff land Thorne', 12 September 2001, https://www.telegraph.co.uk/sport/football/competitions/league-one/3012692/Free-spending-Cardiff-land-Thorne.html
'Division Two Play-off Final: Twist to tale after Stoke end hoodoo', Paul Evans, 11 May 2002, https://www.telegraph.co.uk/sport/football/competitions/league-one/3027559/Division-Two-Play-off-Final-Twist-to-tale-after-Stoke-end-hoodoo.html
'Cotterill unveiled by Stoke', 27 May 2002, https://www.telegraph.co.uk/sport/3028537/Cotterill-unveiled-by-Stoke.html
'Big task confronting Pulis', Neil Goulding, 4 November 2002, https://www.telegraph.co.uk/sport/football/competitions/championship/3037331/Big-task-confronting-Pulis.html
'Stoke prolong their agonies', Nicholas Harling, 28 April 2003, https://www.telegraph.co.uk/sport/2400452/Stoke-prolong-their-agonies.html

The Guardian articles

'The Icemen cometh… to Stoke', Trevor Haylett, 27 November 1999, https://www.theguardian.com/football/1999/nov/27/newsstory.sport9
'Football hooligans raise their game', Vivek Chaudhary, 14 August 2000, https://www.theguardian.com/uk/2000/aug/14/footballviolence.football
'Lewes guns silenced', Mark McGuinness, 19 November 2001, https://www.theguardian.com/football/2001/nov/19/match.sport4
'Stoke steal Cardiff thunder', Paul Rees, 2 May 2002, https://www.theguardian.com/football/2002/may/02/match.sport1

'Cotterill leaves Stoke flapping in vapour trail of ambition', David Alexander and Ian Whittell, 11 October 2002, https://www.theguardian.com/football/2002/oct/11/newsstory.sport6

'Burley set to take over at Stoke', 31 October 2002, https://www.theguardian.com/football/2002/oct/31/newsstory.sport6

'Silver lining for Pulis', Sean Ingle, 4 November 2002, https://www.theguardian.com/football/2002/nov/04/match.sport6

'Turner refusing to wave the white flag at Wednesday', Mark Ogden, 30 December 2002, https://www.theguardian.com/football/2002/dec/30/match.sport8

'Marvellous Marlon', Gerry Cox, 23 February 2003, https://www.theguardian.com/football/2003/feb/23/match.sport5

'It's Brighton and Hope Albion', Jason Thomas, 4 May 2003, https://www.theguardian.com/football/2003/may/04/newsstory.sport6

'Stoke hold their nerve as Akinbiyi bites back', Richard Rae, 5 May 2003, https://www.theguardian.com/football/2003/may/05/match.sport6

'Derby helpless against Stoke new boys', Ian Labourne, 11 August 2003, https://www.theguardian.com/football/2003/aug/11/newsstory.sport4

'Hoddle heading for extended stay at Wolves', Adrian Milledge, 29 April 2005, https://www.theguardian.com/football/2005/apr/29/newsstory.sport

'Boskamp stokes the fires of disharmony', Stuart James, 16 February 2006, https://www.theguardian.com/football/2006/feb/16/newsstory.sport3

Sky Sports articles

'Thordarson praises Petty's action', Alex Livie, May 2001, https://www.skysports.com/football/news/11701/2209603/thordarson-praises-pettys-action

'Oulare out for season', Mark Buckingham, August 2001, https://www.skysports.com/football/news/11701/2229037/oulare-out-for-season

'Greenacre signs for Stoke', Mark Buckingham, June 2002, https://www.skysports.com/football/news/11701/2240478/greenacre-signs-for-stoke

'Bjarni swaps Stoke for Bochum', Adam Marshall and Thomas Zeh, July 2003, https://www.skysports.com/football/news/11701/2265942/bjarni-swaps-stoke-for-bochum

'Stoke clinch Noel-Williams signature', Graeme Bailey, August 2003, https://www.skysports.com/football/news/11686/2266437/stoke-clinch-noel-williams-signature

'Stoke strike permanent Ade deal', Mark Buckingham, September 2003, https://www.skysports.com/football/news/11701/2275761/stoke-strike-permanent-ade-deal

'Stoke snare Sigurdsson', Mark Buckingham, August 2005, https://www.skysports.com/football/news/11701/2347509/stoke-snare-sigurdsson

'Bangoura makes Stoke return', Simon Fudge, February 2006, https://www.skysports.com/football/news/11701/2385862/bangoura-makes-stoke-return

Other information

'KR ræður breskan knattspyrnuþjálfara' KR hire British football manager, *Morgunblaðið*, 27 April 1946, https://timarit.is/page/1259094#page/n11/mode/2up

'Þjálfari K.R. væntanlegur um helgina' K.R. manager expected at the weekend, *Morgunblaðið*, 11 May 1946, https://timarit.is/page/1259259#page/n8/mode/2up

'Knattspyrnumenn æfa upp í sveit' Soccer players practice in the countryside, *Vísir*, 11 July 1946, https://timarit.is/page/1159850#page/n3/mode/2up

'Islendingar verða liðtækir í knaftspyrnu, þegar grasvellir eru komnir' Icelanders will be competent at football when grass pitches arrive, *Morgunblaðið*, 17 August 1946, https://timarit.is/page/1260296#page/n1/mode/2up

'KSI Staða & úrslit' (Iceland rank & results) 1946, https://www.ksi.is/mot/stakt-mot/?MotNumer=10255

'Dawn of the Ssons', Penny Stanley, When Saturday Comes 155, January 2000, https://www.wsc.co.uk/the-archive/30-Clubs/3981-dawn-of-the-ssons

'Reading FC vs. Stoke City', HNA Royals Match Reports, 6 May 2000, https://www.royals.org/matdoc/060500.html

'FA Cup: Lewes are warned to expect Stoke backlash', *The Argus*, 16 November 2001, https://www.theargus.co.uk/news/6770093.fa-cup-lewes-are-warned-to-expect-stoke-backlash/

'Ég er kraftmesta skáld á Íslandi' ('I am the most powerful poet in Iceland' – interview with Hlynur Áskelsson), Dagblaðið Vísir, 30 November 2001, https://timarit.is/page/3025111#page/n9/mode/2up

'Sanchez in hot water after row with Stoke player', *Bucks Free Press*, 17 December 2001, https://www.bucksfreepress.co.uk/news/5185194.sanchez-in-hot-water-after-row-with-stoke-player/

'Kavanagh given a hostile reception', WalesOnline, 29 April 2002, https://www.walesonline.co.uk/sport/football/football-news/kavanagh-given-a-hostile-reception-1979019

'Stoke boss looks to lift "curse"', 10 May 2002, https://www.espnfc.com/england/news/2002/0510/stoke_20020510_bosslookstoliftcurse.html

'Cotterill rejects Dons to join Stoke', 27 May 2002, https://www.irishexaminer.com/breakingnews/sport/soccer/cotterill-rejects-dons-to-join-stoke-51911.html

'Dadason Leaves', Rob Stanway, Footymad, 12 July 2002, http://www.stokecity-mad.co.uk/news/tmnw/dadason_leaves_53631/index.shtml

'Thordarson signs attacking duo', UEFA, 3 January 2003, https://www.uefa.com/insideuefa/news/newsid=48011.html

'Nottingham Forest 6 Stoke City 0: Six goal Forest destroy Stoke', Richard Rae, *The Times*, 23 February 2003, https://www.thetimes.co.uk/article/nottingham-forest-6-stoke-city-0-six-goal-forest-destroy-stoke-90rq03j3k39

'Akinbiyi signs for Stoke on loan', Holmesdale, 26 March 2003, https://www.holmesdale.net/page.php?id=82&story=1538

'Warhurst loan deal confirmed', *The Bolton News*, 27 March 2003, https://www.theboltonnews.co.uk/news/5910304.warhurst-loan-deal-confirmed/

'Further down but staying up', Andy Turner, *Coventry Telegraph*, 26 April 2003, https://www.coventrytelegraph.net/sport/football/football-news/further-down-but-staying-up-3165231

'Albion rely on Palace for favour', *The Argus*, 24 April 2003, https://www.theargus.co.uk/news/6737679.albion-rely-on-palace-for-favour/

'Stoke City 1 Reading 0', HNA Royals Match Reports, 4 May 2003, https://www.royals.org/matdoc/040503.html

'Second signing of the day! Tryggvi Gudmundsson', Rob Stanway, FootyMad, 28 January 2005, http://www.stokecity-mad.co.uk/news/tmnw/second_signing_of_the_day_tryggvi_gudmundsson_202092/index.shtml

'Akinbiyi joins Burnley', *Daily Mail*, 24 February 2005, https://www.dailymail.co.uk/sport/football/article-339100/Akinbiyi-joins-Burnley.html

'Bearing a Rudge', Andy Thorley, When Saturday Comes 226, March 2006, https://www.wsc.co.uk/the-archive/32-Managers/1382-bearing-a-rudge

'Fótboltinn minn: Ceres 4 (Merzedes Club)' Hlynur Áskelsson interview, 22 February 2008, https://fotbolti.net/fullStory.php?id=58426

'Johan Boskamp regrets "every day" quitting Stoke City', Tribal Football, 20 October 2011, https://www.tribalfootball.com/articles/johan-boskamp-regrets-every-day-quitting-stoke-city-1994671#popup-sso

'First Ade: Stoke's Pulis celebrates 10th anniversary of vital Akinbiyi goal against Reading', Jeremy Butler, 8 February 2013, https://www.mirror.co.uk/sport/football/news/stoke-vs-reading-preview-tony-1595025

'150 Memories – Chris Iwelumo', Richard Forrester and Stoke City FC, 8 April 2013, https://www.stokecityfc.com/news/150-memories-chris-iwelumo

'Stoke stunned as Cotterill quits', The World Game, 22 April 2014, https://theworldgame.sbs.com.au/stoke-stunned-as-cotterill-quits

'Stoke sign Crossley', The World Game, 22 April 2014, https://theworldgame.sbs.com.au/stoke-sign-crossley

'Three former top bankers and one broker at failed bank Glitnir sentenced to 2-4 years in prison', *Iceland Magazine*, 3 December 2015, https://icelandmag.is/article/three-former-top-bankers-and-one-broker-failed-bank-glitnir-sentenced-2-4-years-prison

'Peter Coates describes his turbulent love affair with Stoke City: "There were death threats and fans stormed the boardroom but I still came back for more"', Ian Ladyman, *Daily Mail*, 3 December 2015, https://www.dailymail.co.uk/sport/football/article-3344969/Peter-Coates-turbulent-love-affair-Stoke-death-threats-came-more.html

'Stoke 0-8 Liverpool – Relive Reds thumping Potters in League Cup 2000/01', Jordan Chamberlain, Empire of the Kop, 5 January 2016, https://www.empireofthekop.

com/2016/01/05/video-stoke-0-8-liverpool-relive-reds-thumping-potters-in-league-cup-200001/

'A Second Wembley Win', Stoke Loud and Proud, 4 October 2016, https://stokeloudandproud.com/stoke-bristol-city-autoglass/

'The Haunting Tale Of The Millennium Stadium's Curse', Hannah Lichtenstein, The 18, 3 June 2017, https://the18.com/soccer-entertainment/millennium-stadium-curse-champions-league-final

'Icelandic striker explains what it was like at Stoke in their crazy Viking era', Sport and Study, 9 August 2017, https://sportandstudy.org/icelandic-striker-explains-what-it-was-like-at-stoke-in-their-crazy-viking-era/

Defying Expectations: Phil Rawlins and the Orlando City Soccer Story, Simon Veness, November 2017, Publisher: University of Nebraska Press, ISBN-10: 1496201760

'Our House: Gudjon Thordarson', Dave Coxon, #pottersmag and Stoke City FC, 24 April 2018, https://www.stokecityfc.com/news/our-house-gudjon-thordarson

'Ice, Ice, Baby' Toddy Örlygsson interview, *Duck Magazine*, Issue 41, July 2019.

'Thorne in our side' Peter Thorne interview, *Duck Magazine*, Issue 54, October 2019.

Guðjón Þórðarson interview, Kristjana Arnarsdóttir, RUV, 31 October 2019, https://www.ruv.is/frett/eins-og-ad-veida-i-gruggugu-vatni

'Tímavélin: Sigur Stoke í Framrúðubikarnum' The Time Machine: Stoke Victory in the Windshield Cup, Magnús Már Einarsson, Fótbolti.net, 16 April 2020, https://fotbolti.net/news/16-04-2020/timavelin-sigur-stoke-i-framrudubikarnum

About the Author

LIAM BULLOCK is a geologist at the University of Oxford by day, but a full-time Stoke City fan day and night. Liam was raised in Fenton, schooled in Longton and achieved his doctorate at Keele University. His support for the Potters has taken him up and down the country, as well as overseas.

While more accustomed to writing scientific articles, writing a book on his lifelong love for Stoke was not too much of a stretch. Both require rigorous hours of research, the development and review of objectives, plenty of number crunching and analysis of evolution (or devolution) trends, particularly pertinent during the Icelandic years. Most notably – both subjects are highly results-driven. But there is one key difference, and that's the emotion. Supporting a football team, particularly your local team, evokes so much affection, joy, heartbreak, fear, disgust, surprise and anger. Liam, like thousands of others, lived through all these emotions during the Icelandic years of Stoke City. He saw the opportunity to piece together the individual moments into the story of an unforgettable journey, sandwiched between two very contrasting times in the club's history.

ABOUT THE AUTHOR

Liam is now following Stoke from afar in his home in Barcelona with his wife Cris. He makes regular pilgrimages to the Potteries to suffer through yet another 90 minutes at the bet365 Stadium.

Also available at all good book stores

9781785317576

9781785317583

9781785318009

9781785317620

9781785315534

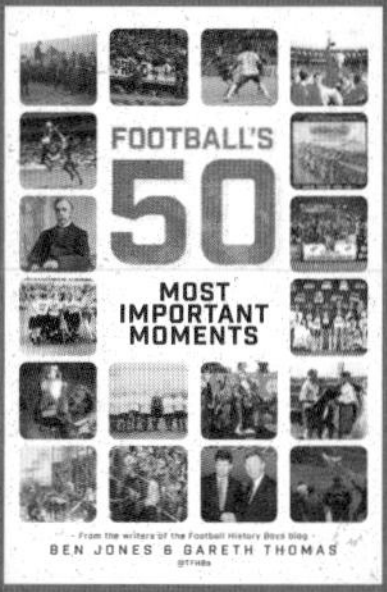

9781785316326

9781785316869

9781785316463

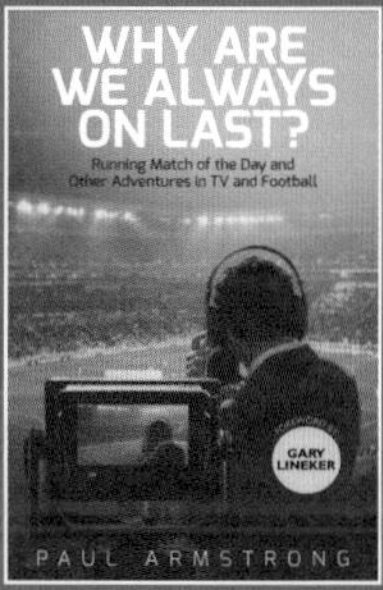

9781785314384

Britannia
Britannia
Britannia
Nat
F O O T B
DIVISION 2 PL
STO